Paris

Paris

Photographs by Hervé Champollion

Notes on the plates by Jean-Paul Caracalla

Foreword by Jacques Laurent

Thames and Hudson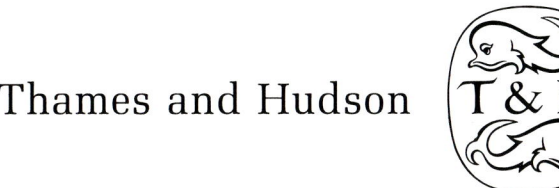

Translated from the French *Vivre Paris*
by Emily Lane

First published in Great Britain in 1988
by Thames and Hudson Ltd, London

© 1987 Editions Mengès
6, rue du Mail – 75002 Paris

All Rights Reserved. No part of this publication may be
reproduced or transmitted in any form or by any means,
electronic or mechanical, including photocopy, recording or
any other information storage and retrieval system, without
prior permission in writing from the publisher.

Printed and bound in Italy

Foreword

New arrivals in Paris often ask where the 'centre' is. There is no answer to that question. The city seems to have been formed, transformed, reformed, and even deformed, with the secret purpose of preventing any simple understanding of its structure. No one square, crossroads, monument or garden is superior to all the rest; none supplies the key to the pattern.

It is of course true that the settlement that gave birth to Paris, Lutetia, was itself born on the Ile de la Cité, and highway milestones giving the distance to Paris reckon it from Notre Dame. But the cathedral cannot be isolated from the forest of spires, towers and domes that surrounds it; it dominates nothing more than the river; and it stands like the needle of a balance, perfectly poised, between the Left Bank and the Right Bank with their equal weights of history and beauty.

As a city grows its geography becomes effaced. The name of 'Lutetia' came from the Gaulish word *lut* meaning 'marsh', but that marsh is unfindable today beneath centuries of building. You would be similarly disappointed if you went in search of the Seine's other arm, which used to curve off near Montmartre and bathe the foot of the hill of Chaillot. Even the names of streets which indicate a rural past are most often spoken without any consciousness of their meaning: who on the Left Bank thinks of meadows in the Place Saint-Germain-des-Prés, or, on the Right, of little fields in the Rue des Petits-Champs?

It is also difficult today to discern particular trades or specialities in particular parts of the city, though there are certain basic distinctions. The Right Bank has always been the home of fashion and consequently of change. The tone of the Left Bank is set by traditional bodies – the University and the Institut de France – and by the publishing houses that cluster round them. For entertainment after dark, though, you can go to Montmartre on one bank or to Montparnasse or Saint-Germain-des-Prés on the other. The museums and galleries on the Right Bank house great masterpieces of art; but on the Left Bank museums are in the process of creation, and experimental art finds display space in avant-garde galleries that rub shoulders with antique shops. The monumental squares laid out by and for kings are on the Right Bank, but government is now shared between the two sides of the river.

French novelists of the nineteenth century, who lived through a time of unprecedented population growth under the smoke-darkened skies of the Industrial Revolution, were often frightened by Paris, which seemed to them a dirty and unfeeling monster. It was from the heights of the cemetery of Père Lachaise that Rastignac, the ambitious hero of Balzac's *Père Goriot*, launched his famous challenge to the city: 'A nous deux, maintenant!' At times to Balzac, filled with a sense of terror and nightmare, the cemetery seemed a microcosm of the city. When he speaks of the countryside, Balzac rhapsodizes about starry skies, golden clouds, blue horizons, lacy trees. In Paris, however, when he wants to describe the hallways of dingy *pensions*, muddy courtyards, shops, the state rooms of ministers, waste ground, he writes economically and chooses precise, harsh words. Nature stirred him to Romanticism; the anti-natural city made him a Realist. One senses a fear of Paris also in the writings of the Goncourt brothers, who were particularly alarmed by the livid hue that the new zinc coverings were spreading over the roofs of the old capital. In *Le Petit Chose*, Alphonse Daudet expressed a similar anxiety about the metropolis: 'I rushed to the door of the train. No houses. Nothing but land scraped bare, a few gas lights, and here and there large coal tips; then, in the distance, a great red glow and an indistinct roar like that of the sea. A man carrying a little lantern went from door to door calling out "Paris! Paris! Have your tickets ready!" In spite of myself I drew my head back, in terror . . . It was Paris.' The intense industrialization of Paris in the nineteenth century had, indeed, greatly widened the gap between it and the countryside; while at the same time the network of rail lines and highways extending outward from the city like tentacles made its dominance over the rest of the nation all too brutally evident. There is no doubt that Paris can be frightening. It is a ruler; and whatever government happens to be in power, France must obey its dictates.

Others have seen the city in more positive terms. To Paul Valéry it was the place where Frenchmen in their great variety and diversity of opinion could come together and understand one another. For the same reason, Montaigne had regarded Paris as the country's chief glory. Vauban, incisively, called it 'a summary of France'.

In the study of history, it is easy to say that a particular situation or event was caused by particular factors, but it is impossible to say that the causal relationship was a necessary one, or that the outcome could have been foreseen. The island of Lutetia was well sited, on a defensible spot in a river which was itself navigable and which gave access to three other navigable rivers, the Marne, Oise and Yonne; it was close to the tin route that ran between Rome and Britain; communication was easy with the Loire region to the south and with the lands to the north. Under the Romans Lutetia was a town of some significance, but it was not the imperial capital, and no one at that time could have guessed its destiny. Under the Franks, Clovis realized its strategic importance and built a large basilica, but although the town was by then called Paris its future role was by no means secured. The Carolingians removed the seat of power to German lands, and left Paris to take its chances with the Norsemen. Then, when the Carolingian Empire collapsed, the newly elected king Hugues Capet considered making his capital at Orléans, but opted for the Seine. Later kings were again tempted by the Loire valley, and even set up a temporary capital at Lyons. Yet the notion had somehow been planted that Paris had a special quality that no rival could match.

No other town could endow a ruler with such authority. The 'King of Bourges' might get himself crowned at Reims; but to be recognized as King of France Charles VII had to enter Paris. It was to the city as key to the kingdom that the future Henri IV referred when, deciding on his conversion to Catholicism, he declared that 'Paris is worth a Mass'.

What lay at the origin of that special character, which Paris still has today? It seems that it was the flowering of intellectual life in the Middle Ages. For Paris was not only the seat of political power: very rapidly, thanks to its university, it became one of the centres of Western thought. The early importance of the university is reflected in the fact that the whole area of the Boulevard Saint-Michel and the slopes of the Montagne Sainte-Geneviève is still known as the 'Latin Quarter'. But the intellectual position of the city – for centuries all French writers and painters have wanted to make their career in Paris – is due to the fact that for a thousand years it has been the capital of a nation state.

Chance decisions sometimes have great consequences. Napoleon had originally intended the Arc de Triomphe to stand on the top of the hill of Montmartre, and the Eiffel Tower was meant to be demolished after the 1883 Exposition. Yet who can imagine Paris without its giant metal idol, a Champs Elysées leading nowhere, or Montmartre without the lunatic whiteness of the Sacré Coeur? It was a present from the Turkish ruler of Egypt, Mohammed Ali, that gave the city the obelisk in the Place de la Concorde, which came to join the Arc de Triomphe as punctuation marks on the longest urban vista in the world.

There are neighbourhoods where the chance visitor might think himself in Africa, and others where he finds Asia all around him. A world city can absorb utterly diverse elements and remain itself: Paris is many, and one. The concrete jungle of the development of La Défense is like a futuristic dream of America conceived by a child in the 1930s, but a short walk will confirm that Paris is still Paris.

Every artist creates his own image of Paris, and that of Bonnard is different from that of Monet. Artists only go wrong when they insist on measuring it by some other standard. Stendhal failed to understand the city because he could never rid himself of the image of his native Grenoble. The two overlapped, like a photographic double-exposure, and it was Paris that he found wanting: Montmartre was not a real mountain, and there were no glaciers reflected in the Seine. Later in his life, he took as his norm Milan, which is equally unlike Paris. Stendhal's refusal to be moved by the metropolis is particularly striking because it is so unusual.

Consciously or unconsciously, each person experiences a Paris that is slightly different from everyone else's, and no one portrait of the city can be definitive. Every artist comes to it afresh, and Hervé Champollion's remarkable photographs show that it is possible to have a new vision of such famous sights as Notre Dame, the Eiffel Tower, the Seine and the Panthéon. Hervé Champollion is a collateral descendant of the great genius Jean-François Champollion, who deciphered Egyptian hieroglyphics; but unlike him he has not attempted to find a single, 'objective' translation. His photographs are a record of his many meetings with this exceptional city, and through them we can share his sensations. No film star can possibly have been photographed as many times as Notre Dame, and yet he has managed to make me see the cathedral with new eyes. Such is the power of art; and such, too, the power of this strange city.

Although I was born on the Right Bank, I have spent most of my life on the Left, so that the Seine to me seems a sort of frontier between childhood and adult life. I remember how excited I used to get, at the age of seven, when the Metro on which I was travelling went between the stations of Concorde and Chambre des Députés, for I knew we were gliding under the river. The Metro station names themselves were full of suggestions: 'Porte des Lilas' evoked a bunch of flowers; 'Blanche' a pretty little girl; 'Muette' a mute about whom I worried, though I was convinced she would recover her speech; I longed to experience 'Gaité' and 'Plaisance'. Gradually I became disillusioned by the reality, and shifted my dreams to far-off places, like Baghdad, Singapore and Hong Kong. Home again now after many journeys, I like to explore Paris, on foot or from the vantage-point of a bus, and go on nostalgic trips through the city which cross and re-cross those made by Hervé Champollion. I like to pause in the middle of the Pont Alexandre III, with its florid streetlamps, facing the Grand Palais as its glass roof reflects the sky. In one direction I have the lacy Eiffel Tower, the only handsome monument to have come out of the second half of the nineteenth century. In the other direction is a tangle of history, of buildings begun by Philippe-Auguste in the late twelfth century and completed by Napoleon III in the nineteenth. All along the river, masses of stone wrought by the hand of taste or of faith lay a trap for you, entice you to linger, through sunset, until darkness has fallen. I suspect it was thus that Hervé Champollion found some of his finest images of Paris.

Those who spend a few days in the city carry away memories of particular things – a palace, an alley, a restaurant, a quai, a scent, a song or a cloudburst. Those who live there all their lives run the risk of becoming blind to it. When you know something 'by heart' your heart is no longer involved in the process. It is only when the Sainte-Chapelle is struck by a ray of sun bursting forth from a dark, stormy sky that you really notice that old, familiar friend. It is one of the merits of Hervé Champollion's photographs that he gives the known the excitement and freshness of the completely new.

Every now and again, for a day, the settled inhabitant of the city should change places with a tourist. The former would no longer pursue his daily round automatically, glimpsing his surroundings only by chance as he passed: he would choose a particular location, walk about there, and observe it at a given hour of the day or night. Jean Giraudoux always used to arrange to meet people late in the afternoon in the Place de l'Alma, at a café terrace from which he maintained that one saw the finest sunsets in the Ile de France. He also used to stand, unobserved, in the Place de Furstemberg, where as soon as three passers-by happened to coincide he felt he was watching a play. My own *penchant* is to go to that temple of the flesh, the Musée Rodin. Here, in a house surrounded by roses, naked bodies embrace. Guidebook in hand, visitors to the museum keep respectfully cool in the face of an orgy of kisses and caresses caught for all eternity in stone and bronze. Sometimes I hesitate before entering my harem, where thighs and breasts await me with submissive pride. After I have left the museum, I go on for a time seeing things with the eyes of an outsider, and as I admire the ornate wrought-iron balconies of neighbouring houses I make plans for a return visit, as though that would require me to come from some distant quarter of the world.

The tourist, on the other hand, should reject the itineraries recommended by guidebooks and follow his nose. Away from famous monuments and well-trodden sites he will come to understand the ordinary life that sustains this enormous city, which is after all not just a collection of monuments but a place of living men. Chance-driven, the wanderer might find himself in the Boulevard Haussmann, where suddenly there are far more people in the street, and it is hard to avoid actually bumping into someone on your way to a crossing, where little armies of pedestrians wait for the light to change. Petrol fumes cloud the air. The Gare Saint-Lazare looms like a battleship out of the mist, escorted by the two great brightly-lit cargo vessels of the big department stores, Printemps and the Galeries Lafayette, which are themselves surrounded by lesser craft in the form of automobiles, moving as slowly as ice-floes. The sound of the city is an aural blur from which no individual note of motor or voice stands out. Illuminated advertisements twitch, multicoloured, on almost every building. In winter the moisture-laden sky is tinted pink with their reflections. On his way back, this traveller without a compass might happen upon something mentioned in his guidebook – perhaps the Place des Victoires, that circular setting for the Sun King, where the concave façades on a bright day reflect the sun's rays back onto the central statue. This is the perfect embodiment of French Classicism, of taste at its most elevated. And perhaps the tourist who has stumbled unintentionally into the Place des Victoires may be stimulated to make his way more purposefully to the other royal squares, to the faceted Place Vendôme, to the Place de la Concorde above which the sky seems immense, or to the Place des Vosges, the only one with lawn and trees. But as soon as he has taken a step or two away from these grand ensembles, he will find his mood changed as he wanders through a maze of smaller streets. There he may skirt butchers' shops with whole ox carcasses hanging alarmingly within reach, sniff the rich scents of Eastern spices, and finally decide for refreshment between North African and Chinese restaurants or a little bar run by a coal merchant from Auvergne.

Like an opera, Hervé Champollion's Paris has both high drama and dazzling spectacle. Paris justifies such a treatment because of its exceptional nature. It is the most northerly city in Europe that is not 'Northern'. The ancient Celtic settlement was poised not only between Left Bank and Right Bank but between the world of the Franks and that of the Romans. Paris is the epitome of France. It is also the epitome of a whole civilization.

JACQUES LAURENT
Member of the Académie Française

The Right Bank

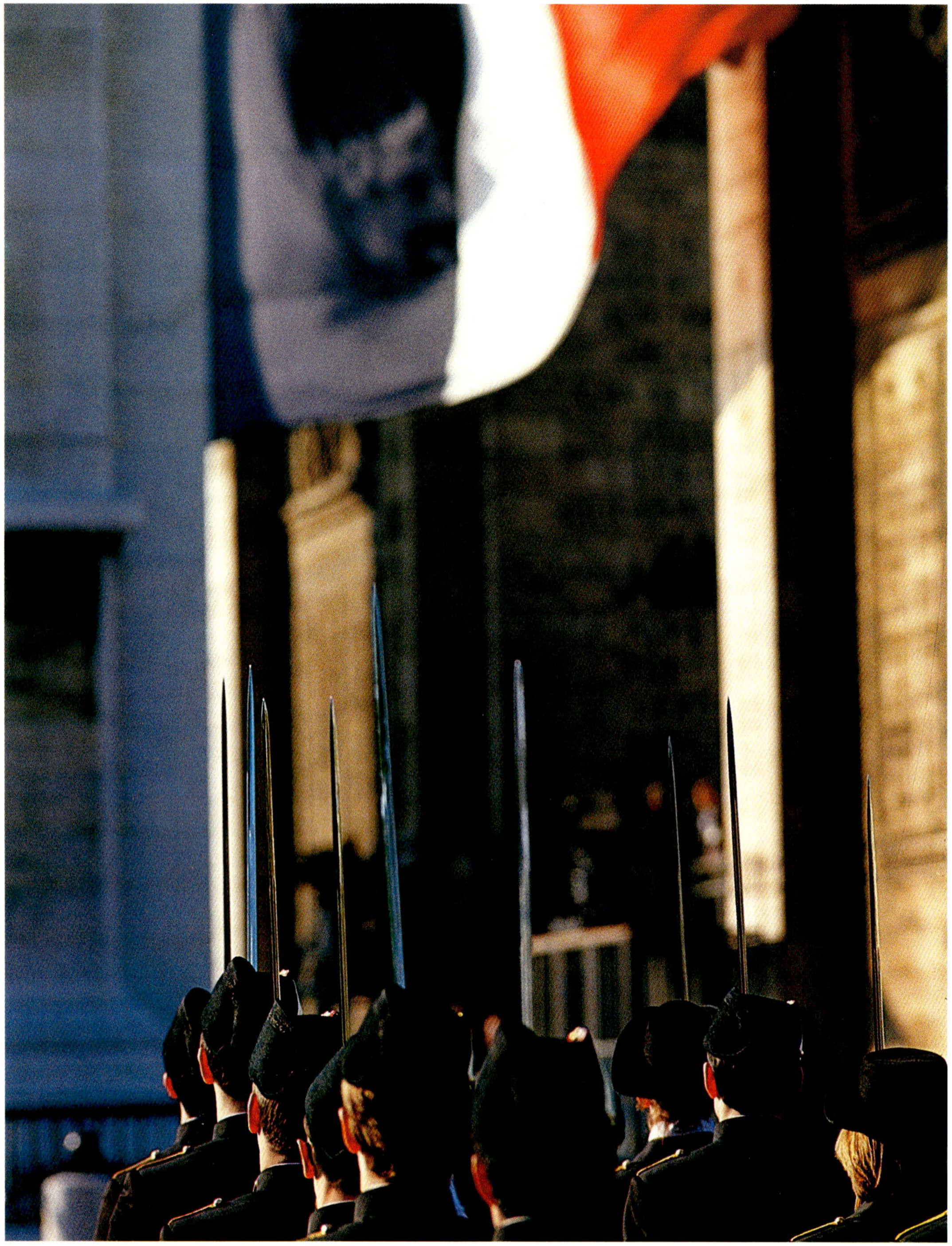

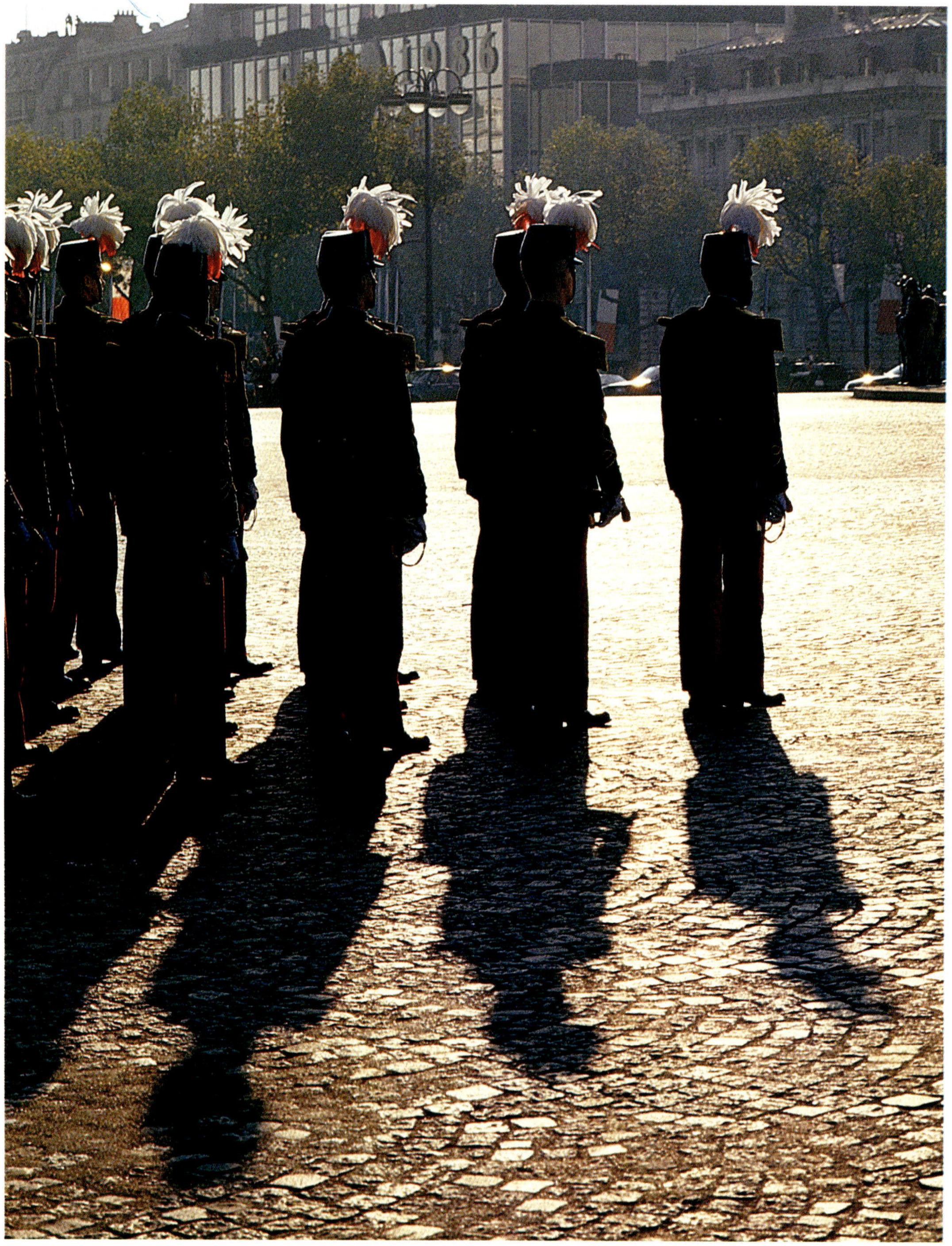

9 10

11 12

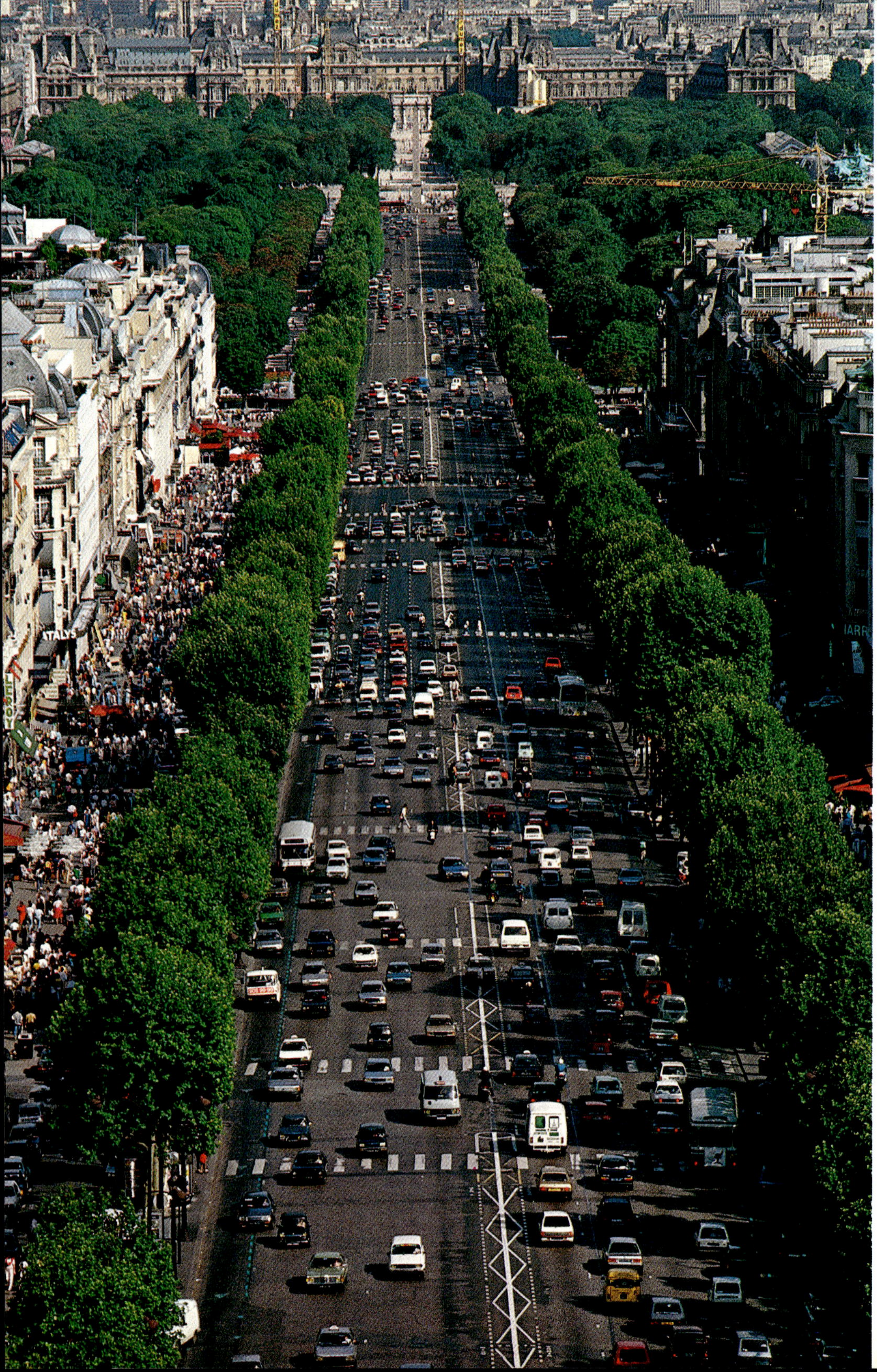

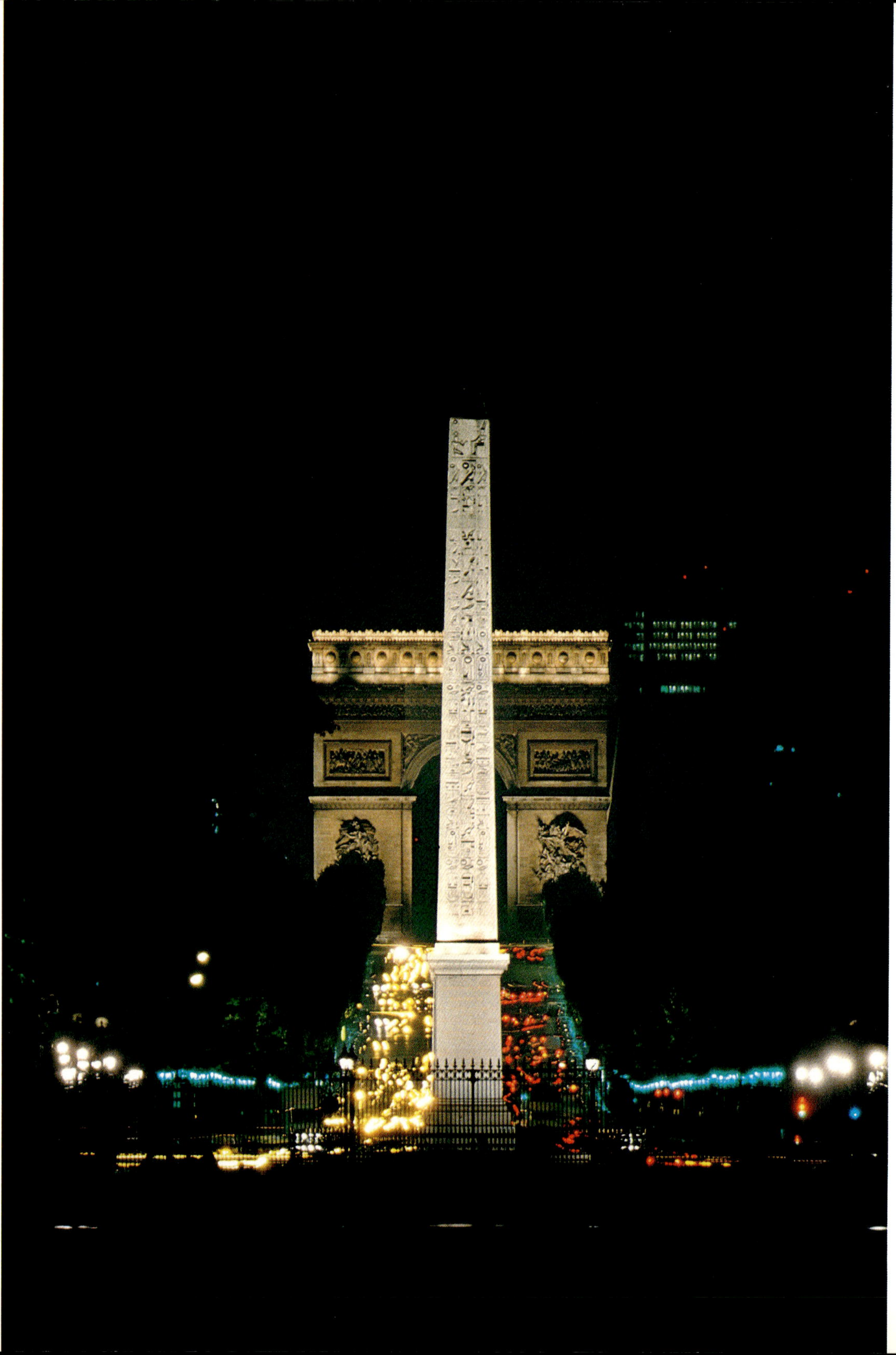

13 14 15

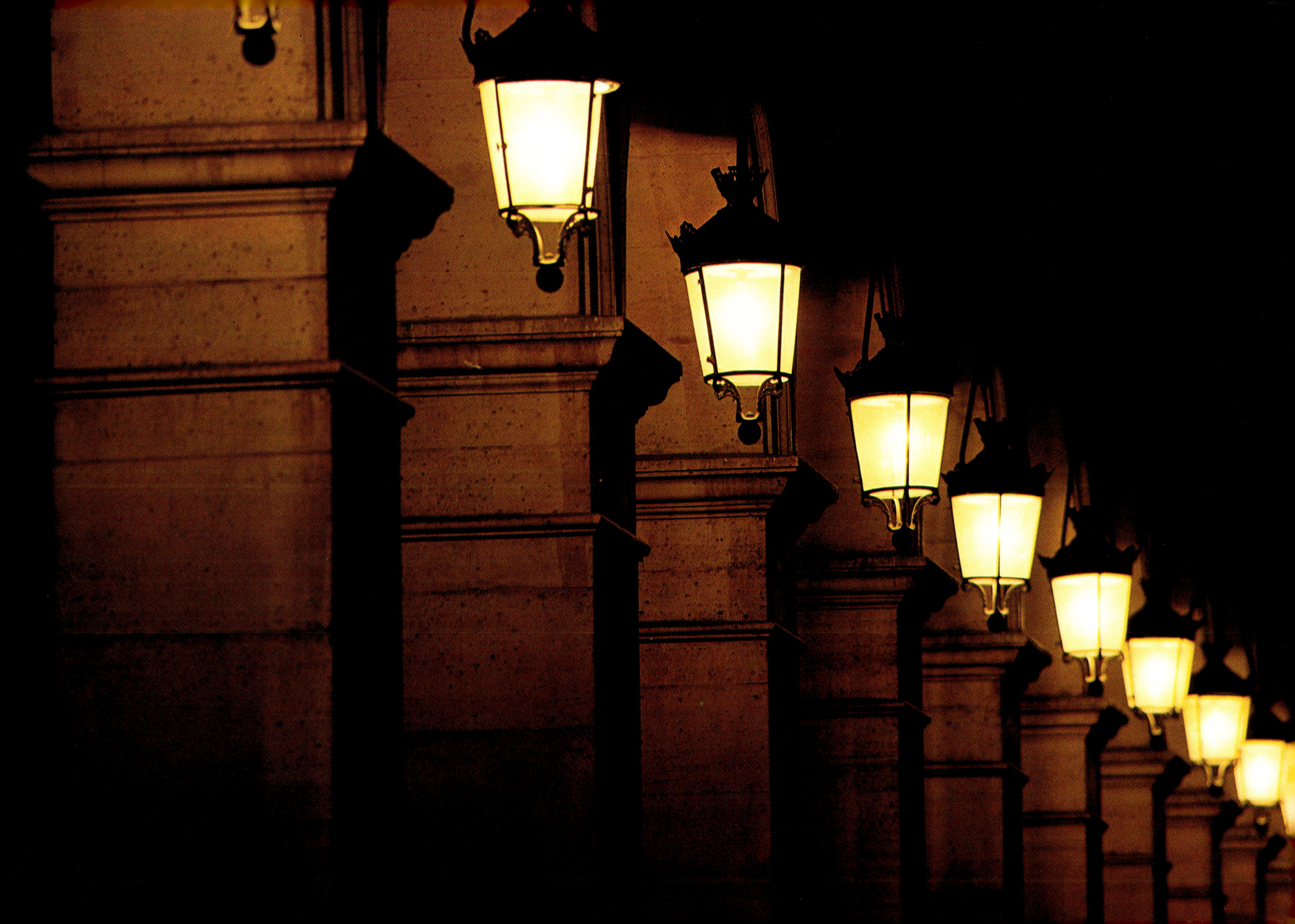

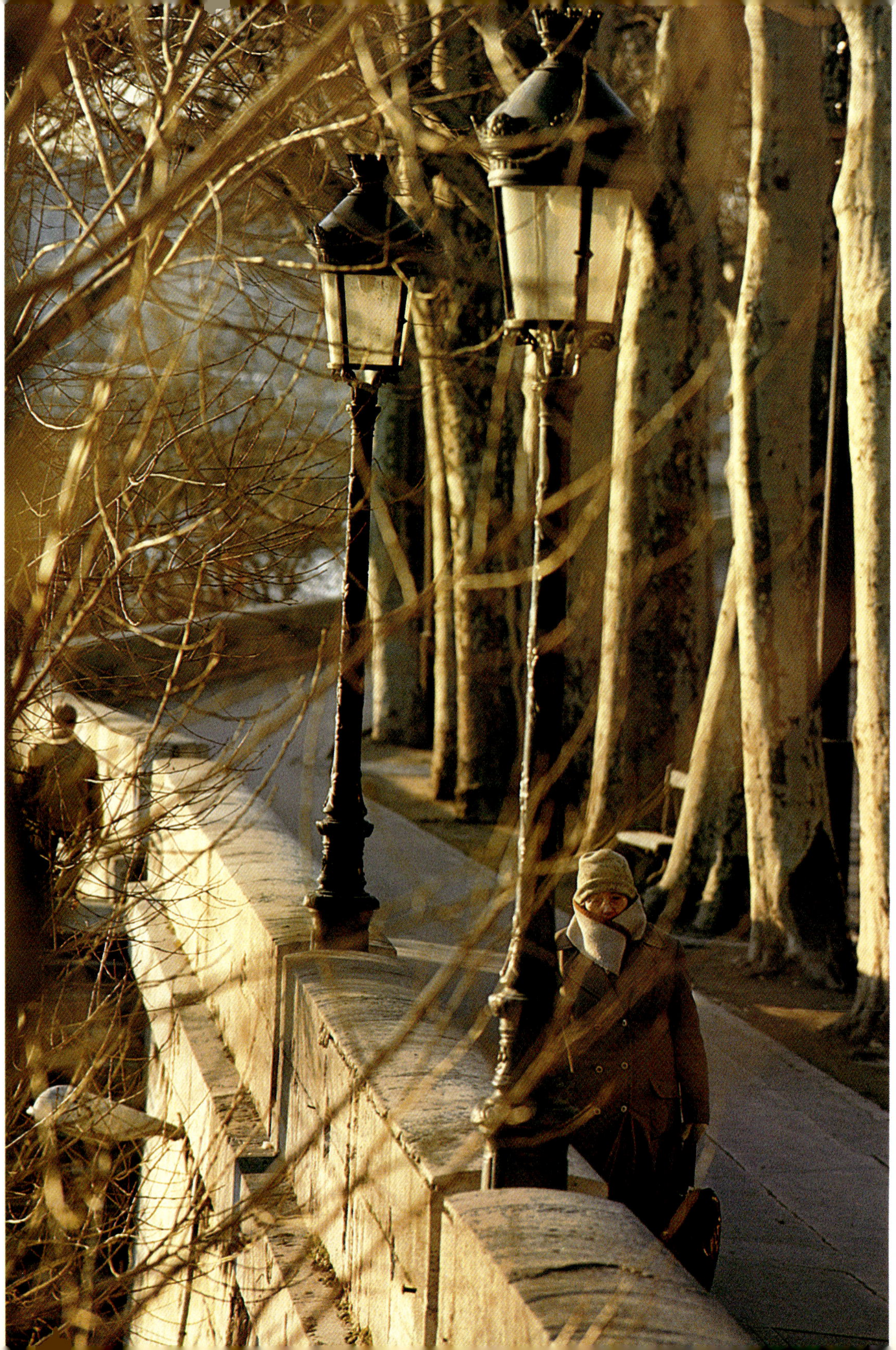

22 23

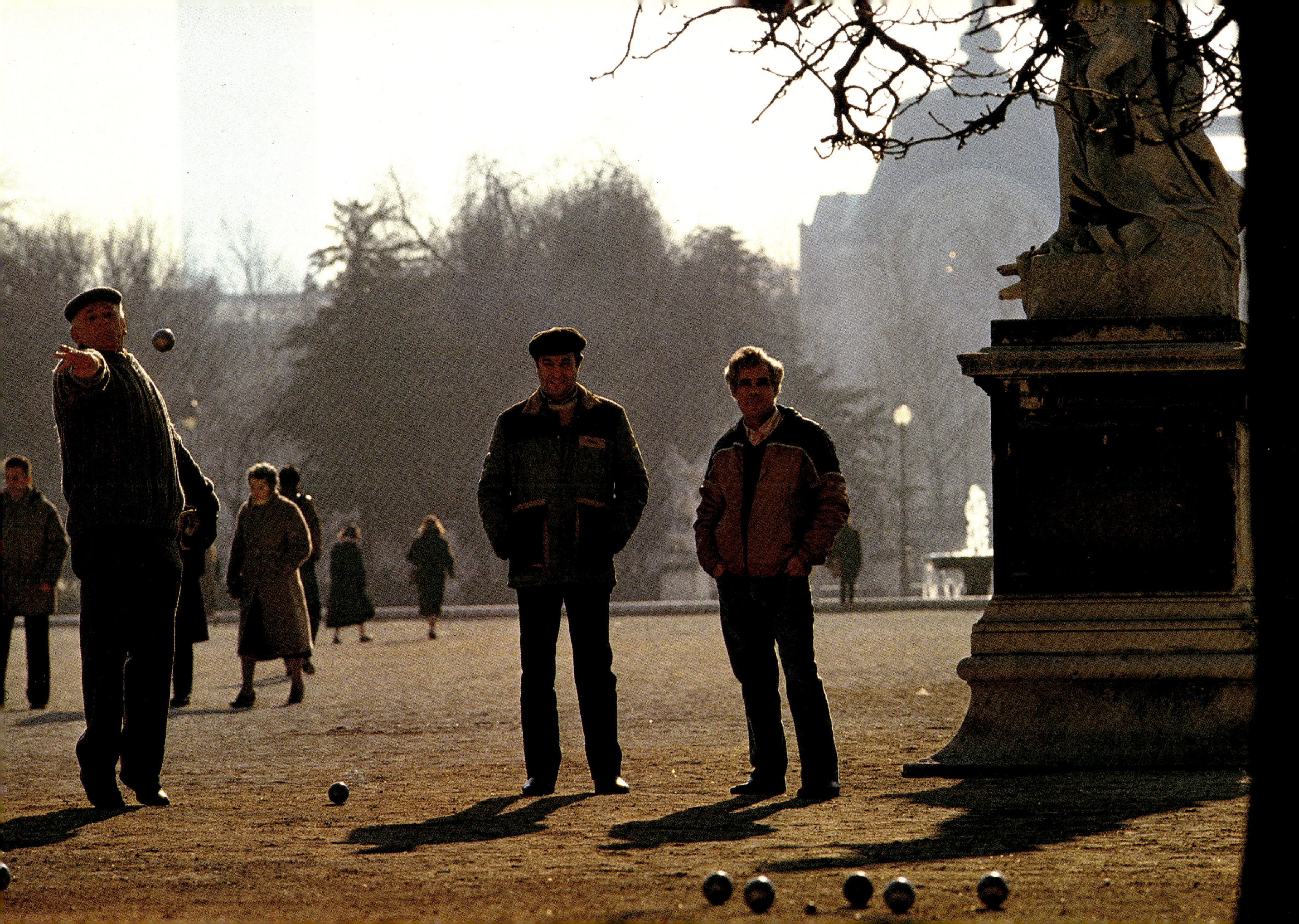

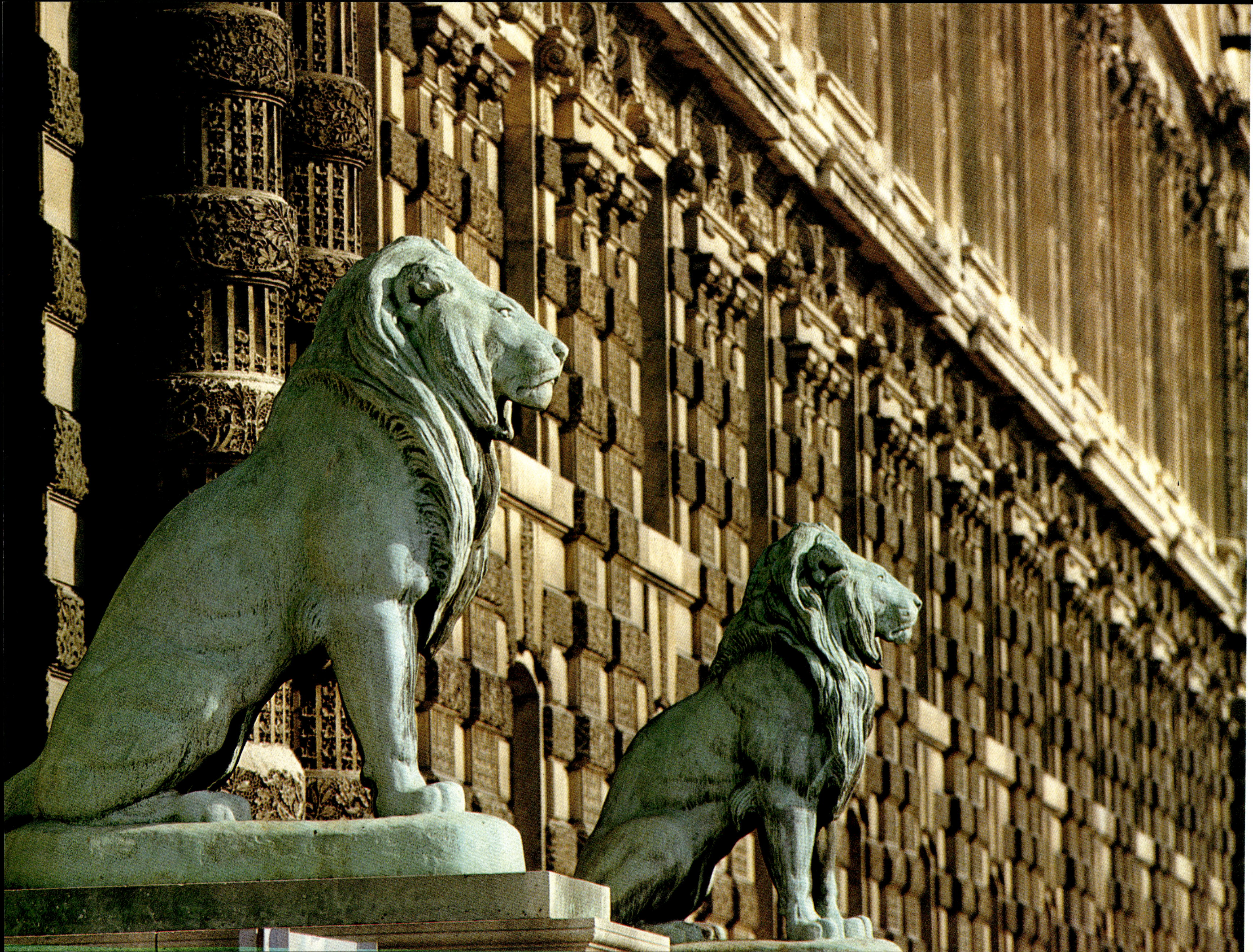

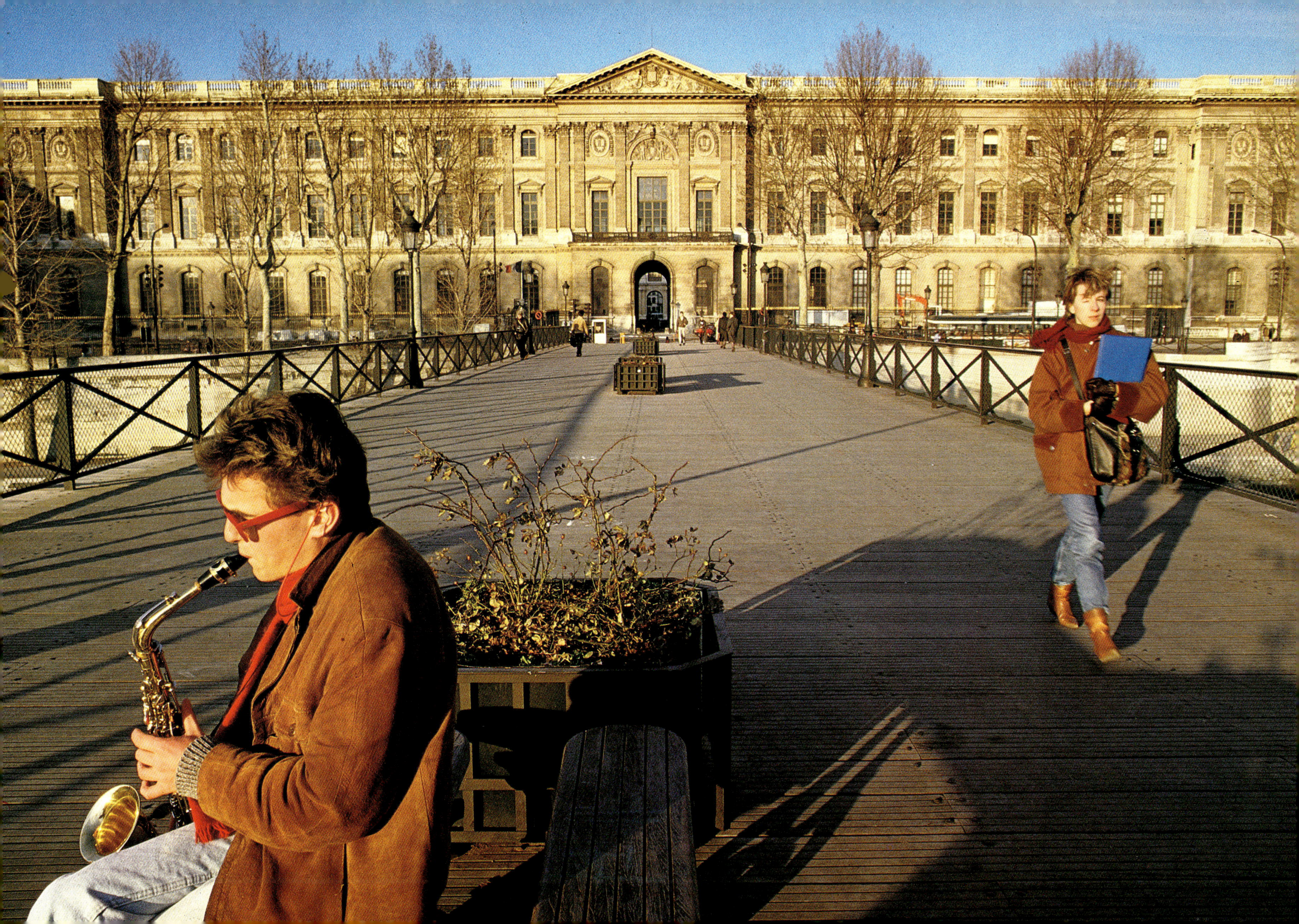

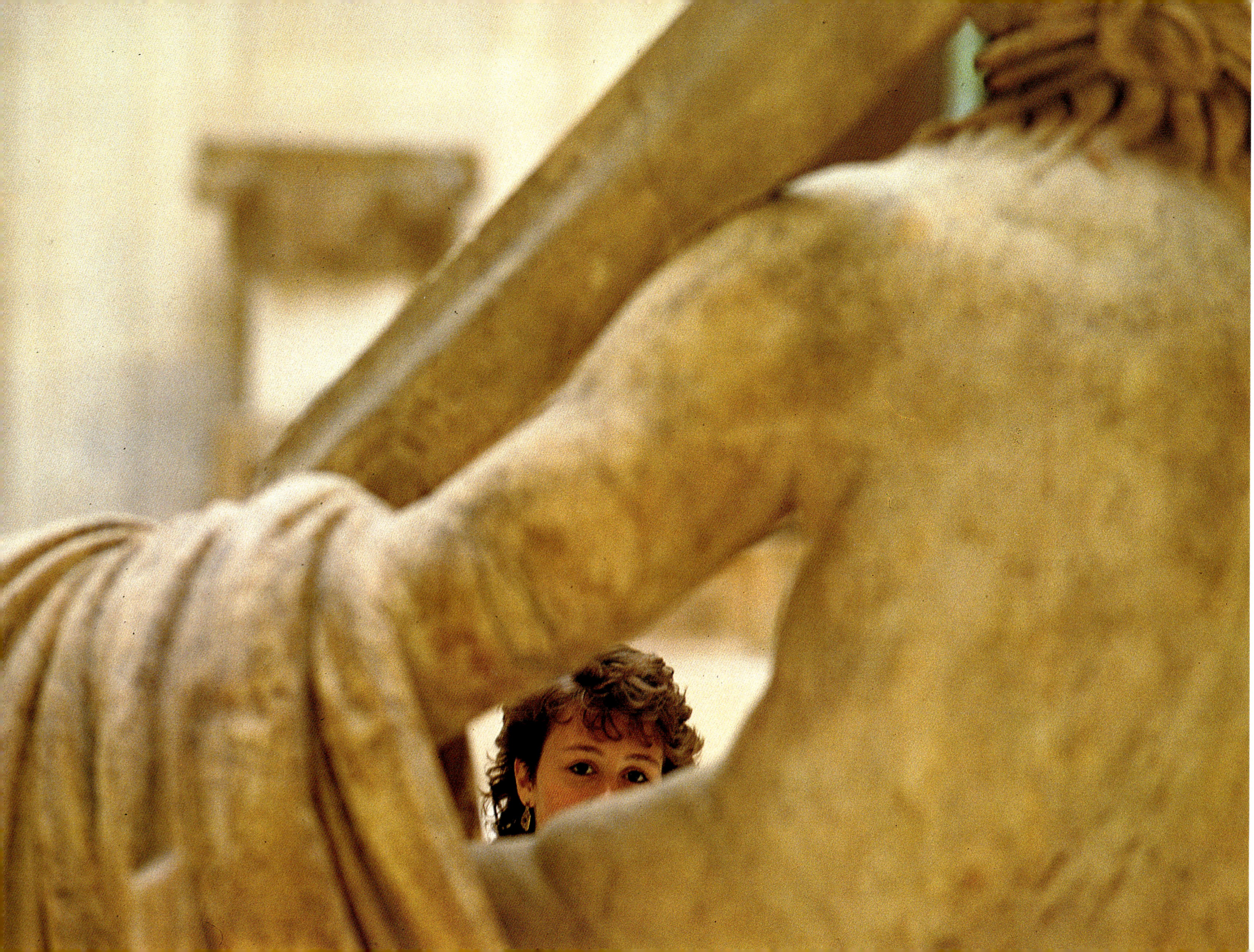

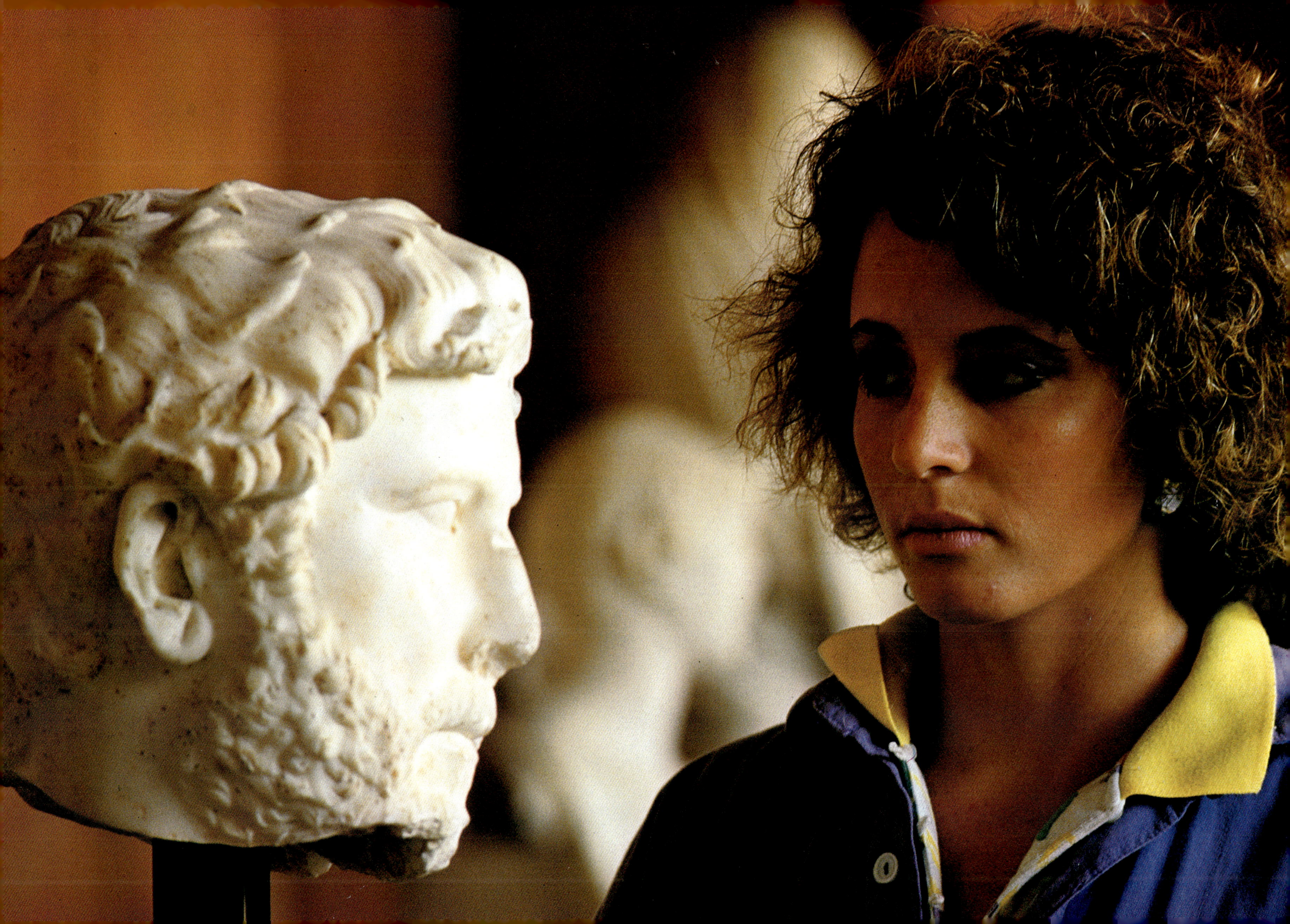

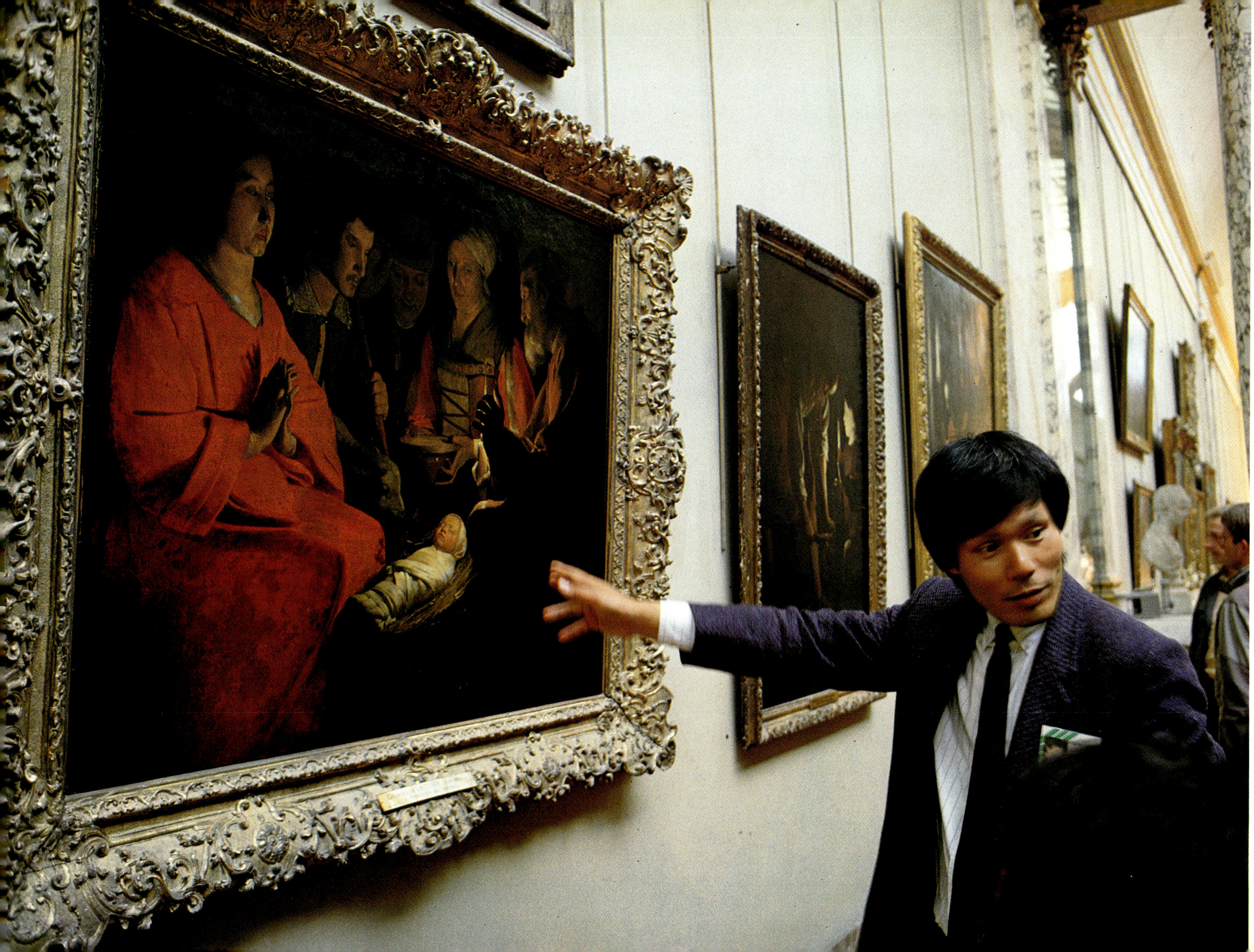

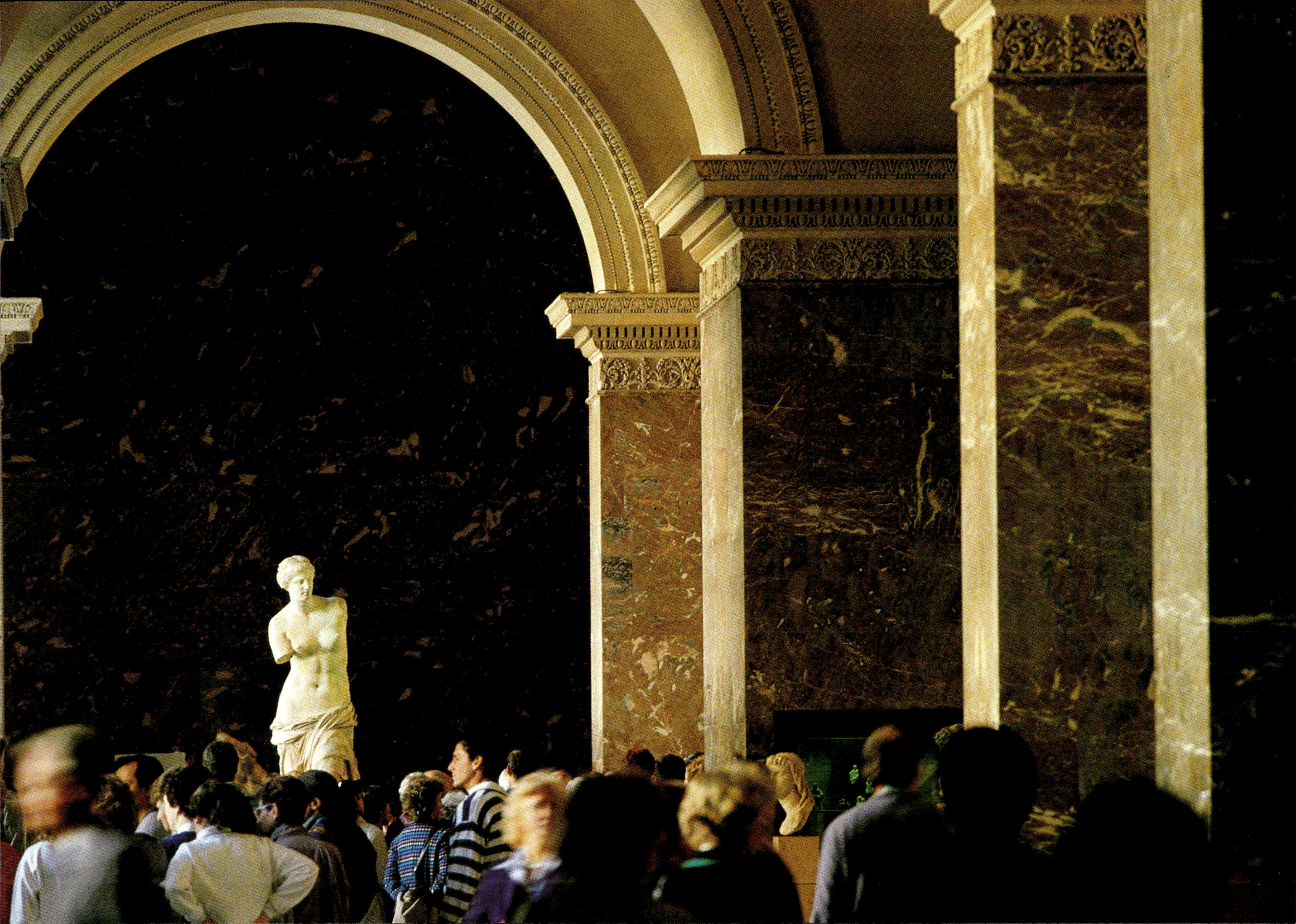

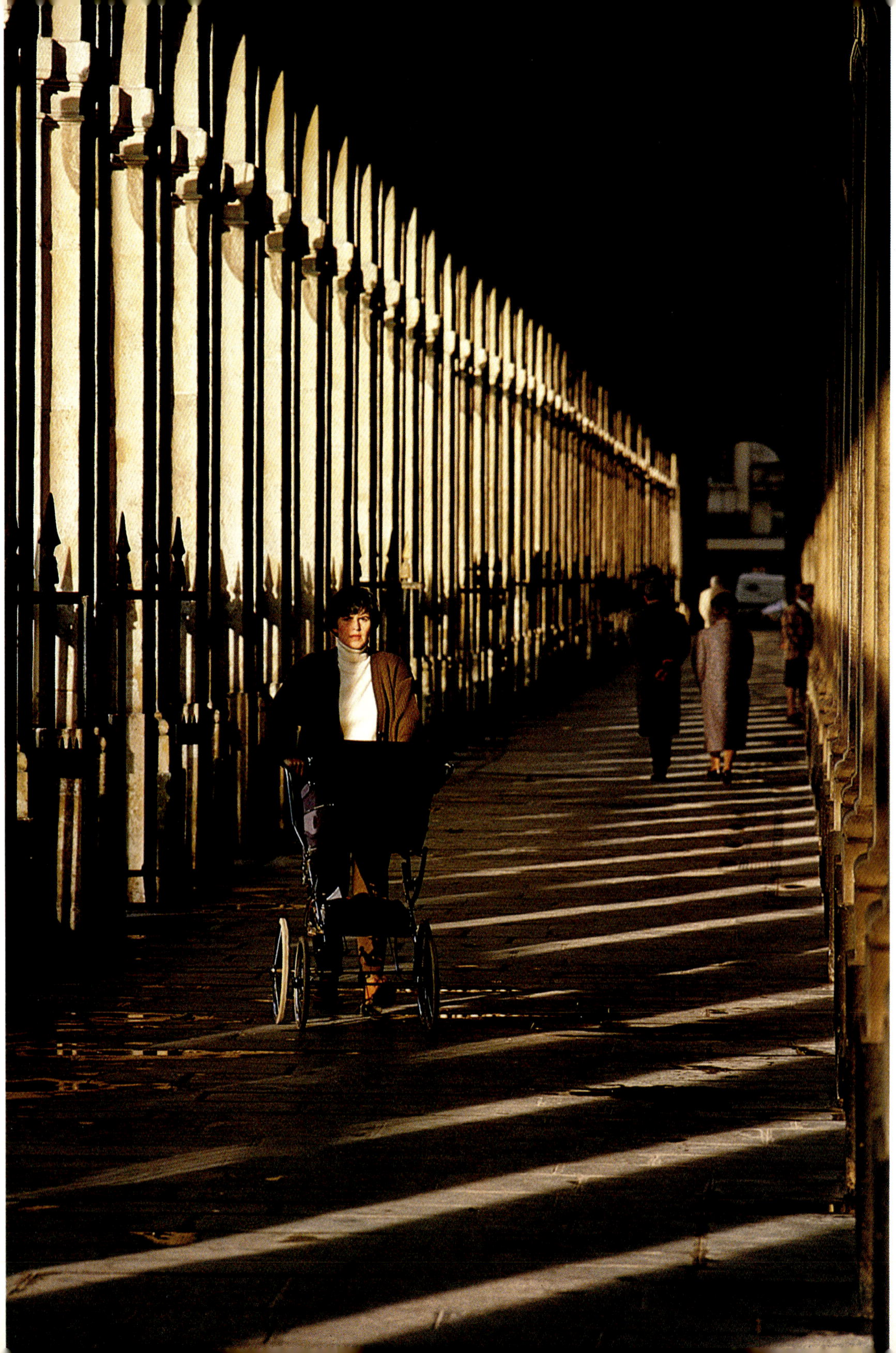

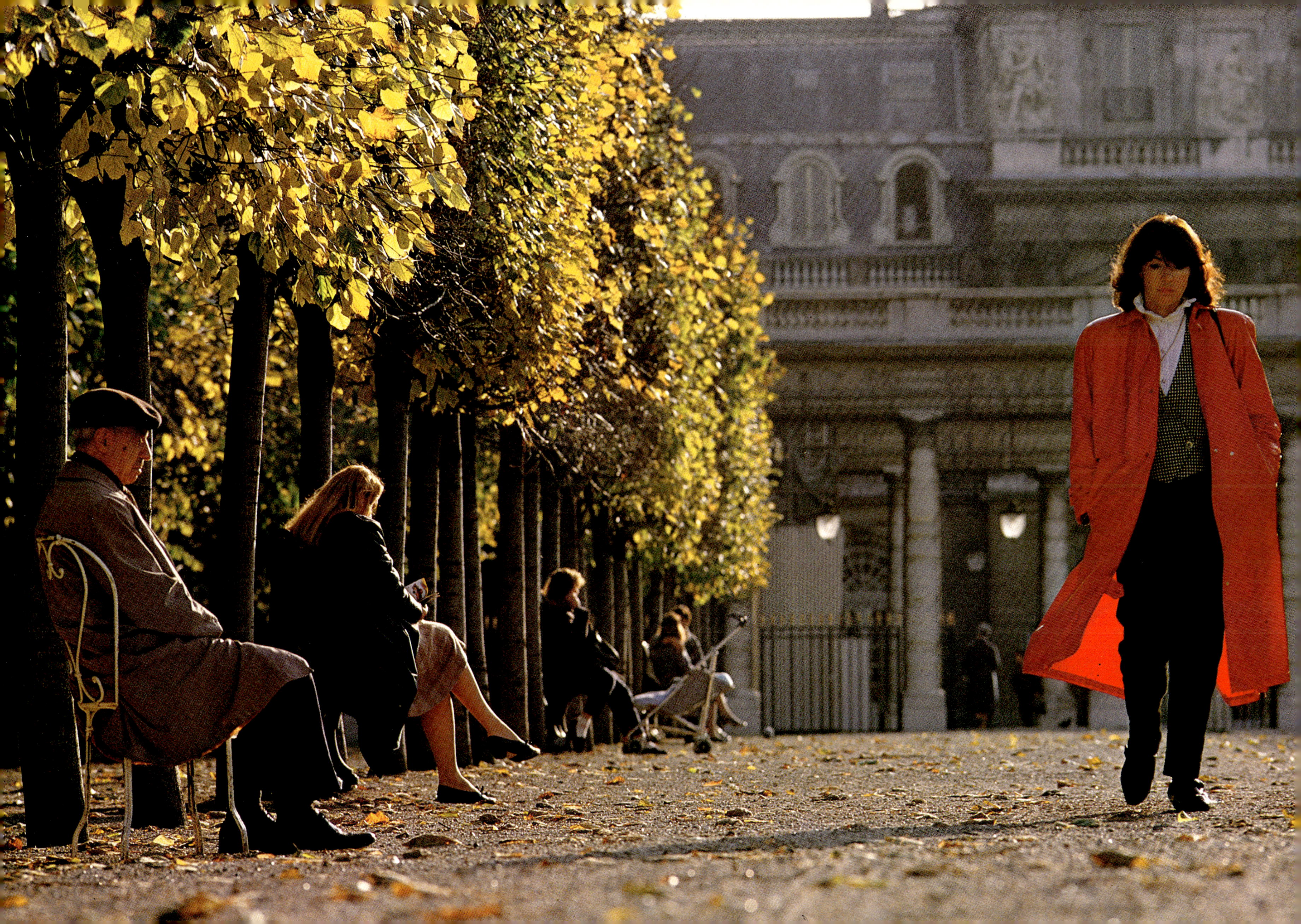

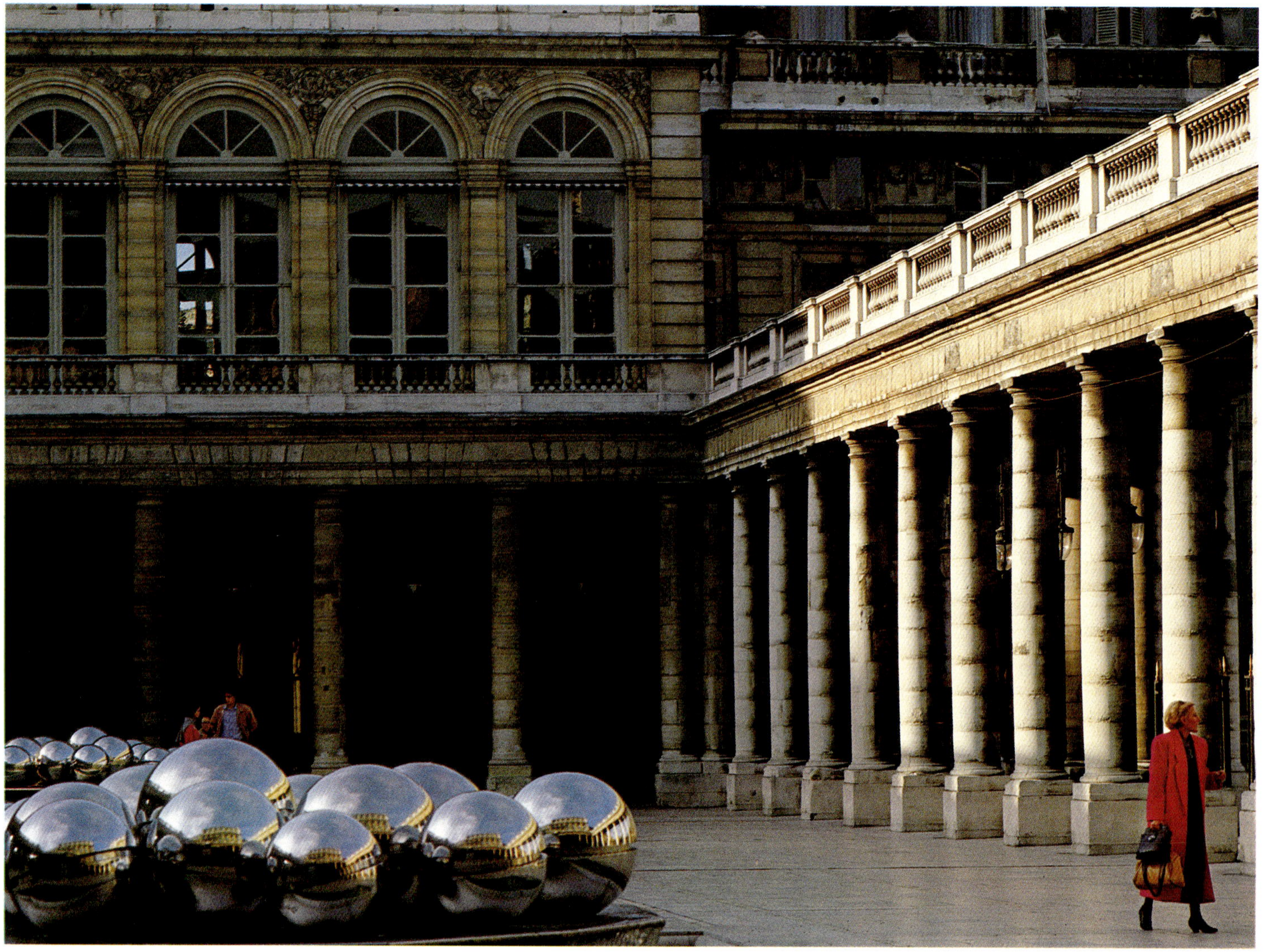

32 33

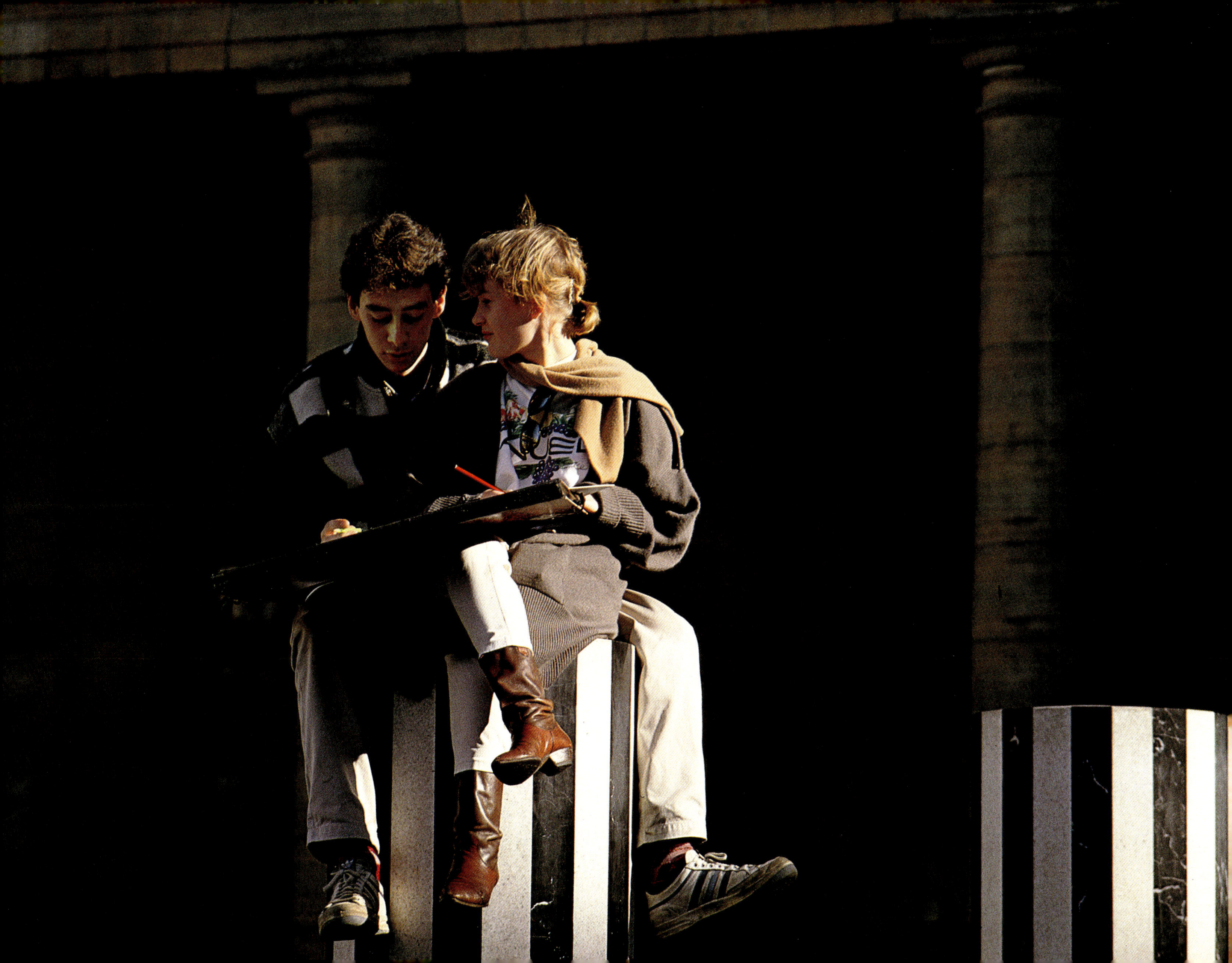

34 35

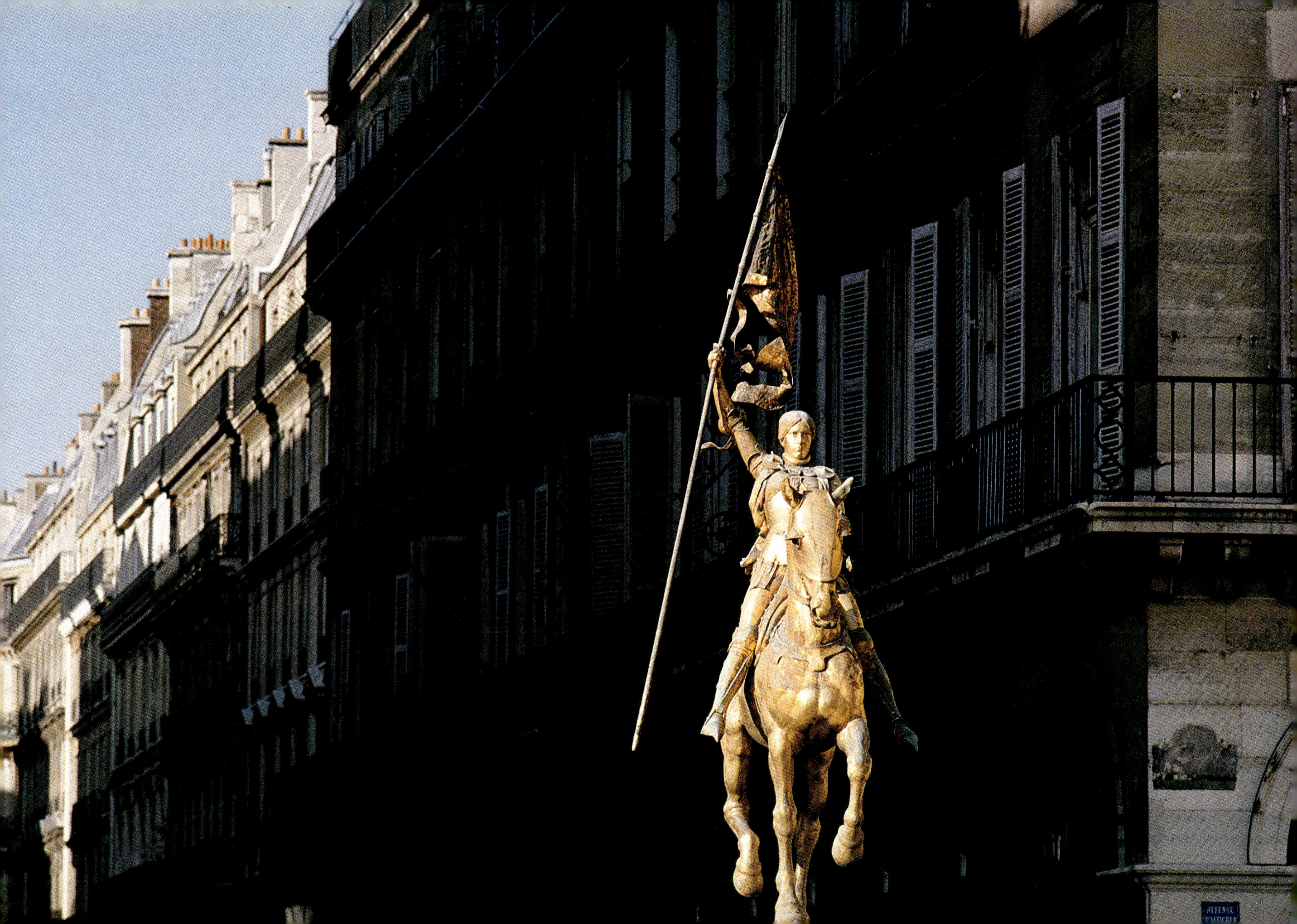

36 37

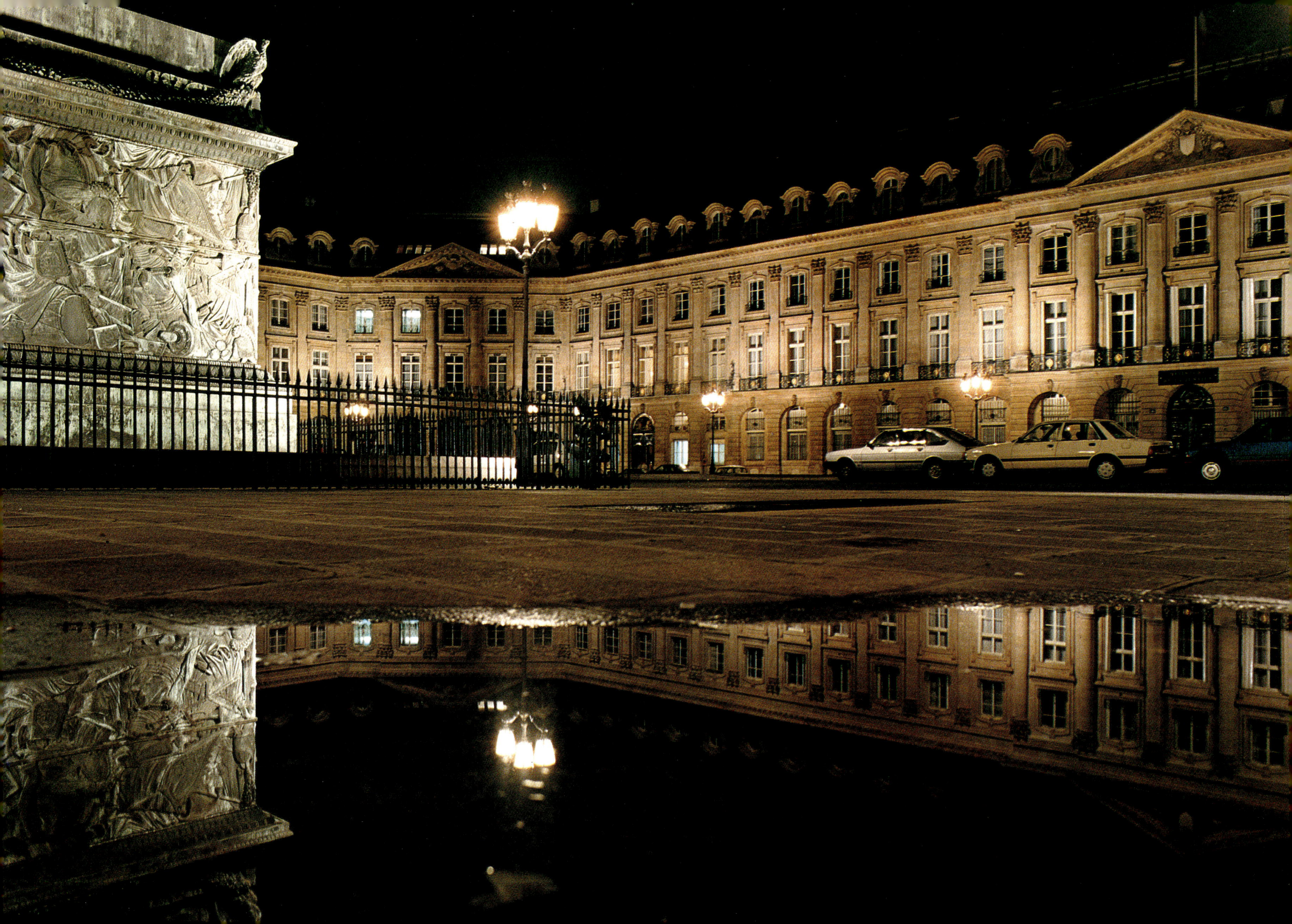

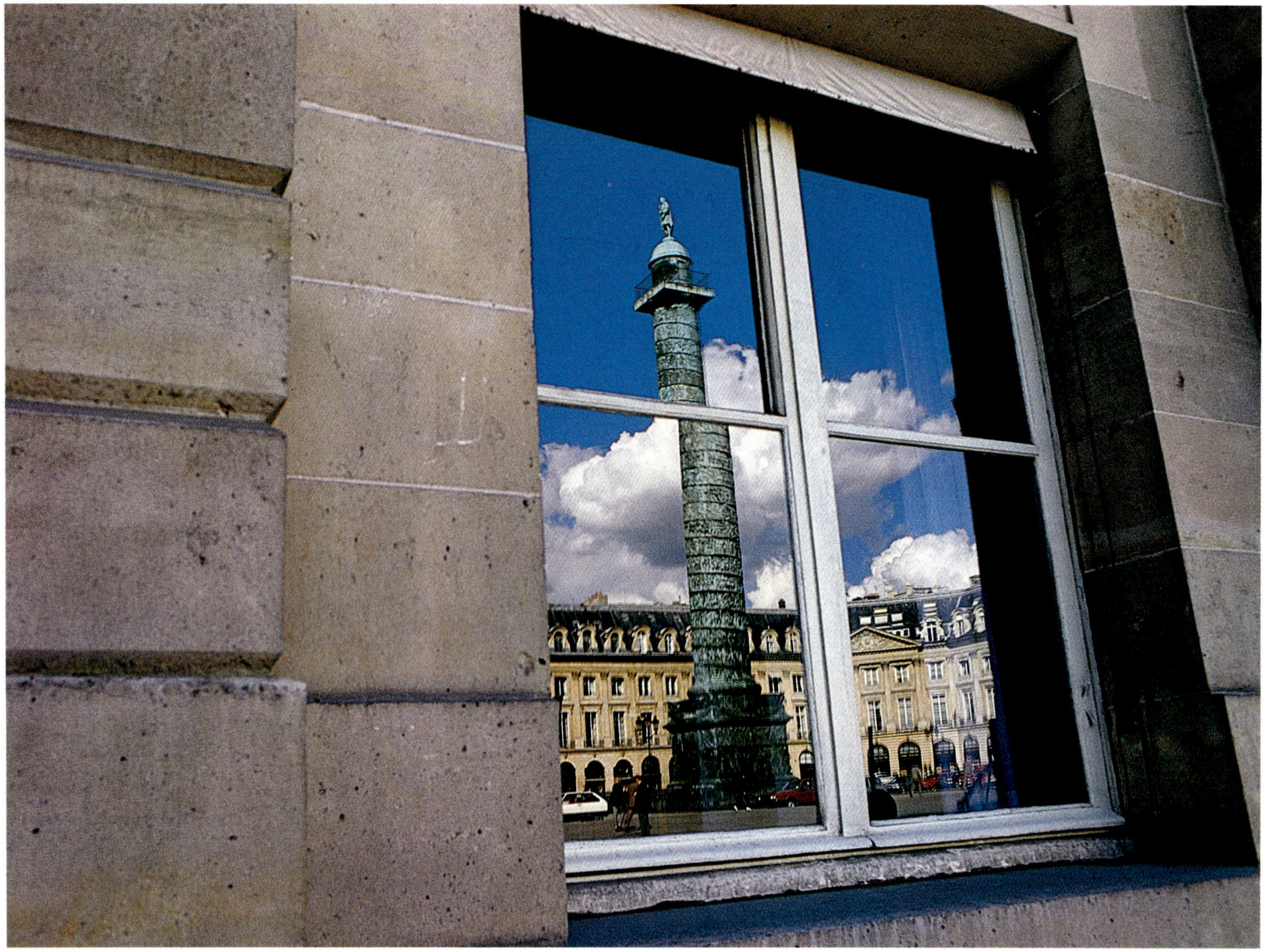

VAN CLEEF & ARPELS

la boutique

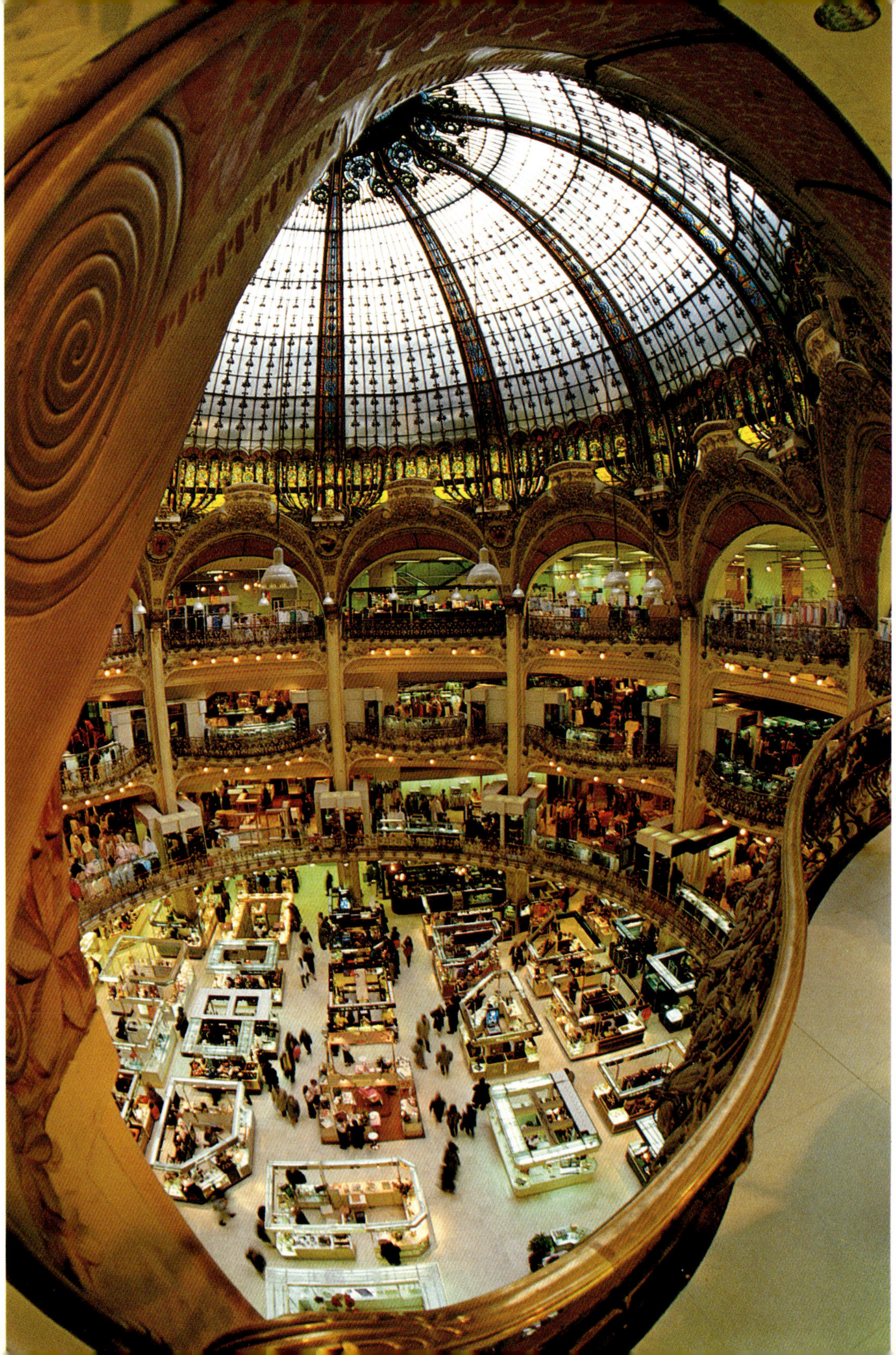

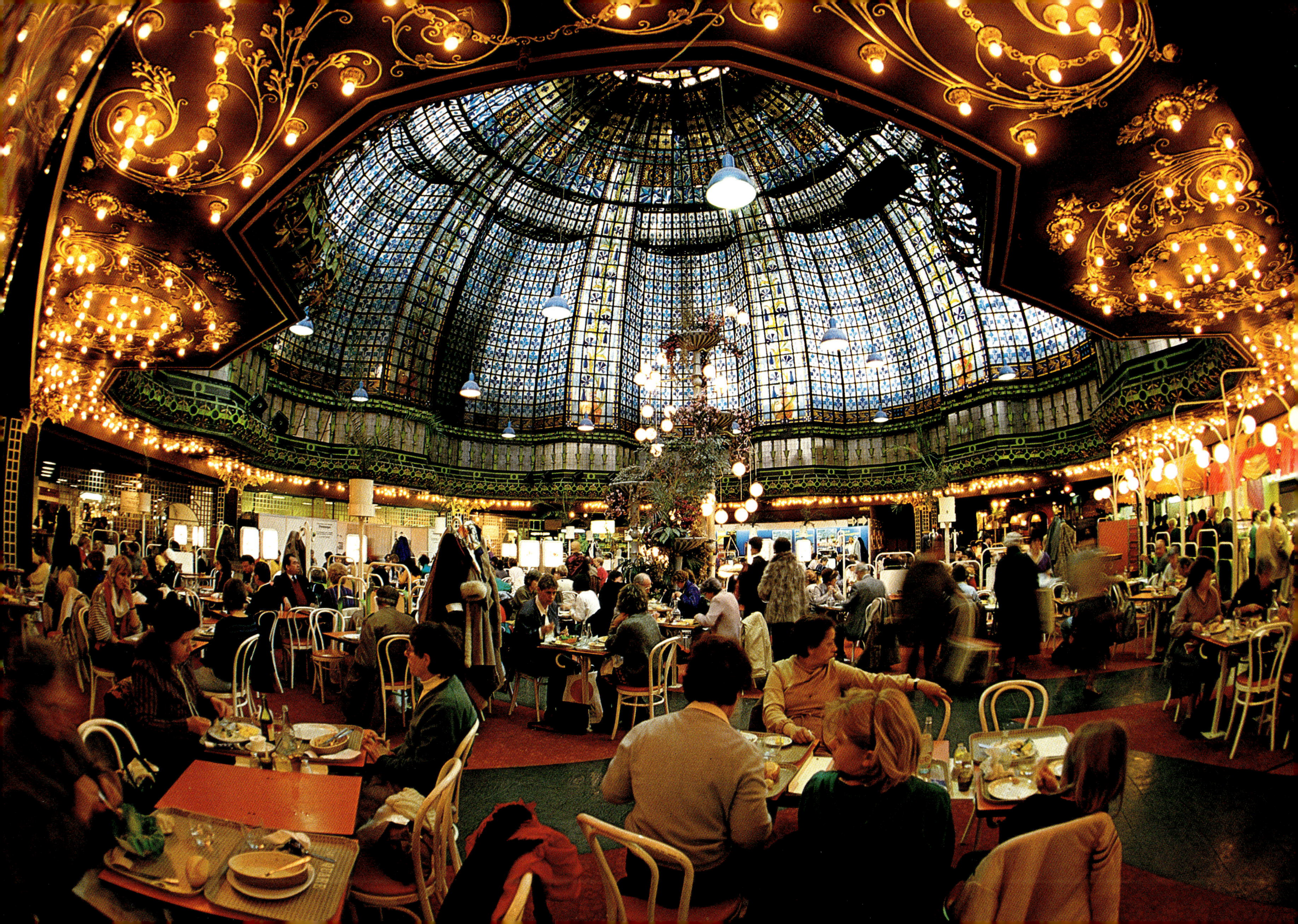

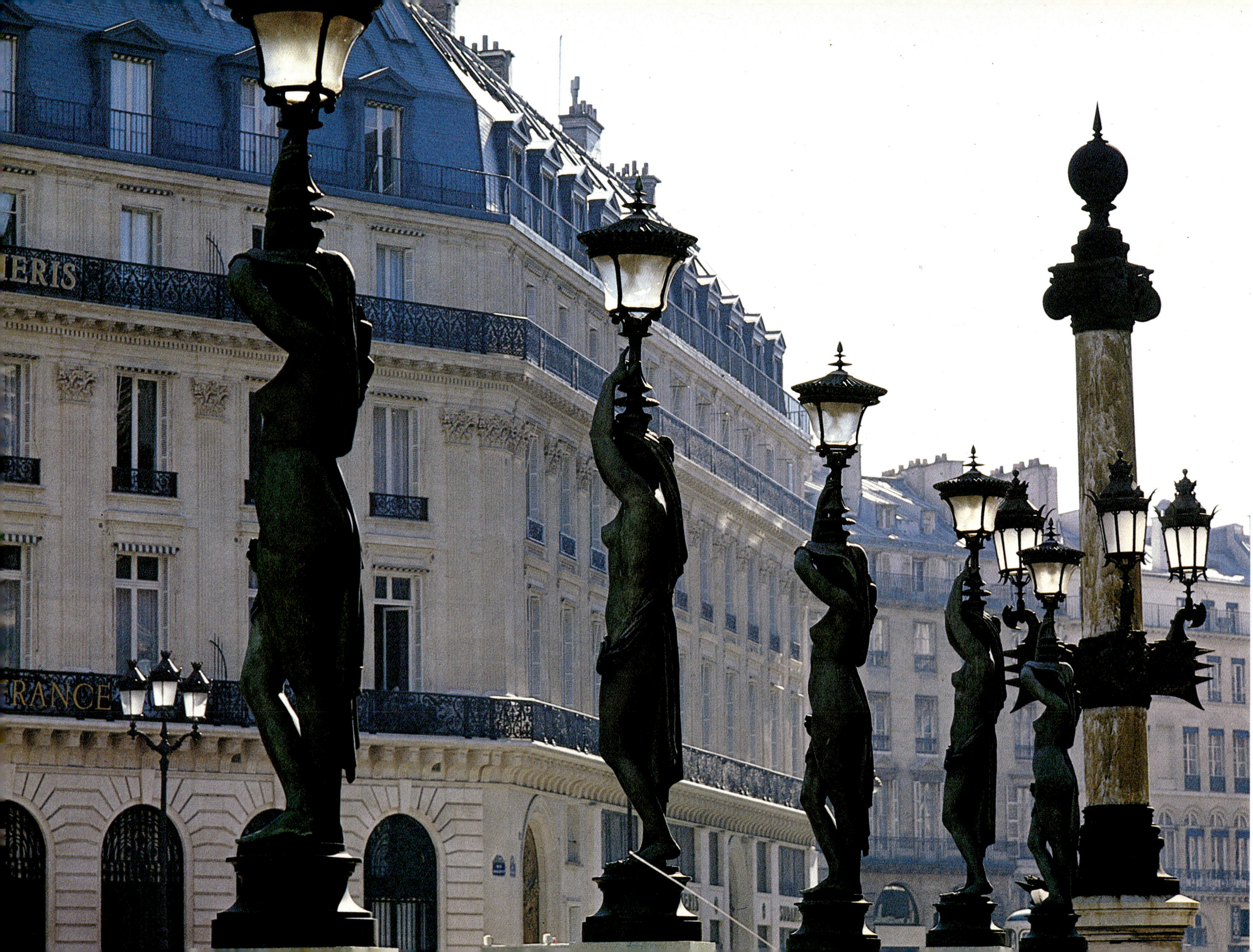
ERIS
RANCE

ACADEMIE NATIONALE DE MUSIQUE
CHOREGRAPHIE
BULGARIE
27 Pte de Vitry
shopping center
BRASSERIE
SALON DE THE
NÉFER
TI PRIX
DARTY

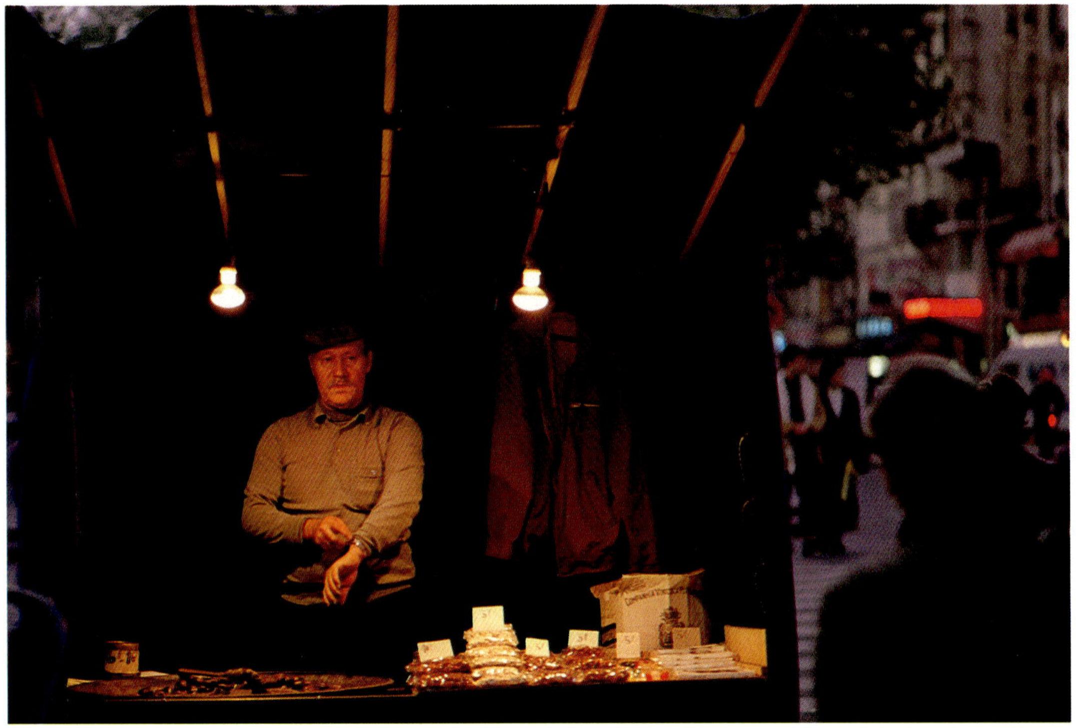

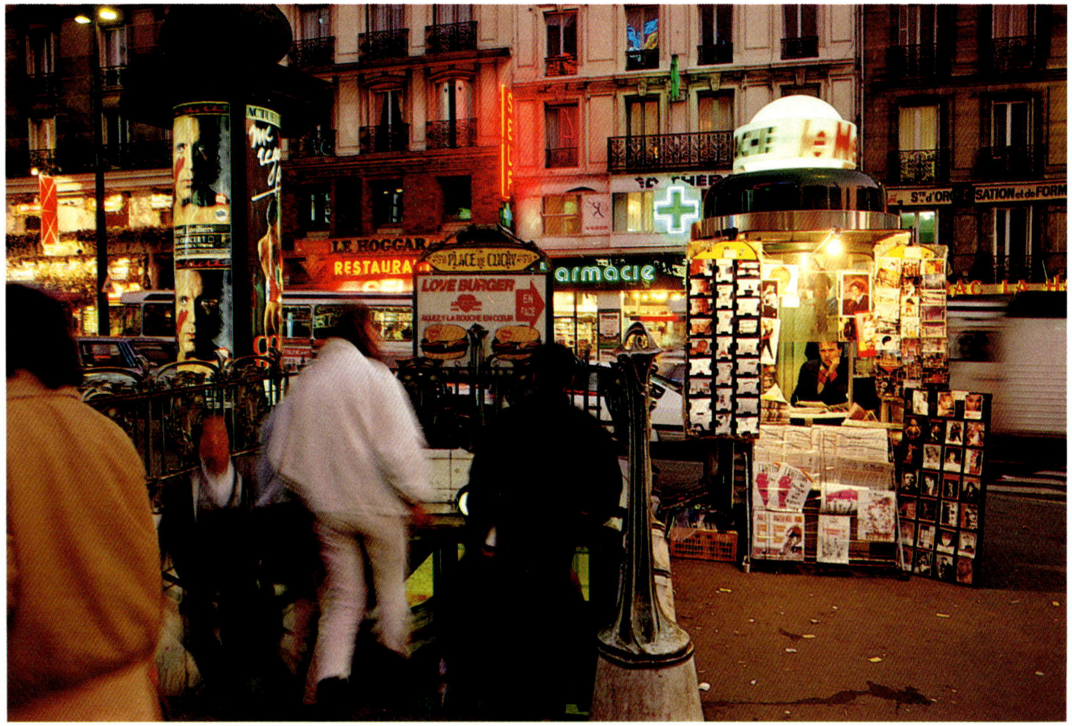

44 45 4

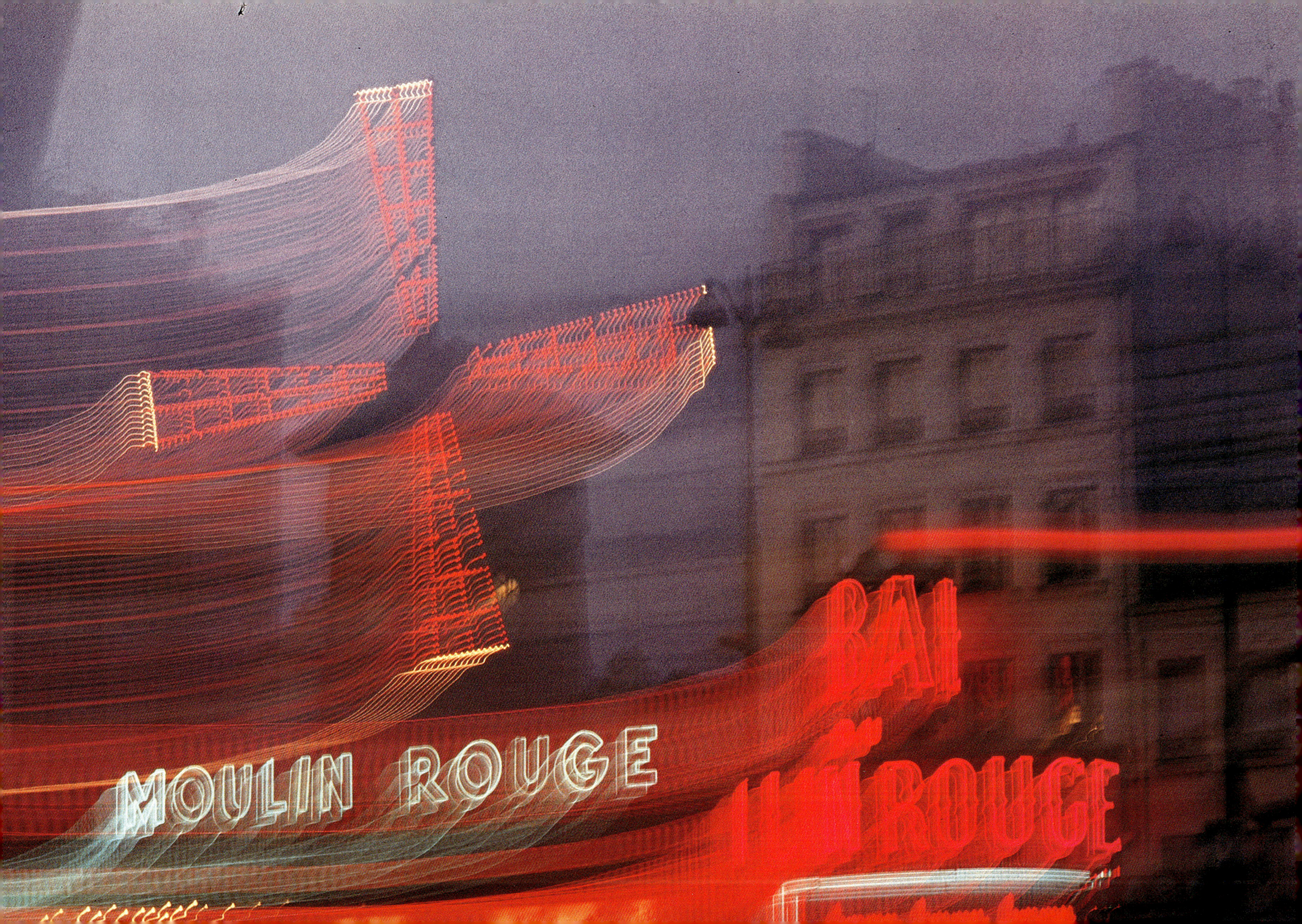
MOULIN ROUGE
ROUGE

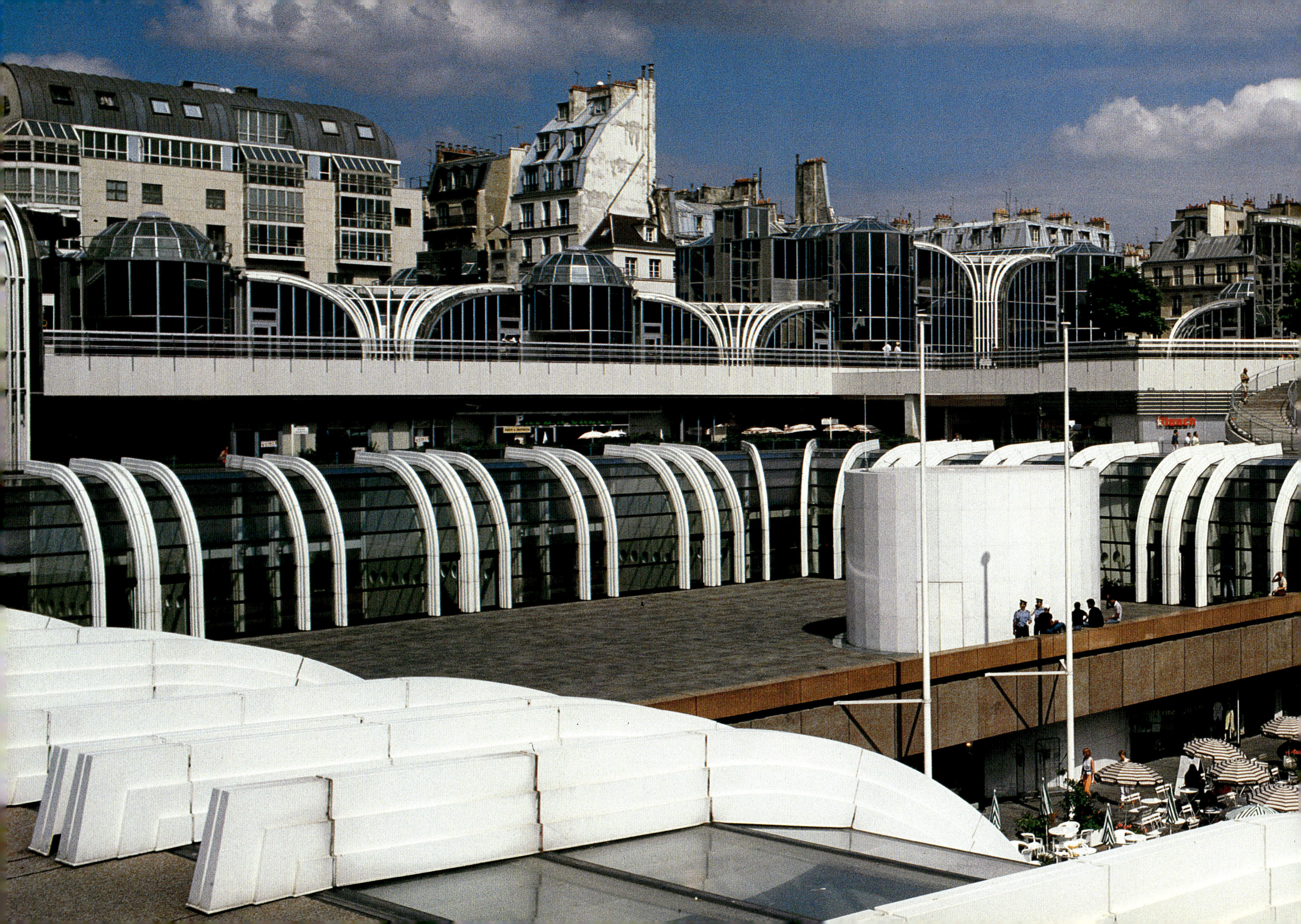

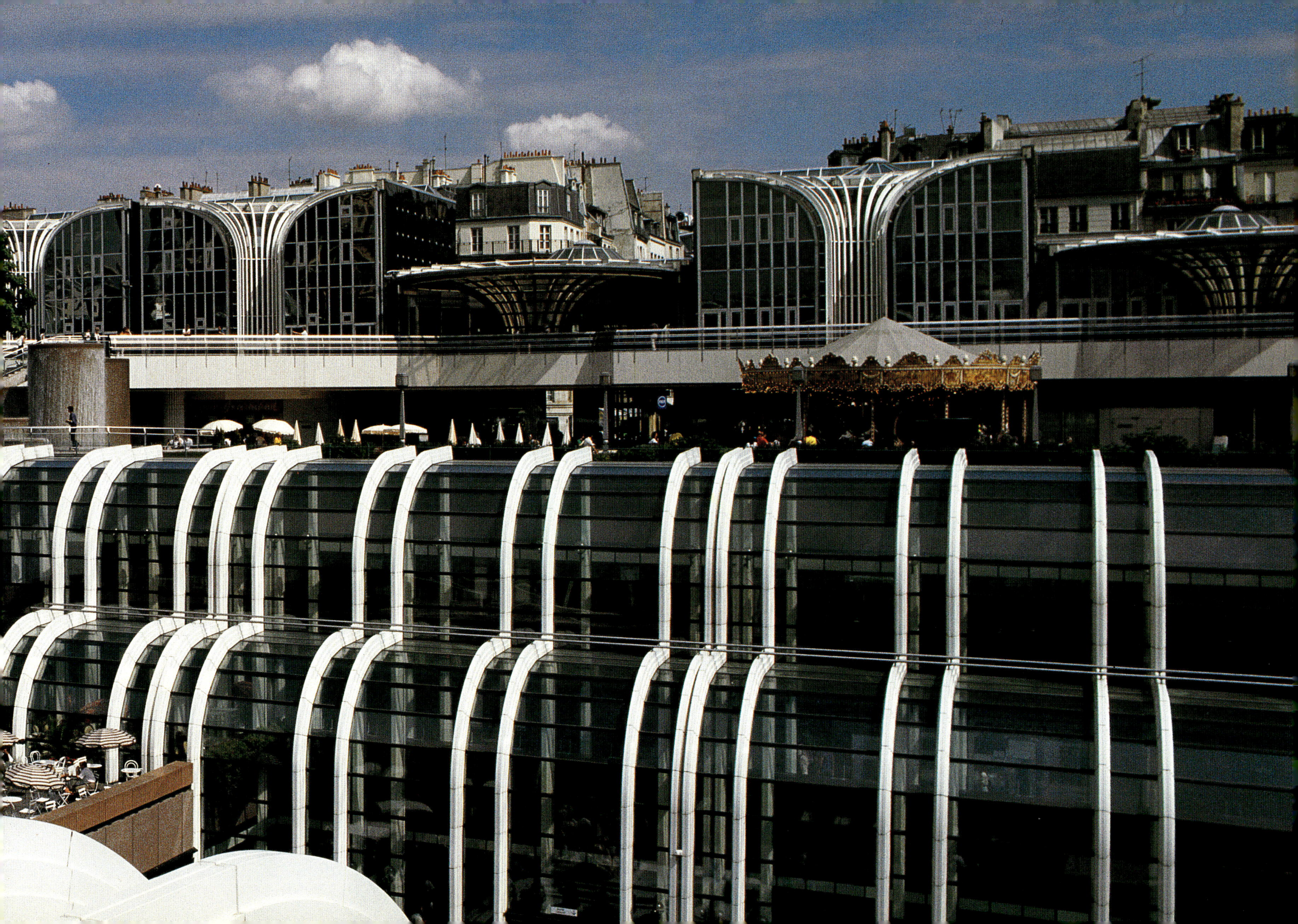

48 49

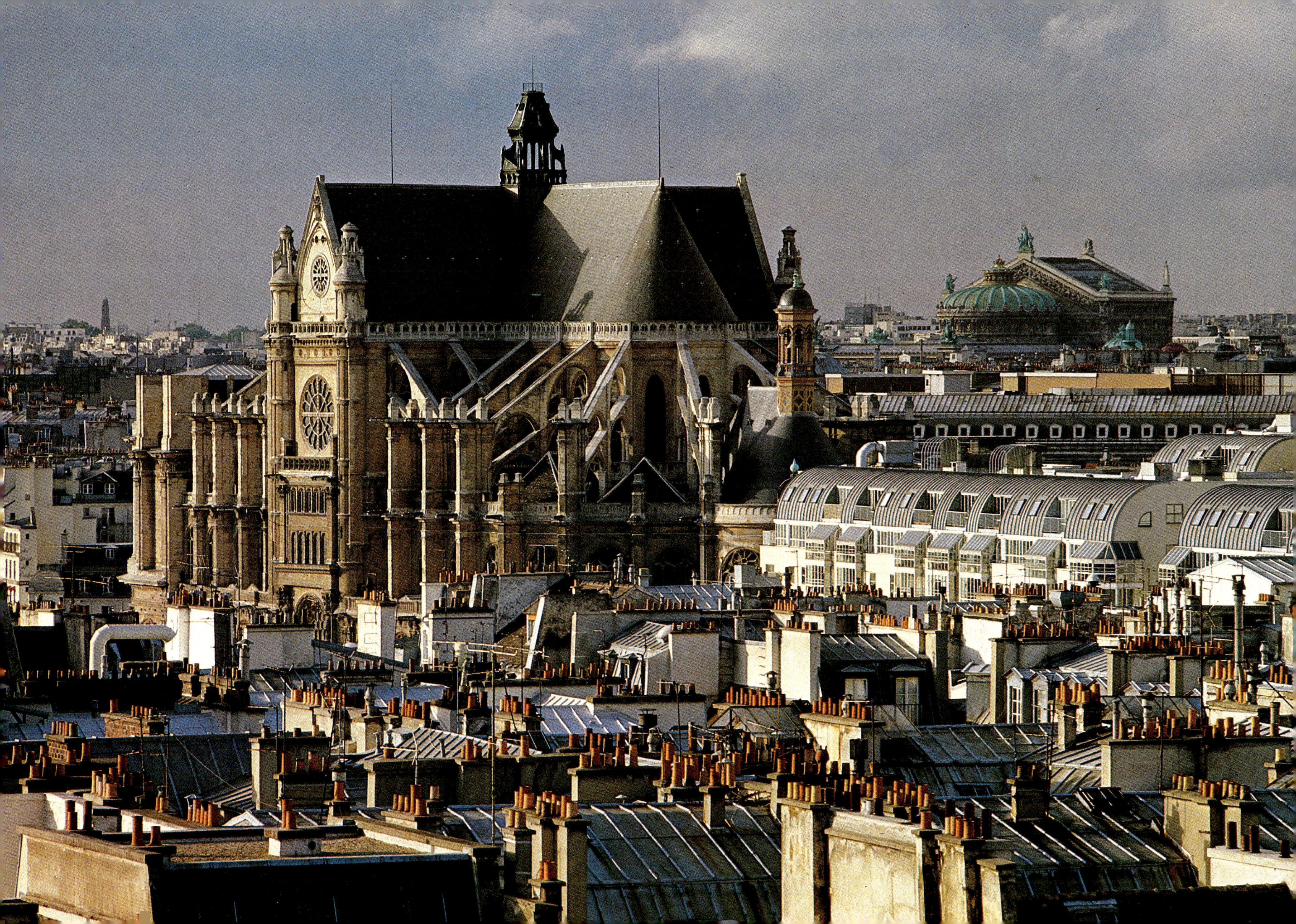

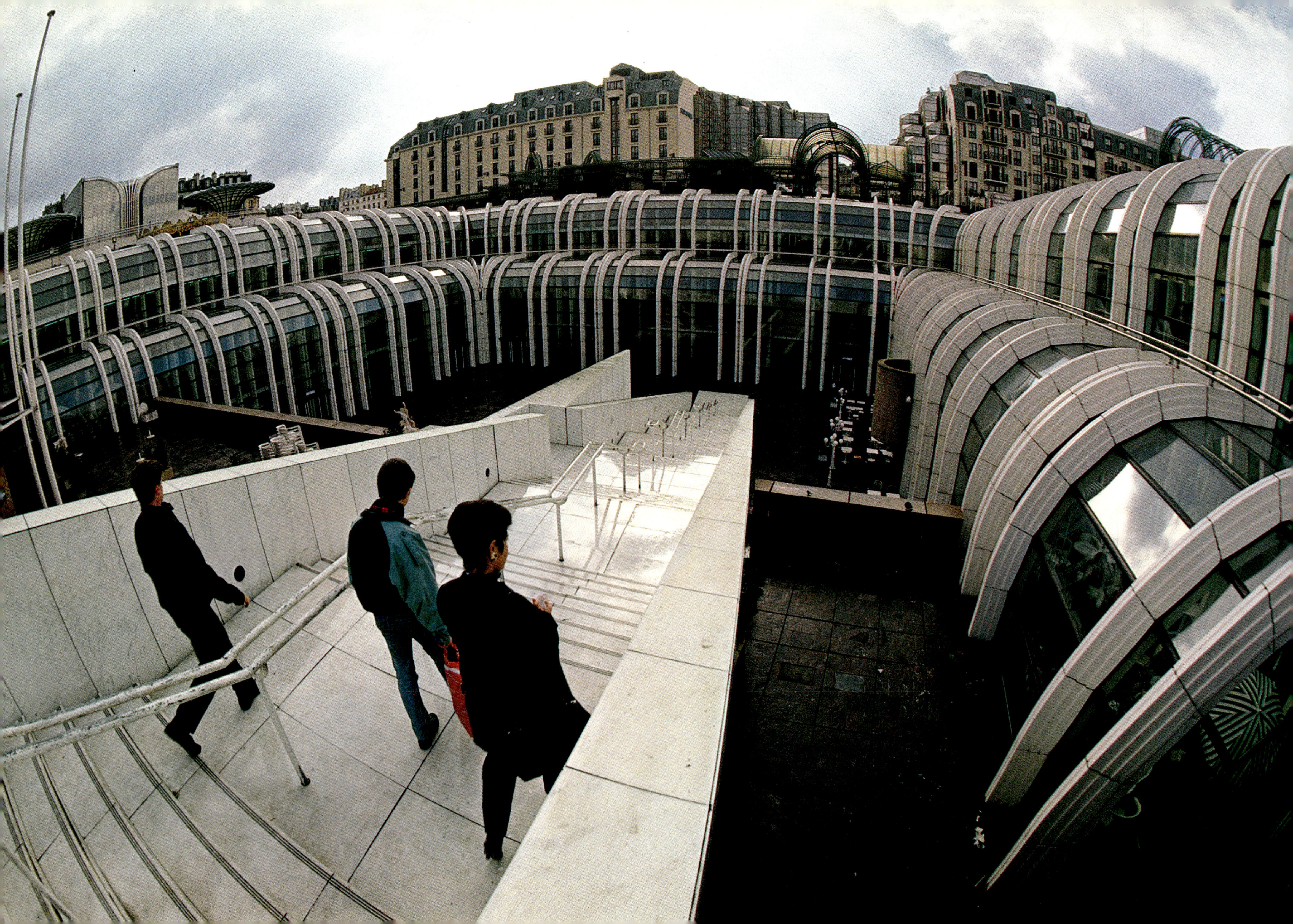

1   Two winged horses flank the entrance to the Tuileries Gardens from the Place de la Concorde. On their backs ride Mercury and Fame (Pl. 18). They were carved in 1701–2 from enormous blocks of white marble 4 m (12 ft) high by Antoine Coysevox, an outstanding sculptor at the court of Louis XIV, who worked at Versailles, Saint-Cloud, the Trianon and Paris, as well as at Marly, where these horses originally stood on a terrace overlooking the horse-pond. They were brought to their present site in Paris in 1719. The horse-tamers on the opposite side of the Place de la Concorde, at the entrance to the Champs Elysées, also came from Marly, where they had taken the place of the winged horses; they were carved by Coysevox's nephew, Guillaume Coustou. All the sculptures that we see here today are copies: the originals were removed to the Louvre to prevent further damage from pollution.

2, 3   A young man on the make today who wanted to follow Balzac's hero Rastignac in challenging the city of Paris to a duel of wits would probably go to the top of the Eiffel Tower, from which the capital – admittedly much changed since the 1830s – appears spread out like a relief map.

4   The Place de la Concorde was conceived as the setting for an equestrian statue of Louis XV by Edmé Bouchardon (of which only a gigantic hand, now in the Louvre, survived the fury of the Revolution). The *échevins* of the city, who had commissioned the statue, held a competition for the square, and designs were submitted by Jean-Nicolas Servandoni, Jacques-Germain Soufflot and Ange-Jacques Gabriel. Gabriel's was chosen in 1755. The vast open space has an octagonal centre, the corners of which are marked by little pavilions which now support nineteenth-century statues representing the major cities of France but which contain staircases that originally gave access to moats surrounding the octagonal centre. On either side of the entrance to the Rue Royale Gabriel constructed splendid palace-like buildings. Above a rusticated ground floor each has a Corinthian colonnade terminating in pavilions with pediments sculpted by Coustou, flanked by carved trophies. The buildings now house the Crillon Hotel and the Automobile Club de France (on the left) and the Ministry of the Navy (on the right).

In 1792 the square's name was changed from the original Place Louis XV to Place de la Révolution. The guillotine was set up on the spot now occupied by the statue of the city of Brest, and some fifteen hundred people fell victim to Dr Guillotin's sinister invention. The Directoire gave the *place* the fine name of 'Concorde', in the hope that this word suggestive of peace and harmony would erase the memory of past divisions among the people of France.

5   To the reader at this stage, a view of Paris from the air is like a giant puzzle or quiz: what are those two contrasting church towers in the distance? can you identify the bridges over the Seine? do you recognize that brightly-lit row of façades at the far right? can you name the quais? to what saints are the churches whose towers you can see dedicated? The answers are all in this book, and you will find them as you turn its pages.

6   The Palais de Chaillot, whose two wings extend on either side of an immense terrace like pincers stretching out to grasp the feet of the Eiffel Tower (on which we are standing), was built in connection with the 1937 Exposition. It stands on the site of the old Moorish-style Trocadéro, itself

constructed for the 1878 Exposition. The name 'Trocadéro' was given to the hill in the 1820s to commemorate a fort at Cadiz captured by the French during an expedition to restore the monarchy in Spain.

From the central platform of the Palais de Chaillot there is a fine view over the Seine and the Champ de Mars (see Pl.95). The fountains surrounding the cascade enliven the Neo-Classical forms of this complex of museums – the Musée de la Marine, Musée de l'Homme, Musée des Monuments Français and Musée du Cinéma. The Aquarium, in a special grotto, displays a selection of the fish commonly found in the rivers and lakes of France.

The Théâtre National de Chaillot, whose large auditorium lies below the platform, knew great days under the direction of Jean Vilar and later of Georges Wilson. Among the company were actors who went on to brilliant careers, and the great romantic film star Gérard Philipe appeared on stage in performances that remain unforgettably vivid to all who saw them.

7, 8   A great triumphal arch in honour of the French armies was commissioned by Napoleon from the architect Jean-François Chalgrin, and begun in 1806. In 1810 when the Empress Marie-Louise made her entrance into Paris it was far from complete, and Chalgrin had a full-scale model made for the ceremony. After the fall of Napoleon work stopped, and it was only resumed in 1836 when Louis-Philippe came to the throne. Four years later, Napoleon's ashes were carried in procession beneath the arch.

The Place de l'Etoile was given its present shape by Baron Haussmann, who created seven new avenues and had Hittorff design a uniform circle of houses.

The Arc de Triomphe itself, which recalls those of ancient Rome, is 50 m (165 ft) high and 45 m (148 ft) wide. The four large sculptural groups on the piers were all to have been executed by François Rude, but resentment and intrigues by other artists led to the commission being divided between Rude, Jean-Pierre Cortot and Antoine Etex. Rude was responsible for the *Departure of the Volunteers in 1792*, which perfectly suits its position and is universally recognized as a masterpiece, although at the time it was rejected by the Academy. The main figure seems to be uttering a great battle-cry, and this gave rise to the name by which the group is usually known, *La Marseillaise*.

For Victor Hugo's funeral the Arc de Triomphe was draped with black crape. On 11 November 1920 the body of an unknown soldier killed in the First World War was buried here, and since 11 November 1923 a perpetual flame has burned, tended by ex-servicemen. It was from here that General de Gaulle set out on 26 August 1944 when, in a triumphant celebration of the liberation of the city from the Germans, he walked down the Champs Elysées amid the cheers of Parisians.

9–12   On ceremonial occasions an enormous flag fills the opening of the Arc de Triomphe. The military parade along the Champs Elysées on 14 July, the national day, has all the precision of a ballet at the Opéra, and crowds strain to see the splendidly dressed students of the *hautes écoles* – those from the Ecole Polytechnique in their black cocked hats (Pl. 9) and those from Saint-Cyr in plumed shakos (Pls. 10, 12).

13   When the allied troops occupied Paris in 1814 cossacks camped under the trees of the Champs Elysées. The City then took the area over and provided it with lamps, pavements and fountains. In 1844 and 1849

it was the site chosen for exhibitions of French manufactures and industry. Under the Second Empire (1858–70) the avenue became extremely fashionable: fine houses were built in the neighbourhood, and patrons arrived in their carriages at elegant restaurants and *cafés-concert*. The Bal Mabille in the Allée des Veuves (now the Avenue Matignon) drew crowds to watch the famous Chicard do the 'cancan', and to enjoy Céleste Mogador, Rose Pompon and Rigolboche. This combination of elegance and amusement made the Champs Elysées world-famous.

Now the houses have given way to office buildings and instead of elegance there are snack bars, fast-food restaurants, dress shops and cinemas. The only survivors of past glory are Fouquet's, the smart restaurant at the corner of the Avenue Georges V patronized by film people, and the *hôtel* built for the high-living Marquise de Païva.

In July each year the Champs Elysées are the scene of great excitement and crowds, for the Bastille Day parade and the finish of the Tour de France cycle race.

14, 15   The obelisk now in the Place de la Concorde was erected by Ramses II at the entrance to the Temple of Amun at Luxor, where its twin still stands. It was brought down the Nile and back to France on a specially constructed vessel, and erected in 1836. An exotic intruder among the eighteenth-century buildings and the statues, it marks the centre of the square, and punctuates the finest vista in the city, from the Louvre to the Arc de Triomphe. It also provides a meeting place where visitors to Paris, exhausted with wonders, can pause to recover between the splashing fountains that surround the great stone needle.

16, 17, 19   The name of the Tuileries Gardens comes from the tile kilns that once occupied the site, making use of clay dug on the spot. Louis XIV's minister, Colbert, gave the task of landscaping the area to the great gardener André Le Nôtre, who created a handsome axial layout, dug large ornamental ponds, laid out parterres and quincunxes, and at the western end constructed two curved ramps leading up to terraces (where the Jeu de Paume and Orangerie stand). Chairs could be hired, and – a great novelty – there were even public conveniences.

The Tuileries Palace, designed by Philibert de l'Orme in the sixteenth century, was gutted by fire during the Commune in 1871 and subsequently demolished. All that survives is two splendidly ornate columns, which were re-erected nearer to the Place de la Concorde.

There are two recent additions to the host of statues in the gardens. Aristide Maillol's *Three Nymphs* (Pl. 16) dates from 1938, when the sculptor from Banyuls was at the height of his powers; it joined his *Homage to Cézanne*, set up here in 1925. Rodin is represented by *Pierre de Wiessant* (Pl. 19), a figure from the group of the *Burghers of Calais* (see Pl. 139).

18   Coysevox's *Fame* forms a pendant to his *Mercury* (see Pl. 1), at the entrance to the Tuileries Gardens.

20, 21   The Rue de Rivoli, with its long row of arcades and hanging lamps, was conceived by Percier and Fontaine in the early years of the nineteenth century as an elegant street facing the Tuileries Gardens. Here, sheltered from the weather, you can stroll, buy souvenirs, or browse in fine shops.

22   The leafy quais of the Ile Saint-Louis are old-fashioned and quiet. From them massive wooden doors, decorated with panels and heavy metal bosses, open onto the courtyards of imposing seventeenth-century houses.

23   On the Terrasse du Bord de l'Eau at the edge of the Tuileries Gardens children's games have been replaced by the southern game of *pétanque*. Players show the same concentration and ritual formality as on the Place des Lisses at Saint-Tropez, though here they speak with a Parisian accent. Many of them are elderly, and they do not always welcome the comments of their casual audience. When one game is finished they start all over again, with infinite patience, to show how they understand the science of ballistics. Visible in the background, across the river, is the Gare (now Musée) d'Orsay.

24   The Galerie du Bord de l'Eau of the Louvre was erected in the late sixteenth century by Métézeau and extended in the early seventeenth century by Du Cerceau. Its rich surface had become seriously decayed by the nineteenth century, and it was refaced by Félix Duban. The lions guard one of the entrances to the Louvre Museum.

25   The Pont des Arts, constructed entirely of iron and reserved for pedestrians, was a novelty when it was built in 1804. To cross it, you had to pay a toll of one *sou*. There were benches placed along the sides between orange trees in tubs, which in winter were moved into two specially provided greenhouses at the ends of the bridge. The Pont des Arts became unsafe and was closed for a long time, but it was reopened a few years ago, and now once again you can cross between the Louvre and the Institut de France and, whichever way you look, get some of the finest views in Paris.

26, 27   Silent confrontations in the Classical sculpture galleries at the Louvre.

28, 29   The world's museums contain an artistic heritage that belongs to all mankind. Paintings, sculptures and *objets d'art* become the mental furnishings of our lives, and the *Adoration of the Shepherds* by Georges de La Tour and the injured Venus from the island of Melos occupy more than their confined space in the Louvre; they are part of the memories and pleasures of visitors from distant lands and different cultures.

30–33   The Palais Royal was built as the Palais Cardinal for Richelieu, but he had little time to enjoy it. At his death he bequeathed it to Louis XIII, who scarcely outlived him. It then became the residence of Anne of Austria and her young son Louis XIV, but they moved out during the uprising known as the Fronde and never returned, the King thenceforth preferring the comfort and relative security of the Louvre. Louis did revisit the palace, however, when he became enamoured of Mademoiselle de Lavallière, one of the ladies in waiting to Henrietta Maria, widow of Charles I of England, who was living in exile in the Palais Royal. His attentions bore fruit: the child was delivered, it is said, by a doctor whom Colbert had summoned – blindfold, to ensure his discretion. The palace was then inhabited by the King's brother, Monsieur, and later it was the scene of riotous suppers given by Philippe d'Orléans, Regent for the young Louis XV. In 1780 the Palais Royal became the property of Louis-Philippe d'Orléans, who launched into property speculation. On the grounds surrounding the palace he laid out new streets, whose names he took from the titles of junior branches of his family – Valois, Montpensier, Beaujolais. A little later, he built the present Théâtre Français and Théâtre du Palais-Royal. Napoleon, when he came to power, suppressed the gambling establishments that had moved in during the Revolution, and installed the Bourse and Tribunal de Commerce. Louis XVIII handed the palace back to the Orléans family, and it was from here that Louis-Philippe set out in 1830 for the Hôtel de Ville to be crowned king. Today the Palais Royal is the seat of the Council of State.

The gardens where mothers and babies now take the air were not always so peaceful. At the end of the eighteenth century they were a place for gaming, drinking, and sexual encounters: indeed, Napoleon is supposed to have had his first adventure with a woman here, when he was eighteen. Under the arcade that surrounds the gardens is the famous Grand Véfour restaurant, formerly the haunt of the writers Colette, Jean Cocteau and Emmanuel Berl, who all lived in flats in the Palais Royal.

The front quadrangle, which had become a car park, was recently given a new layout. Public opinion was passionately divided over Daniel Buren's striped column stumps, though young tourists find them not without their uses. Pol Bury's fountain made of glistening spheres clashes less aggressively with the eighteenth-century colonnade.

34   The Tour Saint-Jacques is all that remains of the church of Saint-Jacques-la-Boucherie, from which pilgrims set out for the shrine of St James at Compostela in Spain. Although there is a weather station on its Flamboyant Gothic top, the statues still keep a keen eye on the sky.

35   The sculptor Emmanuel Frémiet started out with an advantage, as the nephew and pupil of the great François Rude (see Pl. 8), and his *Joan of Arc* set up in the Place des Pyramides in 1874 is infinitely more popular than Paul Dubois's version of the same subject dating from 1895 in front of Saint-Augustin. Frémiet's dazzling golden Maid of Orleans is also a genuine object of pilgrimage: every year on the Sunday following 8 May (formerly the French national day) flowers are placed at its base.

The square, surrounded by arcades like those of the Rue de Rivoli off which it opens, leads to the Rue des Pyramides, which was extended in 1876 to the new Avenue de l'Opéra.

36–39   The Place Vendôme was intended by Louvois for the mint, academies, embassies and a library, all in honour of Louis XIV. Louvois died, and the project lapsed until the architect Jules Hardouin Mansart created the present octagonal *place* surrounded by classical façades behind whose Corinthian pilasters houses were gradually built.

The Vendôme Column, modelled on Trajan's Column in Rome, was erected in 1810 by Vivant Denon, Napoleon's Director-General of Museums, using the bronze of 1,200 cannon captured from the Germans and Austrians. Its reliefs depict the campaigns of 1805–7, in a spiral that ascends to a colossal statue of Napoleon in the guise of a Roman emperor. The figure was thrown down in 1871 by a group of Communards; among them was the painter Gustave Courbet, who spent six months in prison for his revolutionary gesture. (That bronze Napoleon had been in position only since 1863: it replaced a poor replacement of the original figure, which had been melted down after 1818 to make a new Henri IV on the Ile de la Cité (Pl. 121).) Eventually a new figure of Napoleon was cast for the Column.

In and near the Place Vendôme you will find the finest jewellery shops in France, and the most sumptuous jewels in the world. While the customers make up their minds, their liveried chauffeurs wait with gleaming limousines.

40, 41 Department stores at the end of the last century were a place where architects could show off their boldest structural inventions. At the Galeries Lafayette (Pl. 40), by Chanut, a skeleton of metal and reinforced concrete allowed the store to open out below an immense stained-glass dome. Behind hundreds of counters, women in black uniforms provided clients with a bewildering range of goods, under the stern eye of floorwalkers in morning coats. Le Printemps (Pl. 41), built by Paul Sédille in 1899, had a similar vast skylit hall; recent rationalization subdivided the space, leaving the stained glass vault to light a restaurant on the top floor.

42, 43 As part of his plans for Paris, Baron Haussmann set aside a site for a great opera house, which was to be the finest in all France. A competition was announced, and 171 architects submitted designs. The winner was Charles Garnier, then aged thirty-five and relatively unknown. Reacting against the prevailing classicism of his day, he produced a new, more ornate type of architecture, which he diplomatically called the 'Napoleon III Style'. The great auditorium and the façade are equally matched in richness and luxury.

Ten steps lead up to a terrace from which seven arched openings give access to the building. Here on the right is Jean-Baptiste Carpeaux's famous sculptural group representing the spirit of dance (the original, now in the Musée d'Orsay, has been replaced by a copy by Paul Belmondo). In the loggia above, paired Corinthian columns frame busts of famous composers. At roof level the copper-covered dome that marks the position of the auditorium is flanked by figures of Poetry and Harmony; behind rises a vast pediment crowned by Apollo between Poetry and Music.

Inside, a colonnaded space leads to the grand staircase, then the lobbies, and finally the auditorium, where the original ceiling by Lenepveu is now concealed by a design painted on canvas by Chagall.

All around the Opéra, vestal virgins hold lamps to light the shrine of Euterpe and Terpsichore. In front is a square bordered by buildings in the style typical of Haussmann's new developments, from which the Avenue de l'Opéra leads down to the Palais Royal. Seen at night, the floodlit 'Palais Garnier' glows like a sumptuous Baroque shrine.

44, 45 Place Clichy and Place Pigalle were formerly the haunt of artists; writers, painters and sculptors gathered in cafés like the Nouvelle Athènes, where the 'Incohérents' met to discuss *salons* at which they would show works calculated to shock bourgeois taste. Between the two squares is the Moulin Rouge, in Place Blanche (Pl. 46), where tourists are fed a jumble of stories about the days of the Belle Epoque – of Aristide Bruant's cabaret Au Chat Noir, of the cancan dancers who fascinated Toulouse Lautrec, and of the ruffians celebrated by Francis Carco. Those days have gone forever, and have left no trace behind. Today the Boulevard de Clichy is lined with blue movie houses, sex shops, stripteases and peepshows. Only the little fountain of the Place Pigalle remains to evoke a gentler past.

46 In Place Blanche the sails of the Moulin Rouge slice through the blue of the evening sky. Once they were the sign of the dance hall famed for La Goulue, Grille d'Egout, Nini Patte en l'Air, la Môme Fromage, Jane Avril and Valentin le Désossé, the shrine of the cancan, opened in 1899. In 1903 it became a music hall where Parisians crowded to hear Max Dearly, Mistinguett and Maurice Chevalier. Then it became a cinema. Now the Moulin Rouge is a branch of the Paris Lido, and stages spectacular shows featuring the Blue Bell Girls, that sternly drilled regiment of charmers. The old dance hall lives on, immortal, in the posters of Jules Chéret and Toulouse Lautrec and in Lautrec's paintings.

47, 50   Paris lost its belly when the old Halles were demolished. Nightcrawlers, no longer attracted by the onion soup available at all hours in the market men's restaurants, drifted away to other neighbourhoods. The old quarter that Zola celebrated in his novel *Le Ventre de Paris* is unrecognizable: Baltard's great iron and glass market halls have been replaced by a pedestrian 'Forum' on four levels where glazed galleries surround an open space. Here, in semi-subterranean shops, stores, restaurants and cafés the curious, avid for novel experiences, rub shoulders with the sinister drifters that are common to all great cities.

48   Thousands come to the Pompidou Centre (see Pls. 51–53). Many pass by its proffered attractions and let themselves be carried up the escalators to see the view out over the city, as though from the cockpit of a giant airship.

49   A curiously foreshortened view of the mixture of styles in Paris: the church of Saint-Eustache, itself half Gothic and half Renaissance, rises between the Opéra built under Napoleon III and the ultra-modern Forum des Halles. Nearby (not visible here), the futuristic Pompidou Centre jostles the Flamboyant Gothic church of Saint-Merri. The metropolis yields to the whims of men; yet it has retained a distinctive harmony through the centuries.

City of art and of life

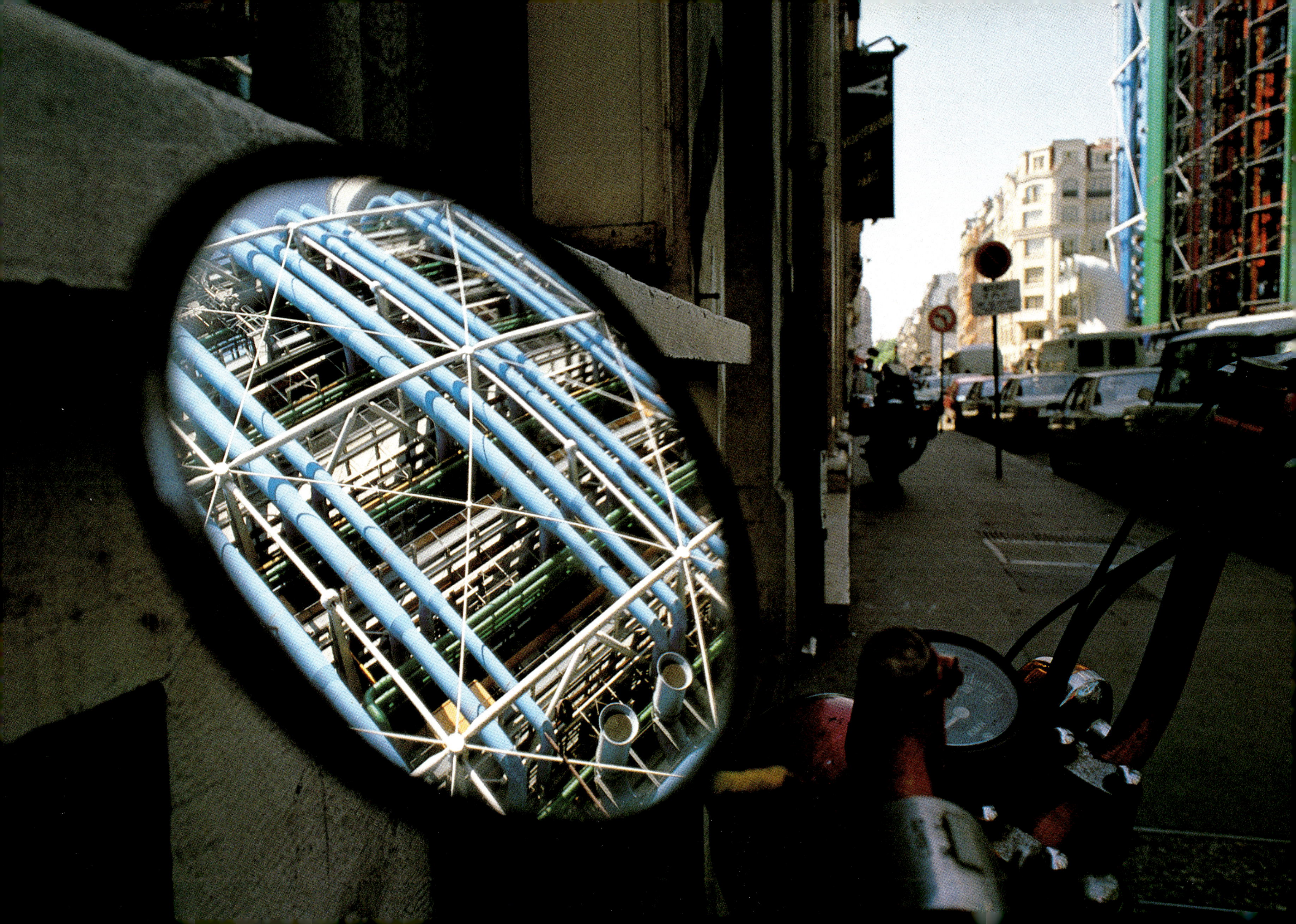

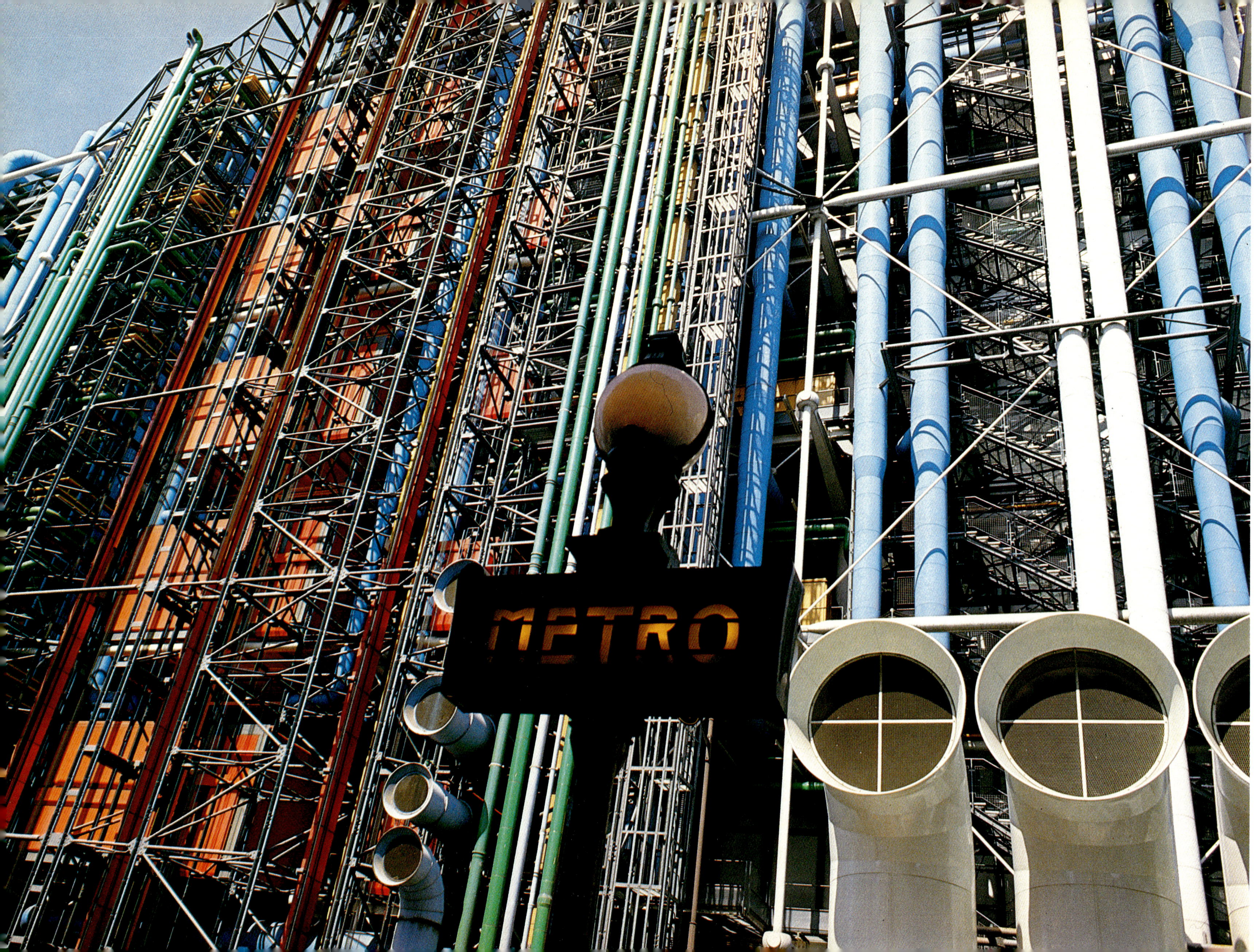
METRO

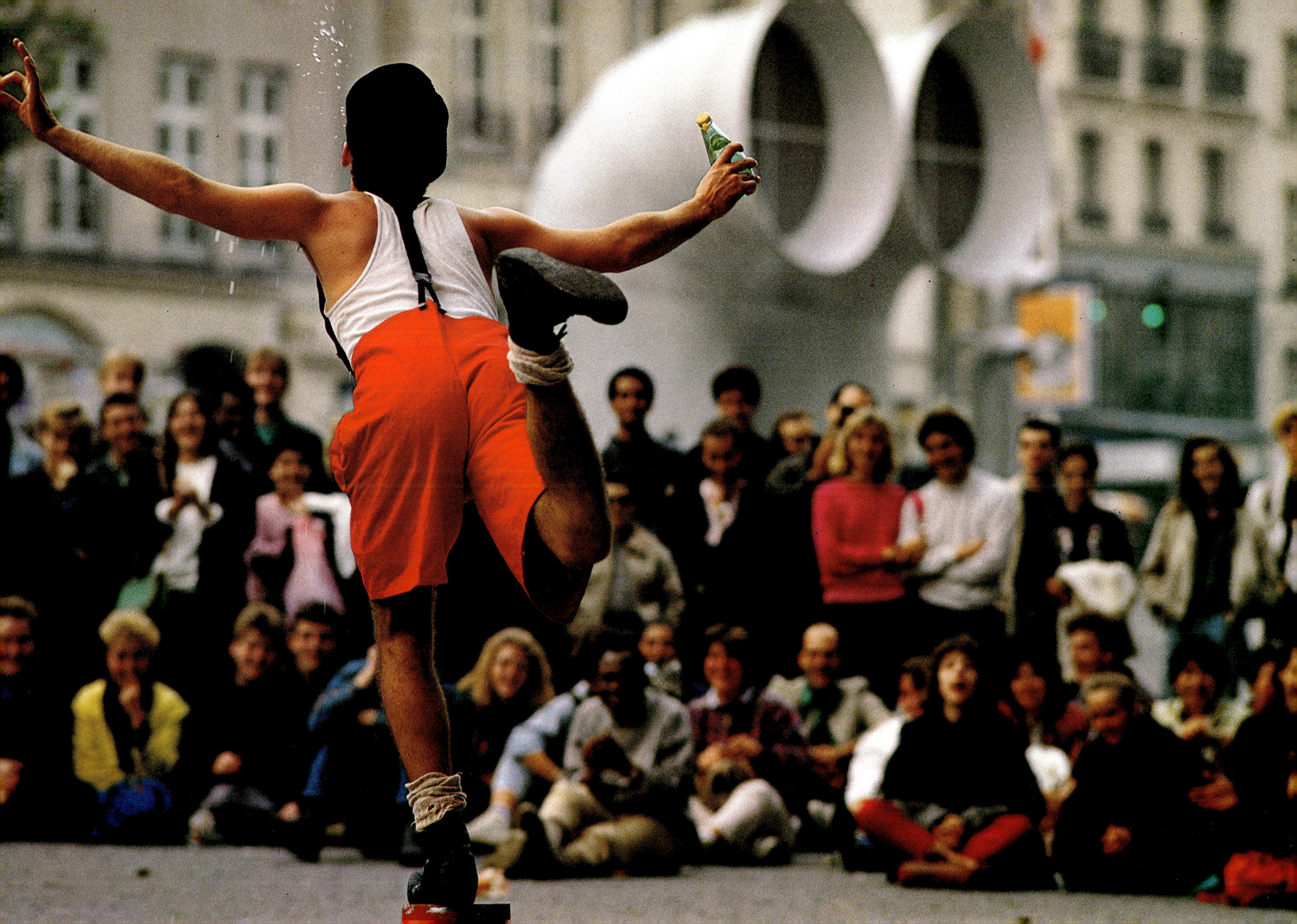

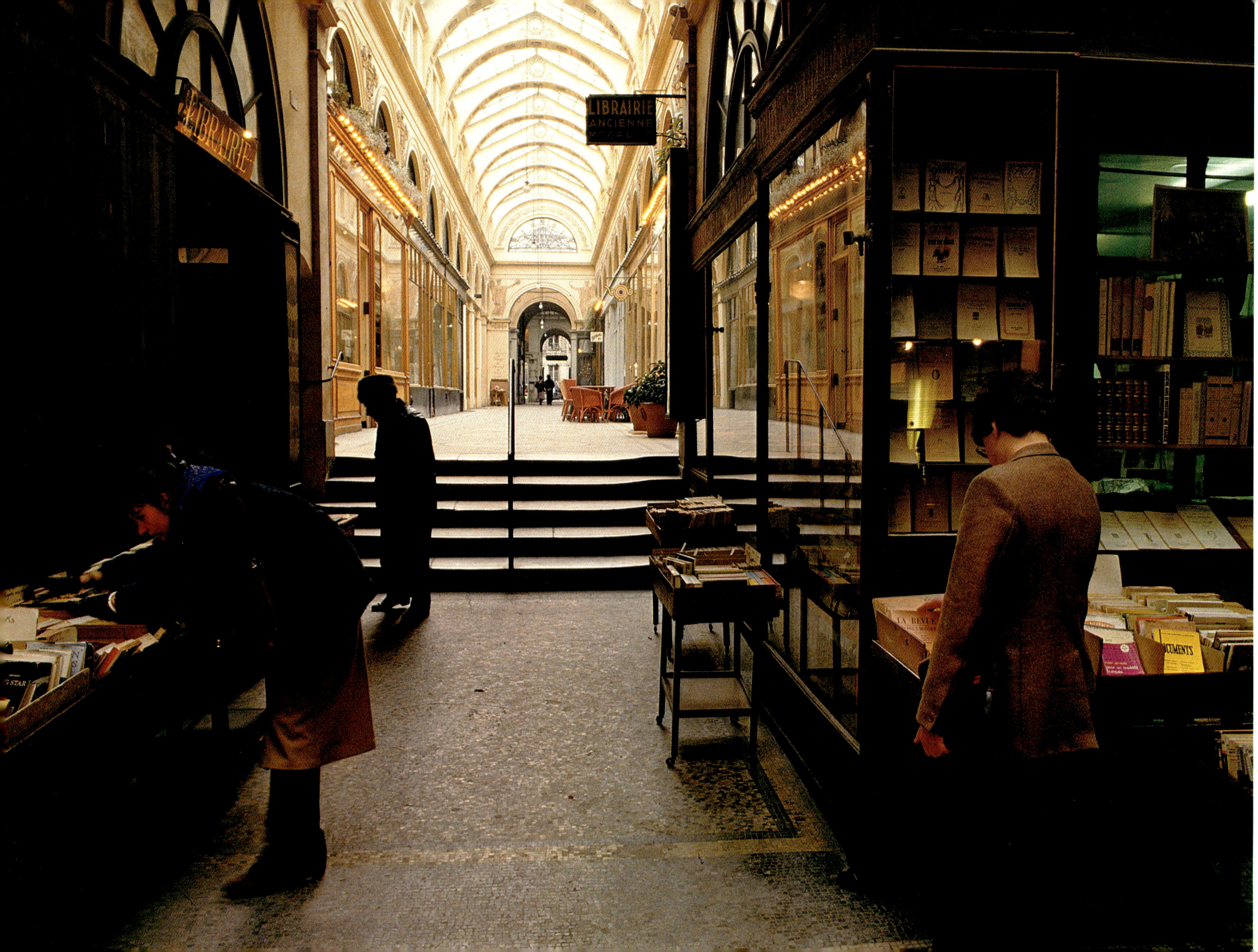
LIBRAIRIE
ANCIENNE
LIBRAIRIE
LA REVUE
DOCUMENTS

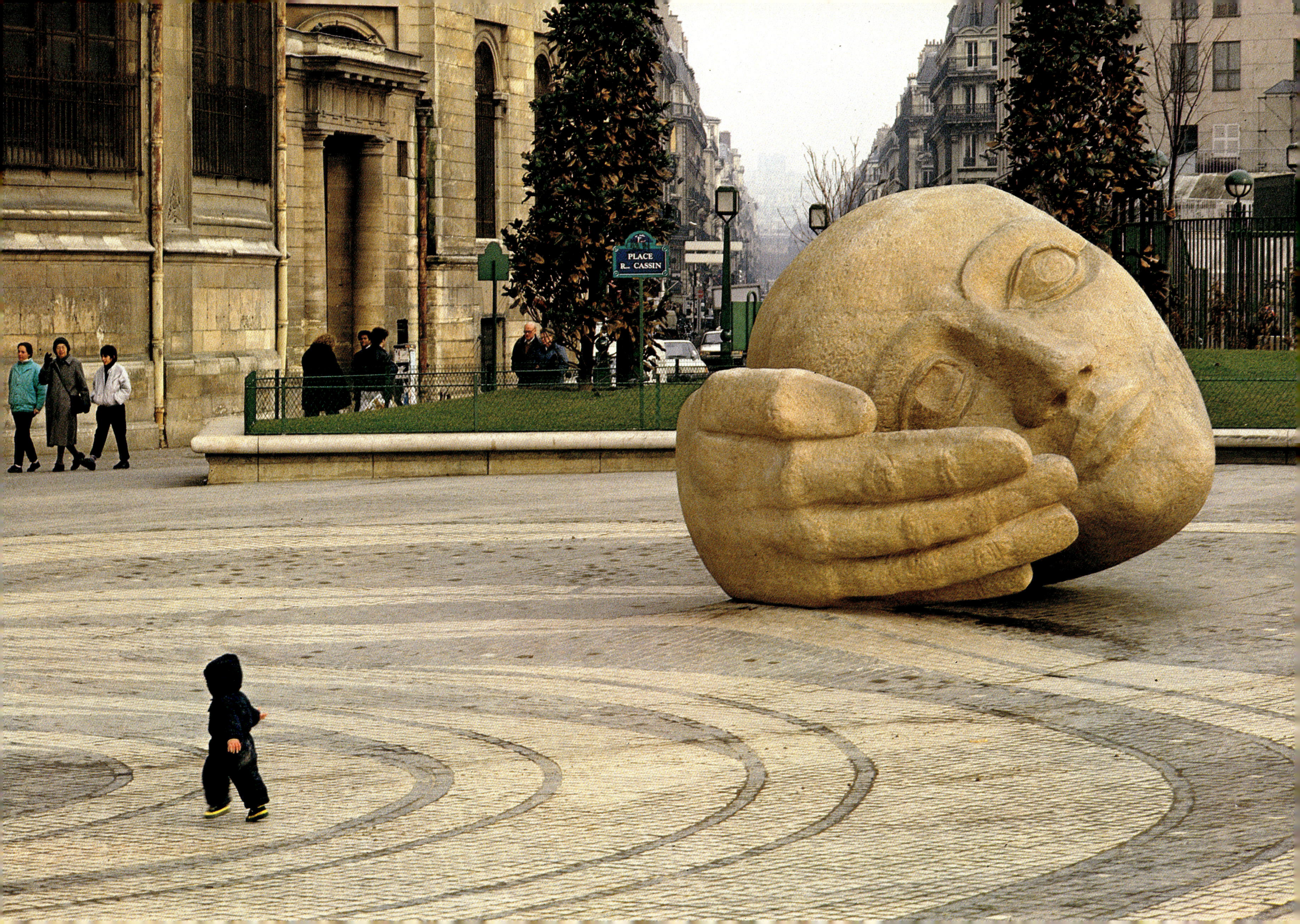
PLACE
R. CASSIN

56 57

RT CAPIA
POUPÉES ANCIENNES
DES EXPERTS SPECIALISES
ABLEAUX

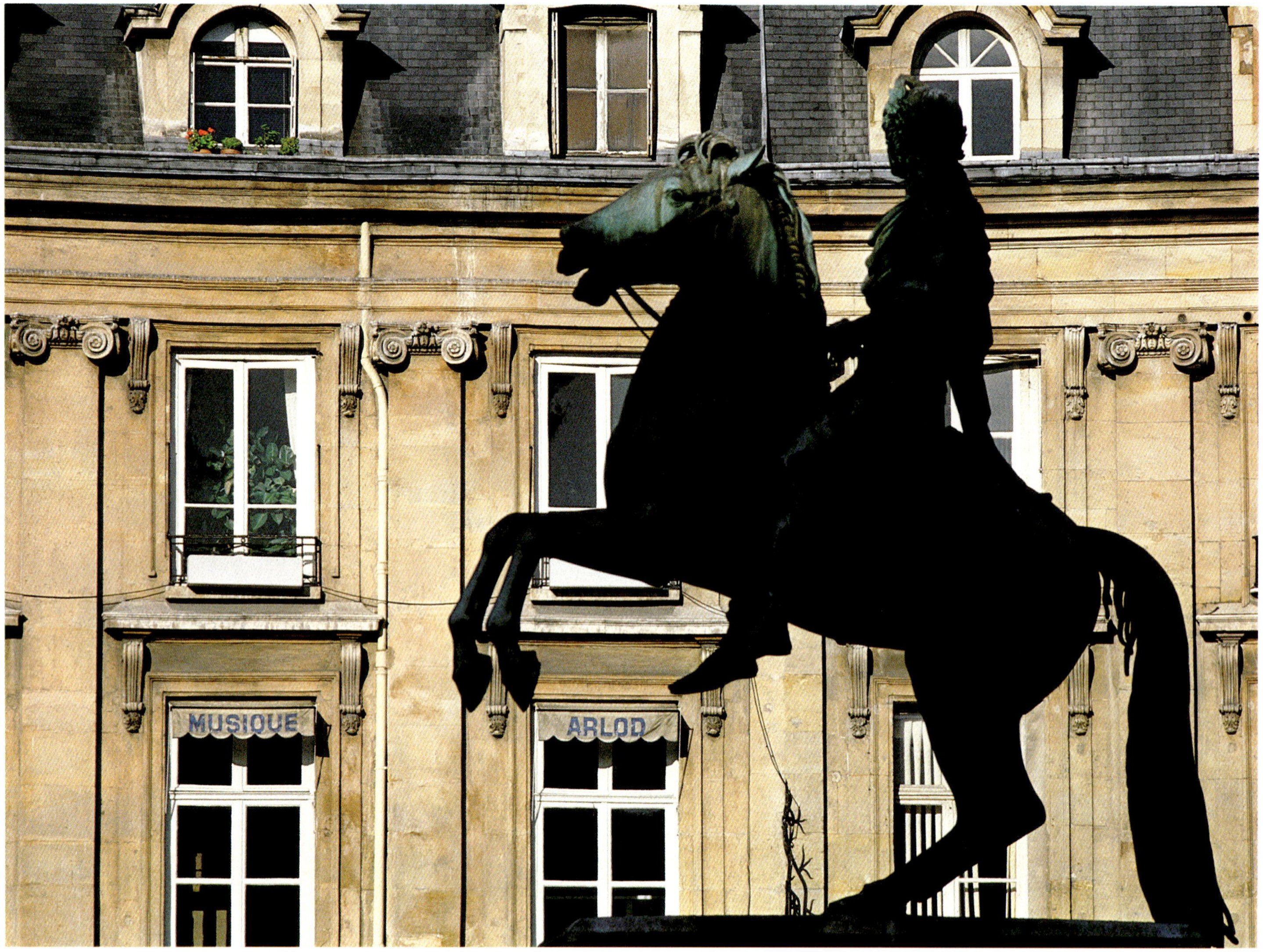

58 59

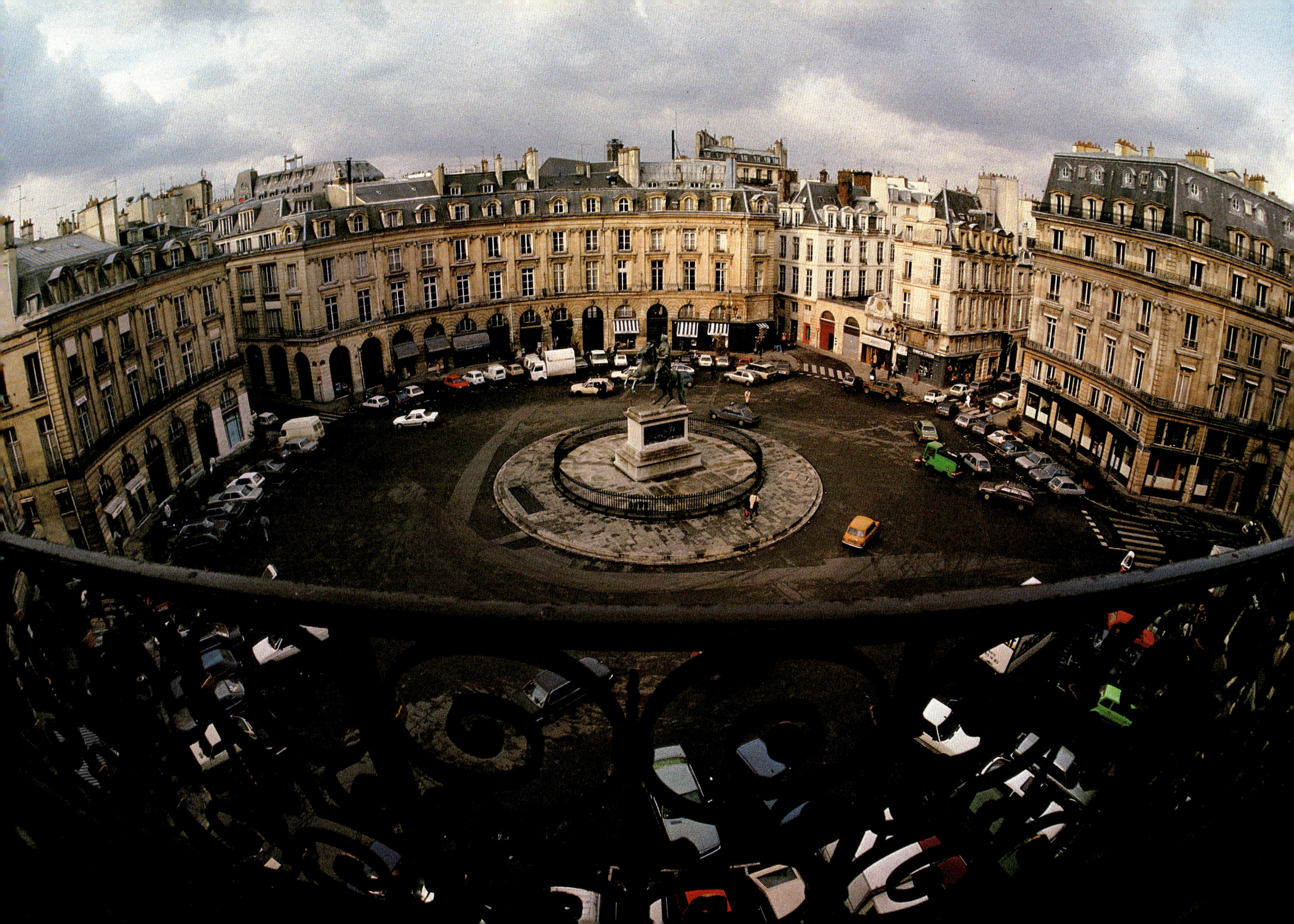

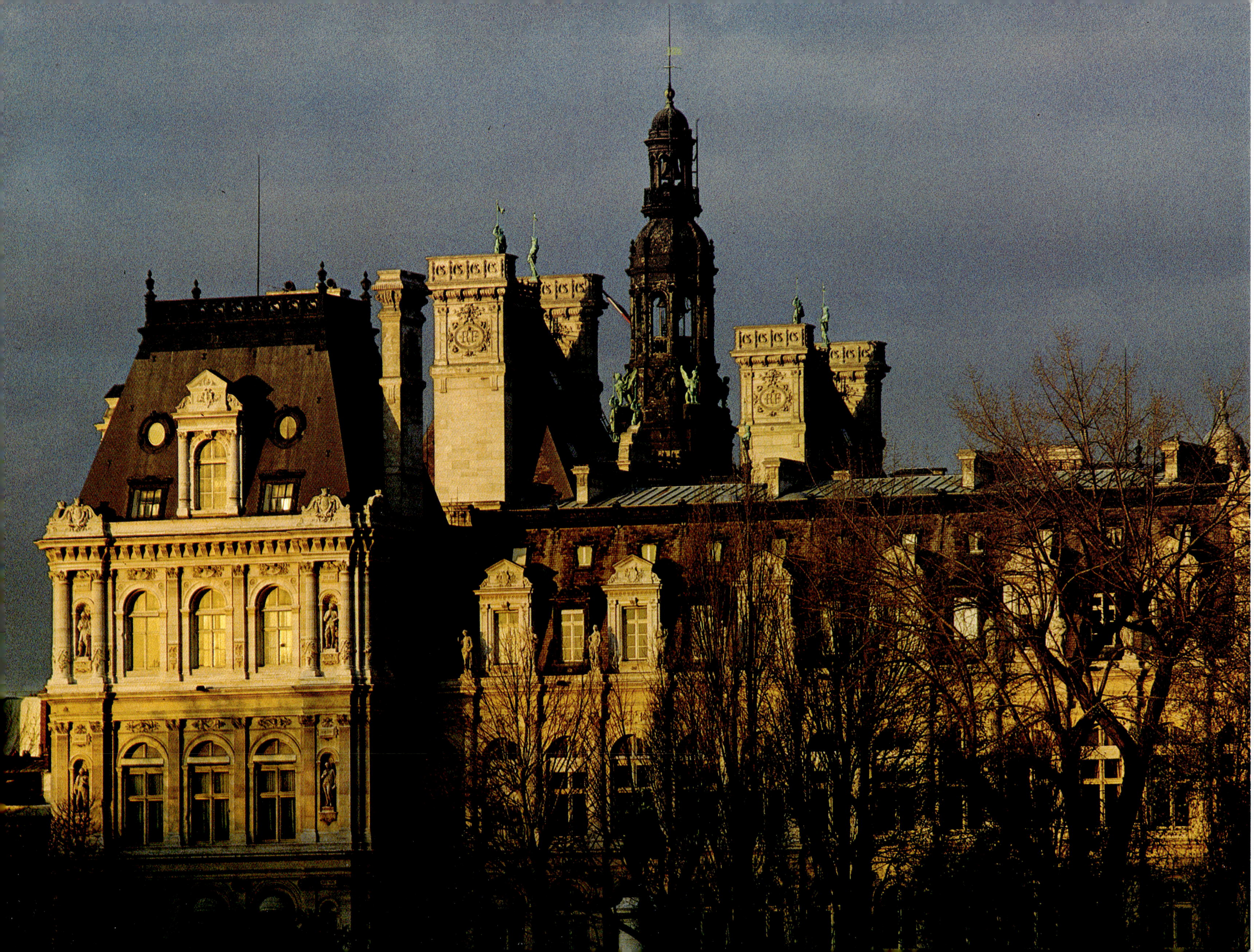

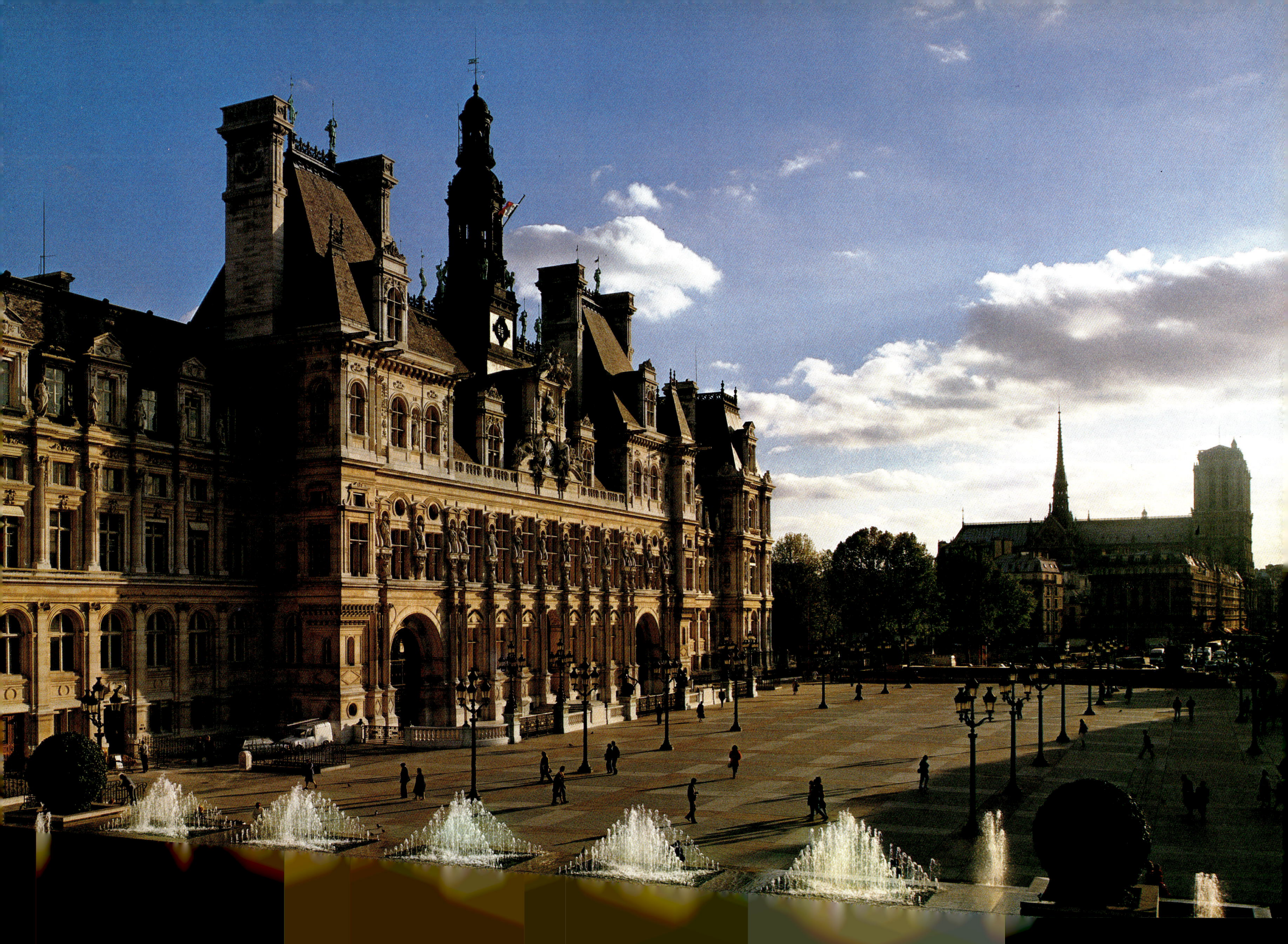

62 63

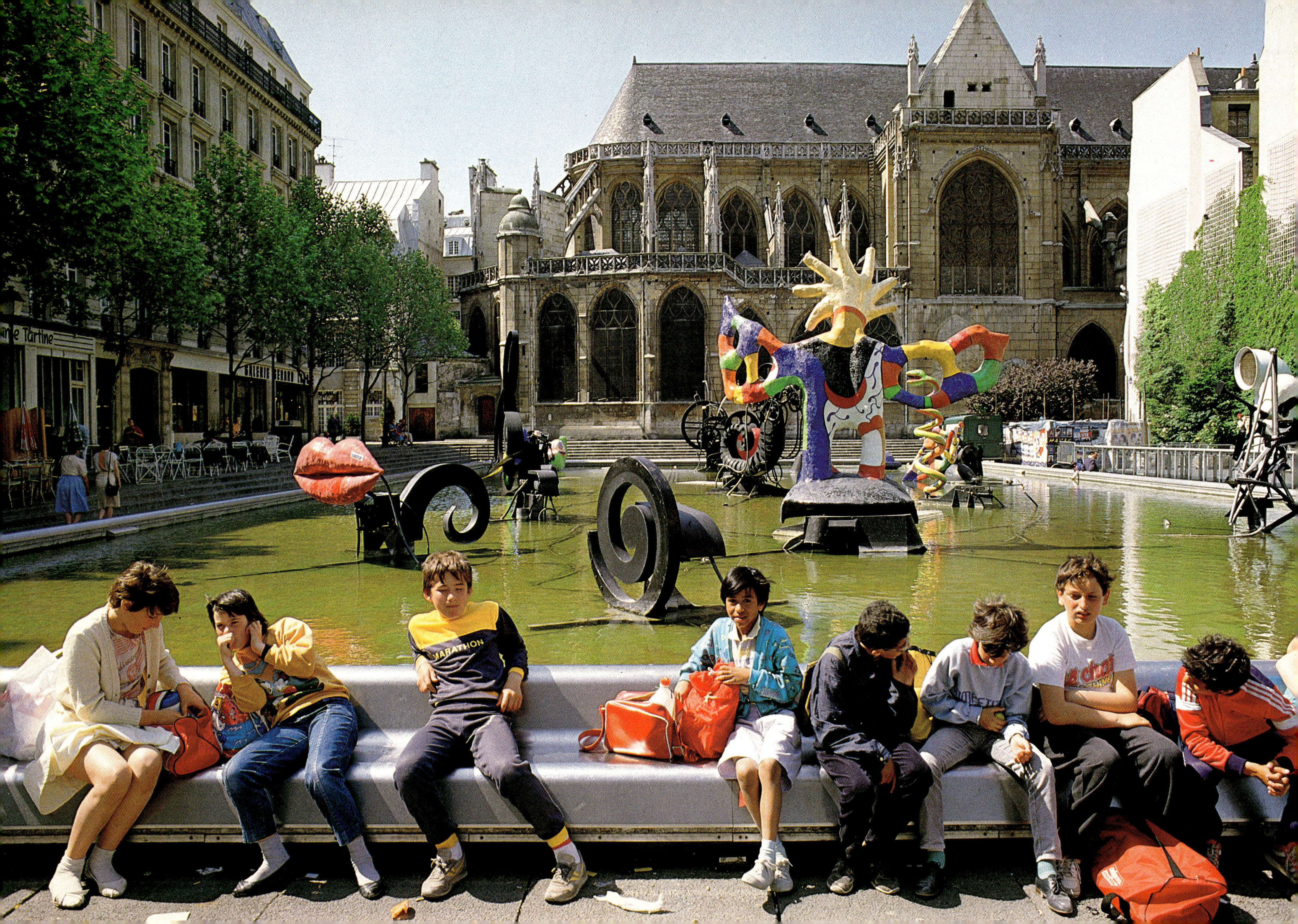
MARATHON

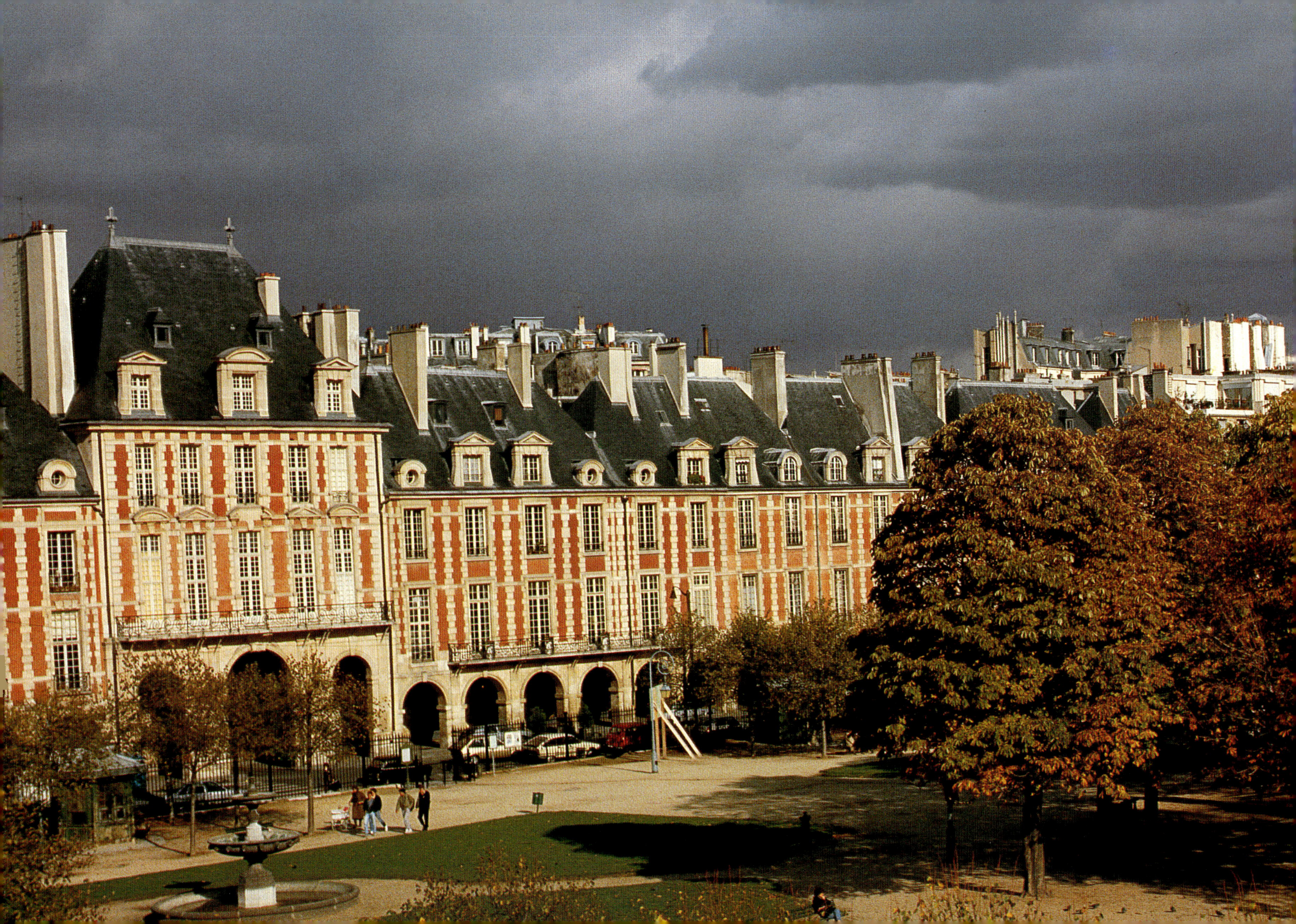

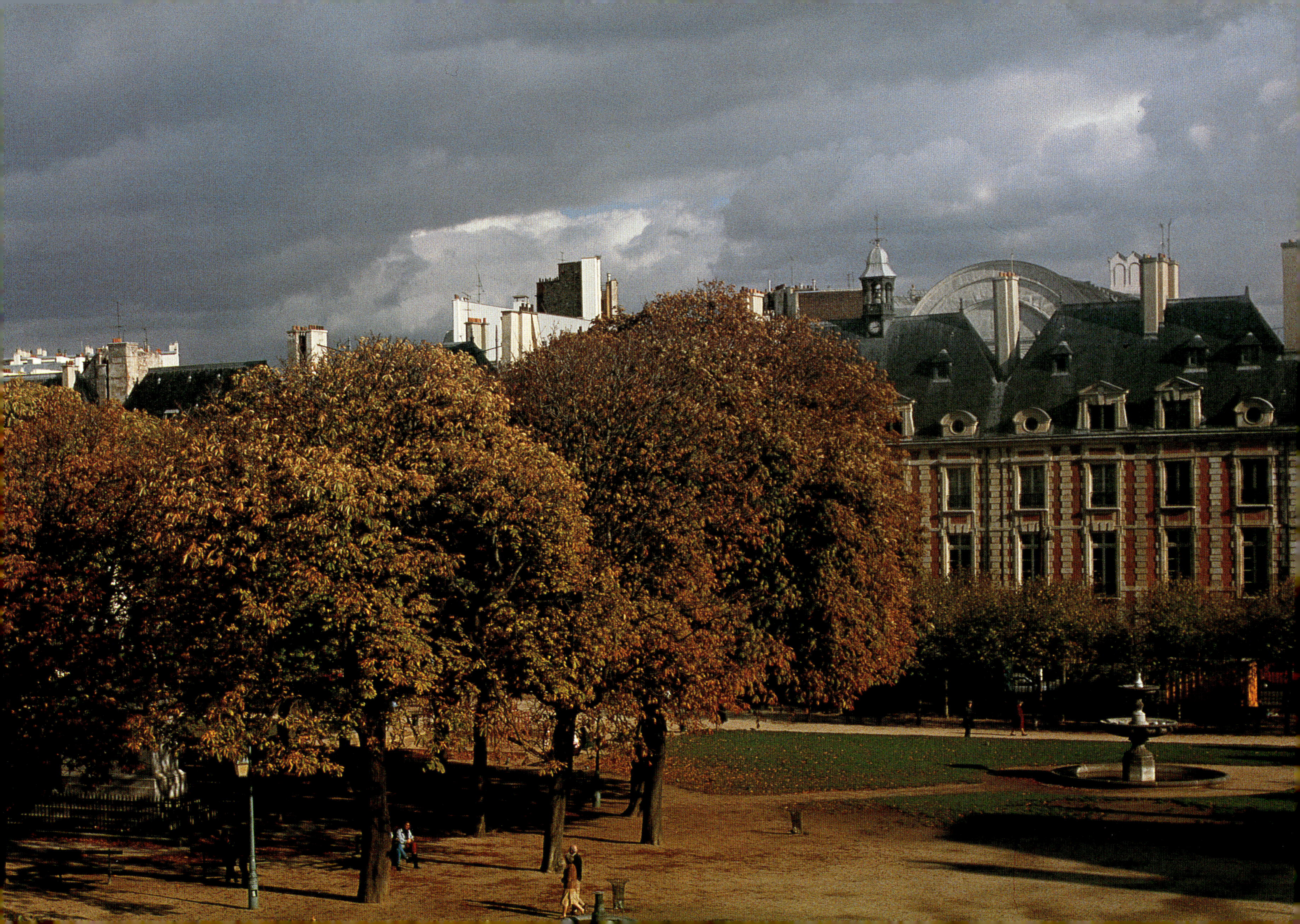

65 66 67

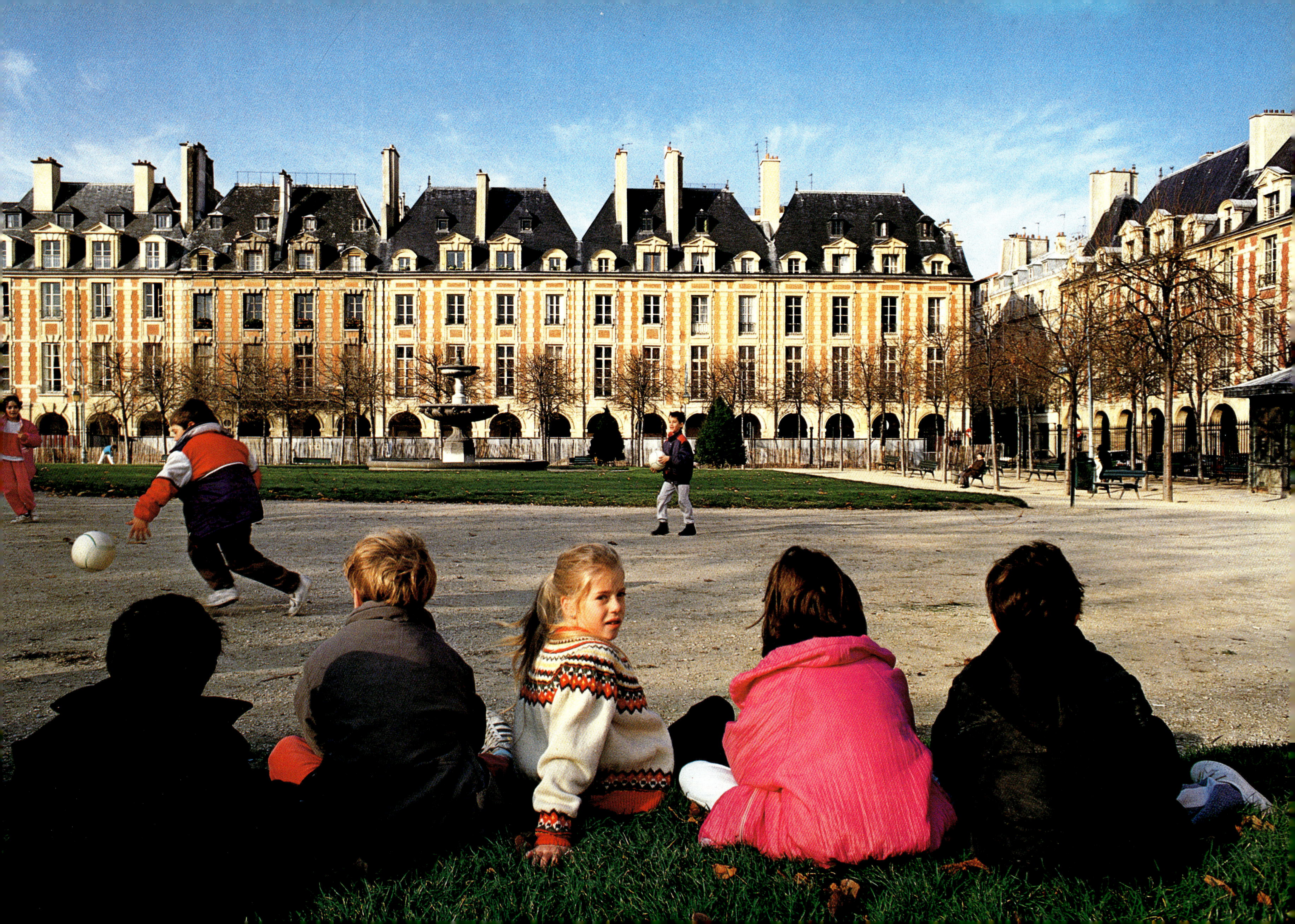

68 69

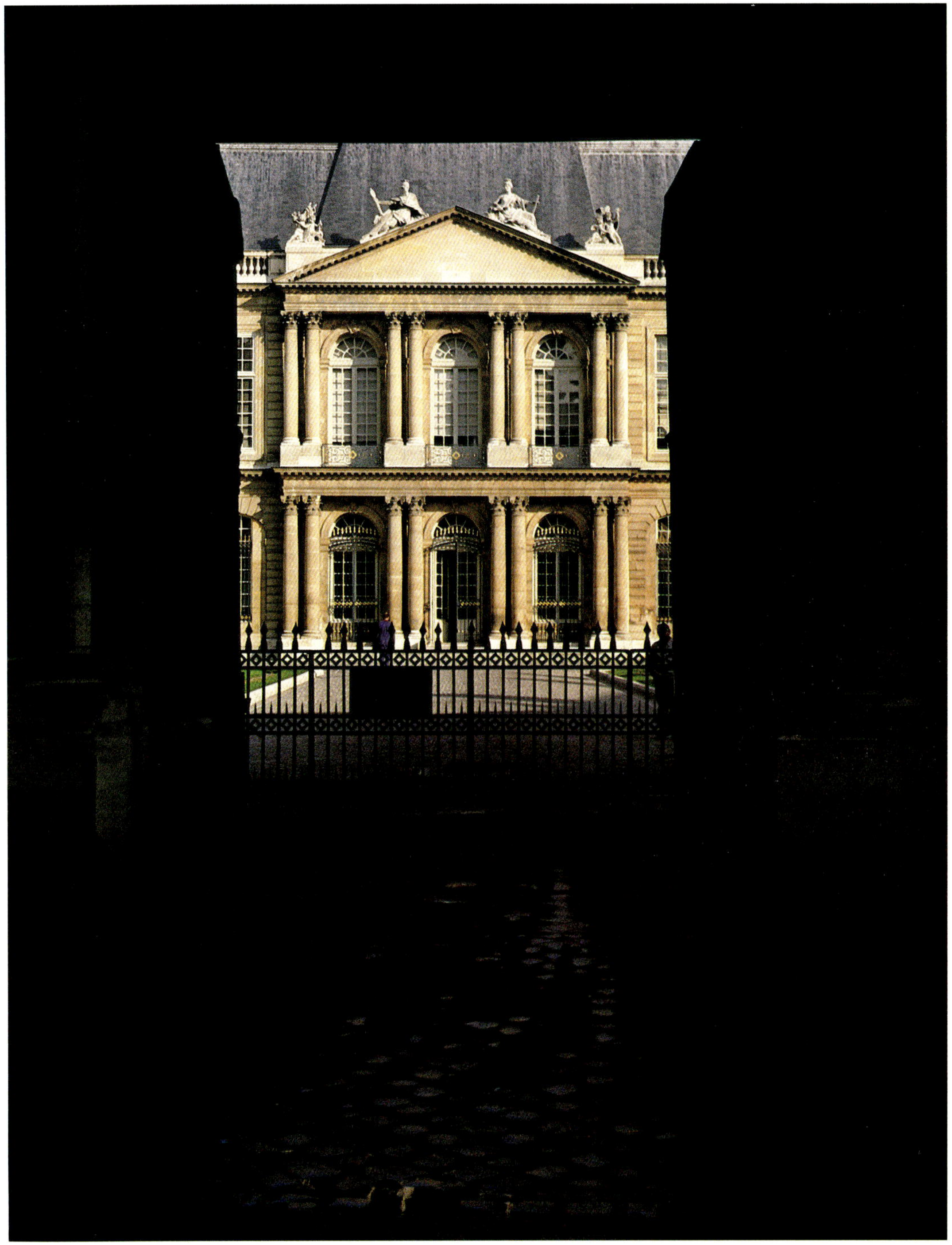

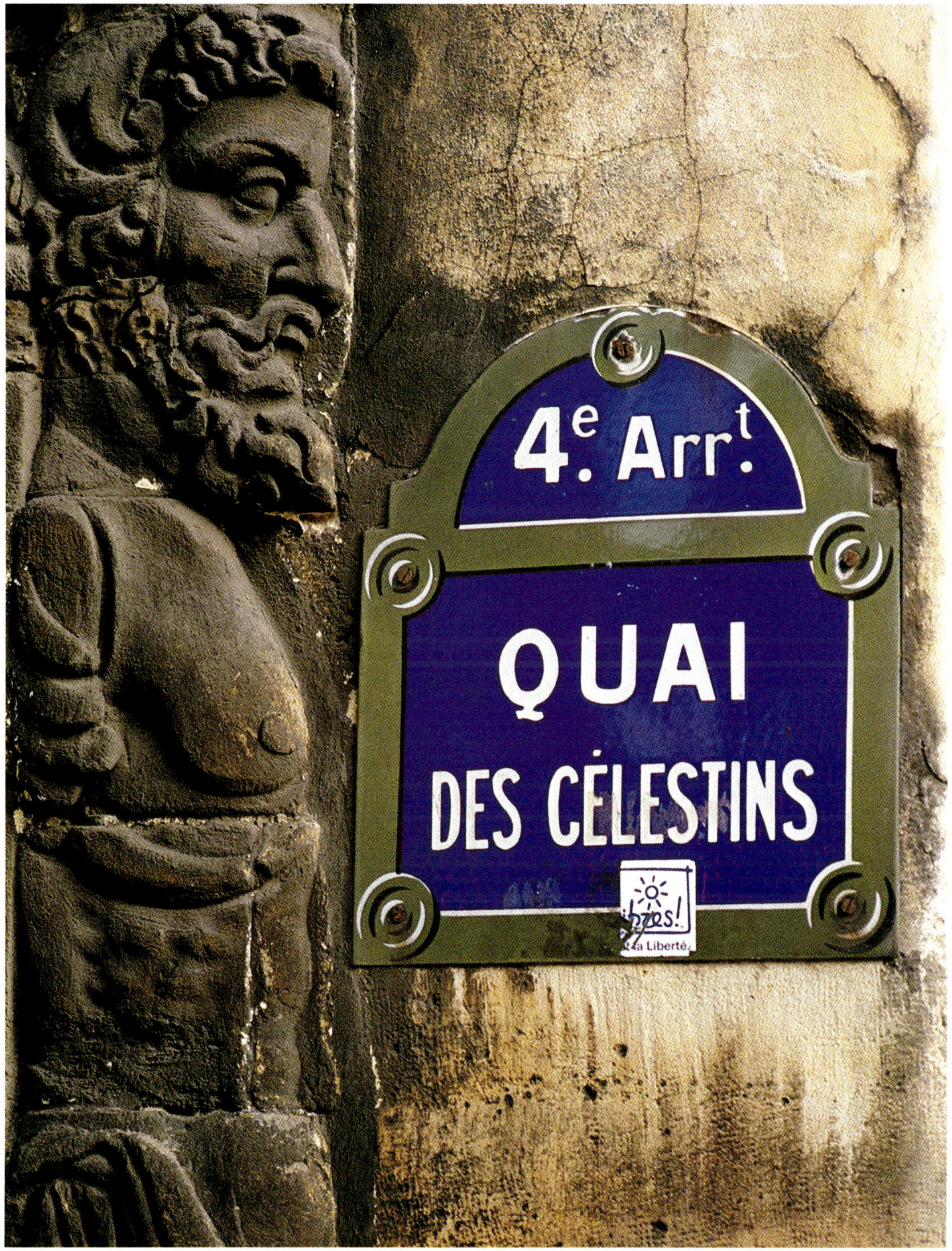
4e Arrt
QUAI
DES CÉLESTINS

72 73 74

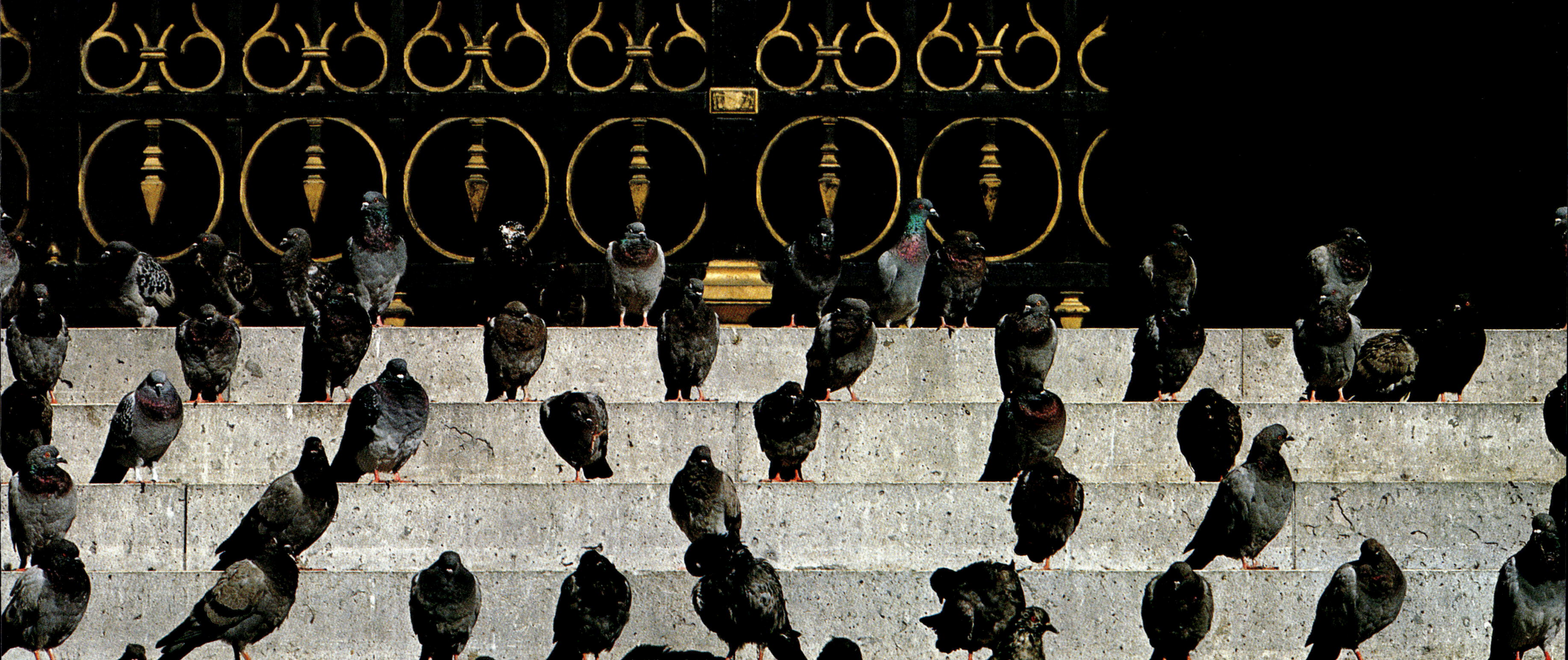

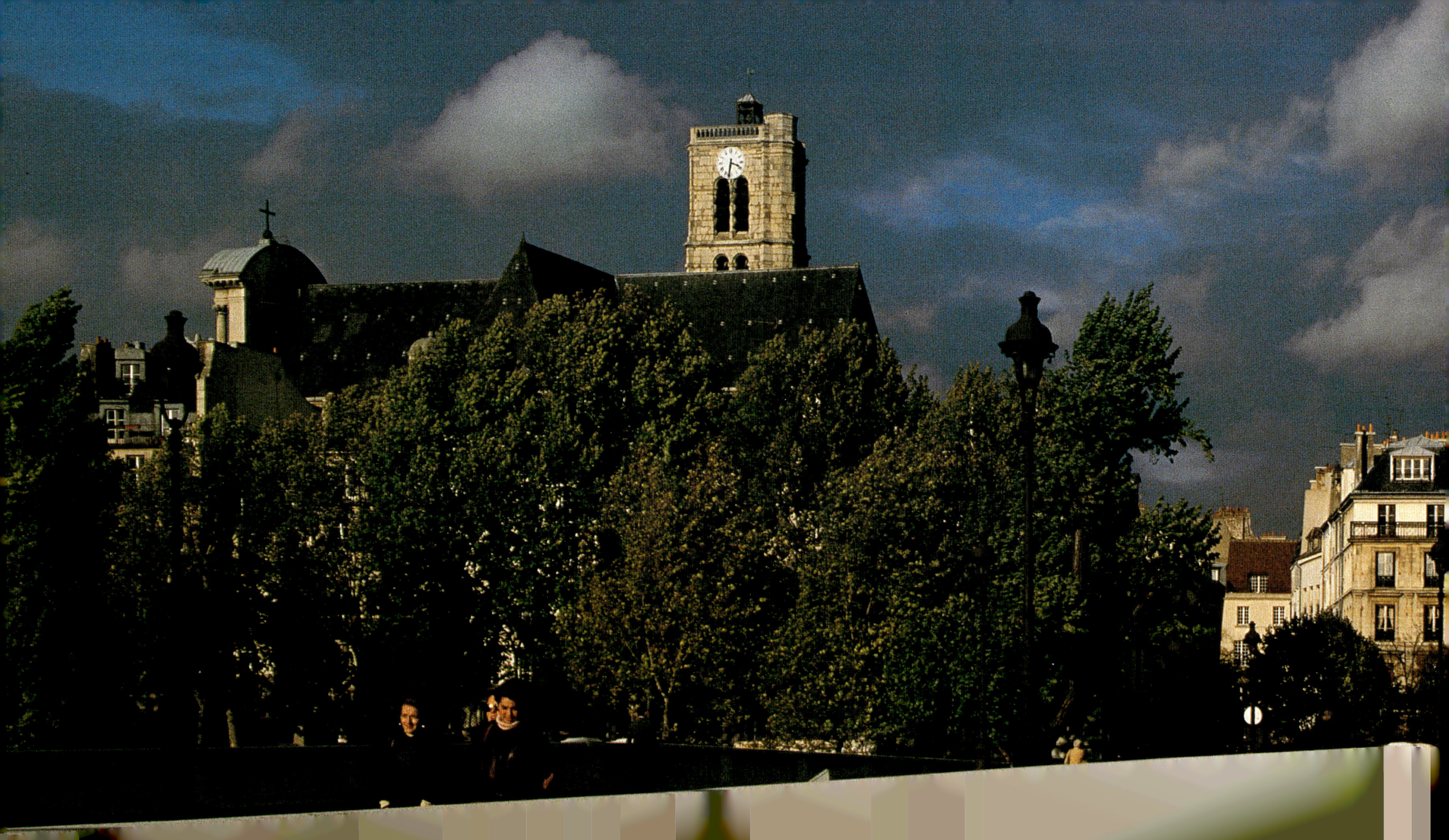

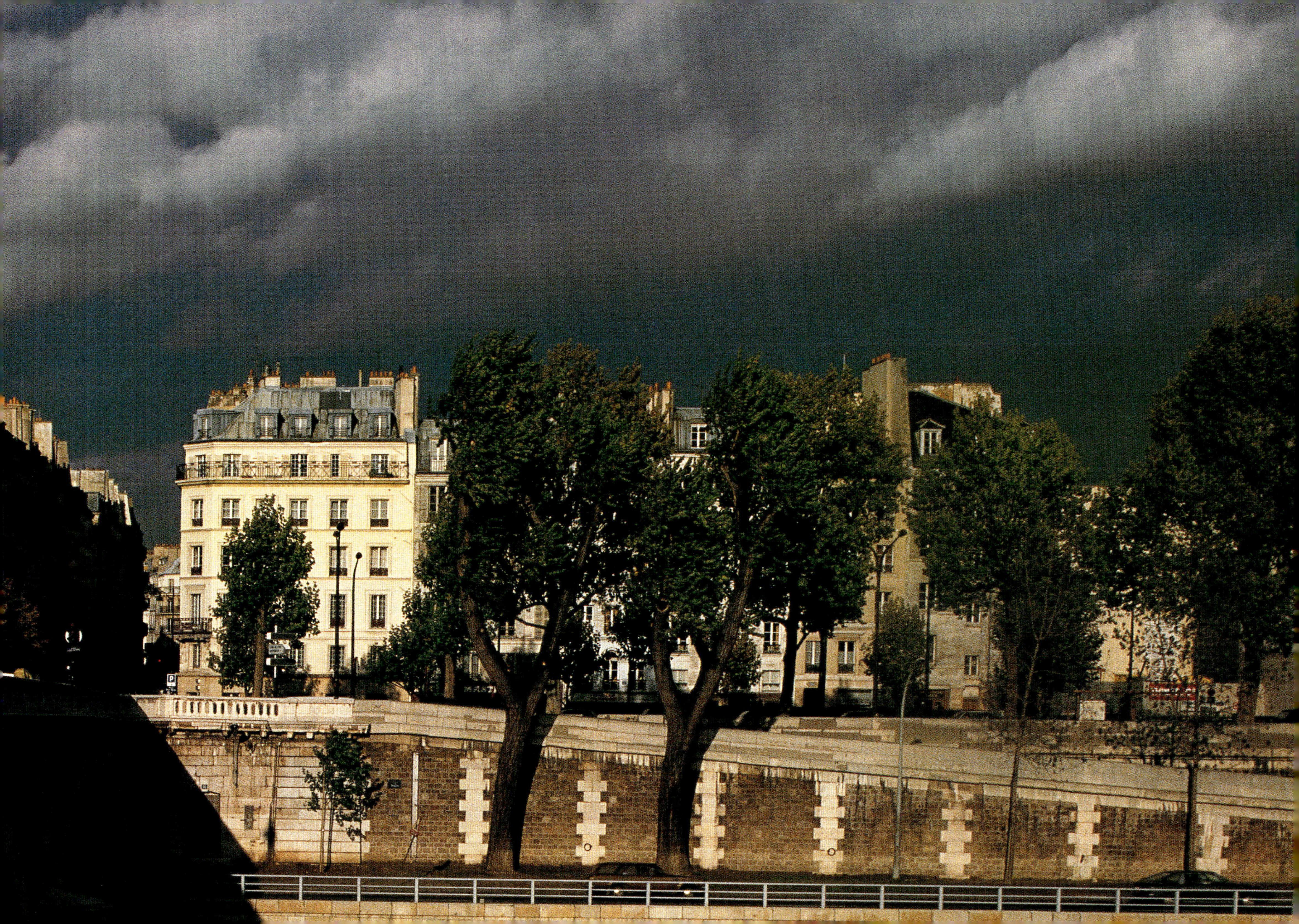

76 77 78

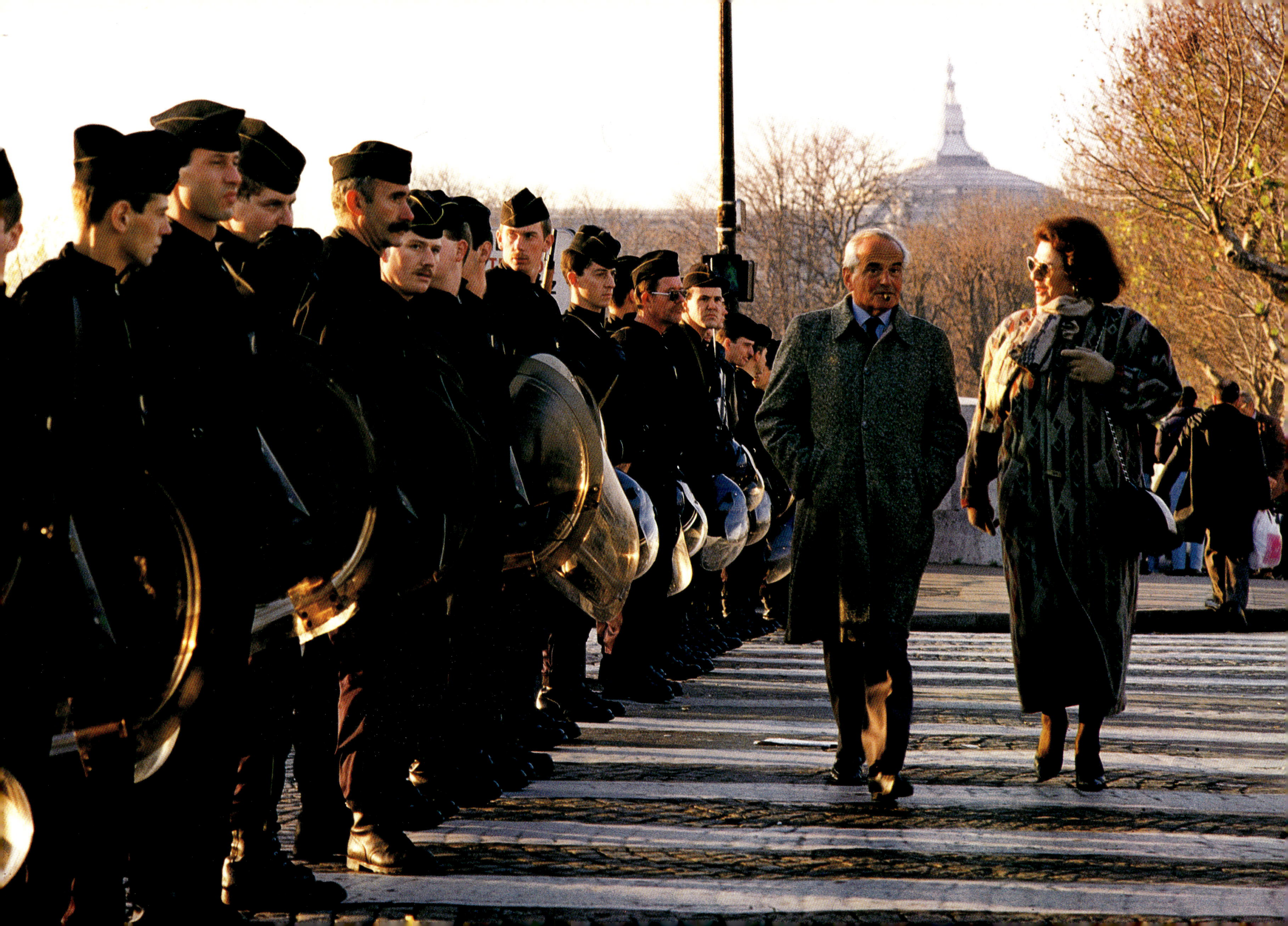

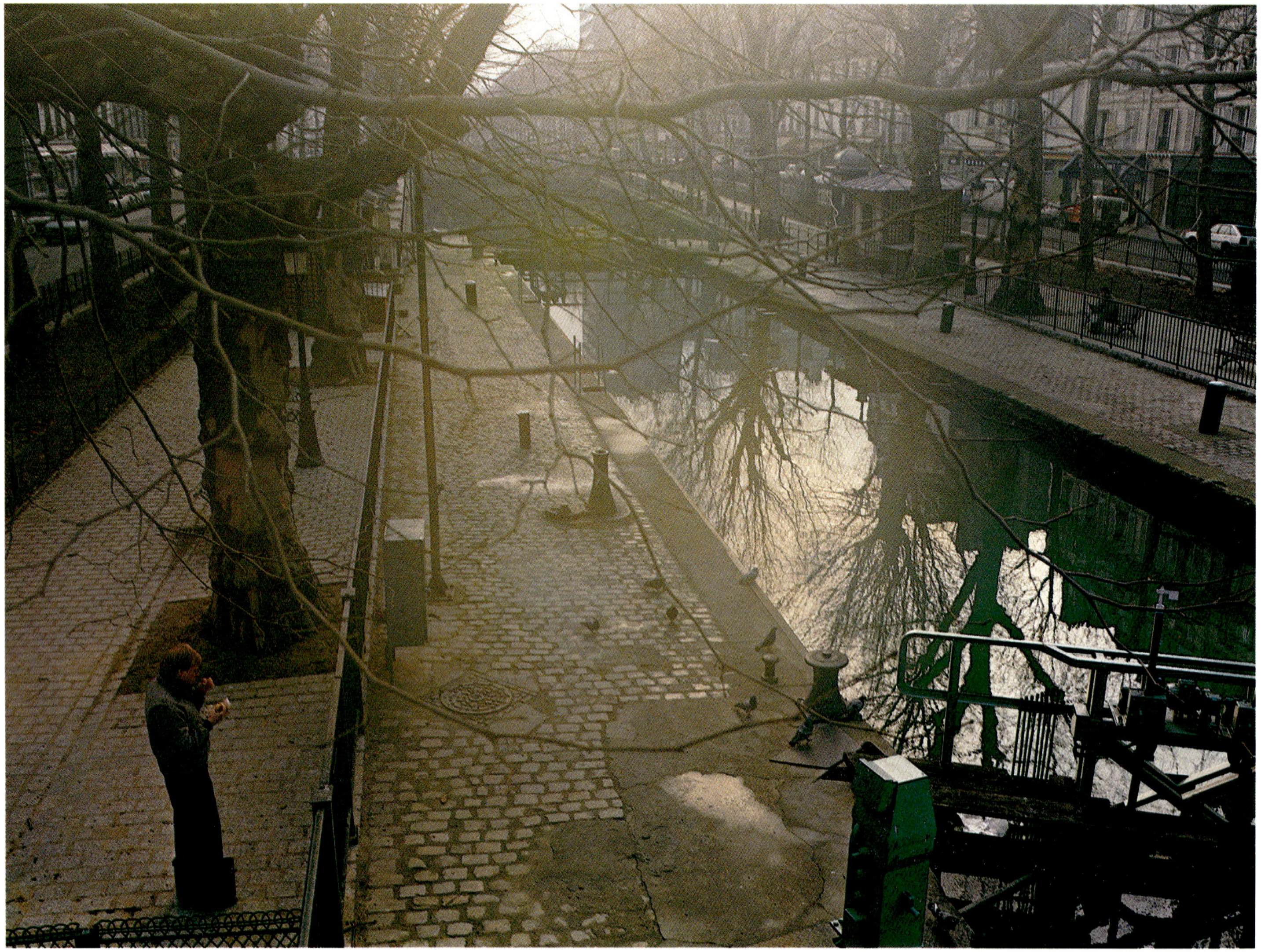

79 80

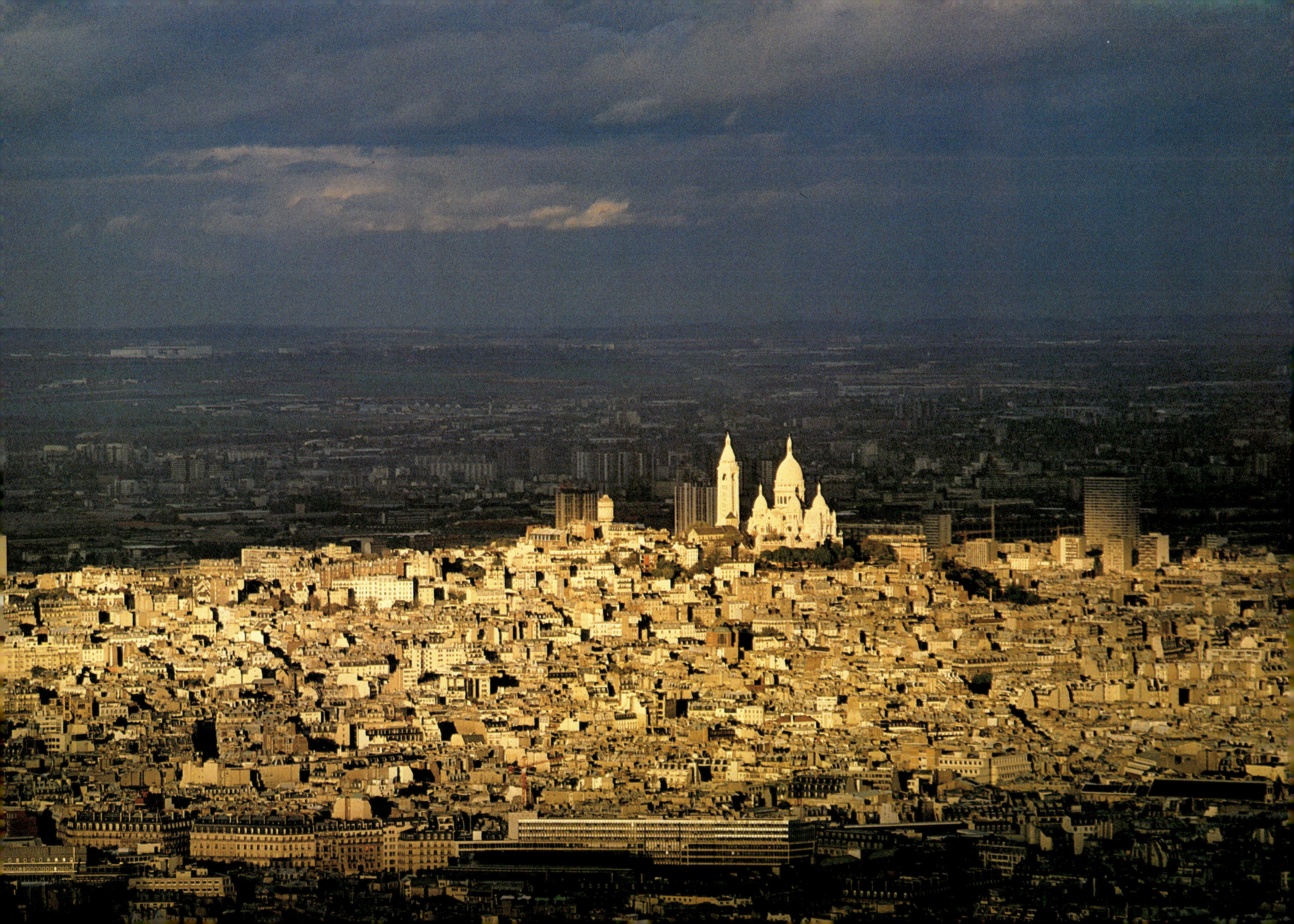

81 82

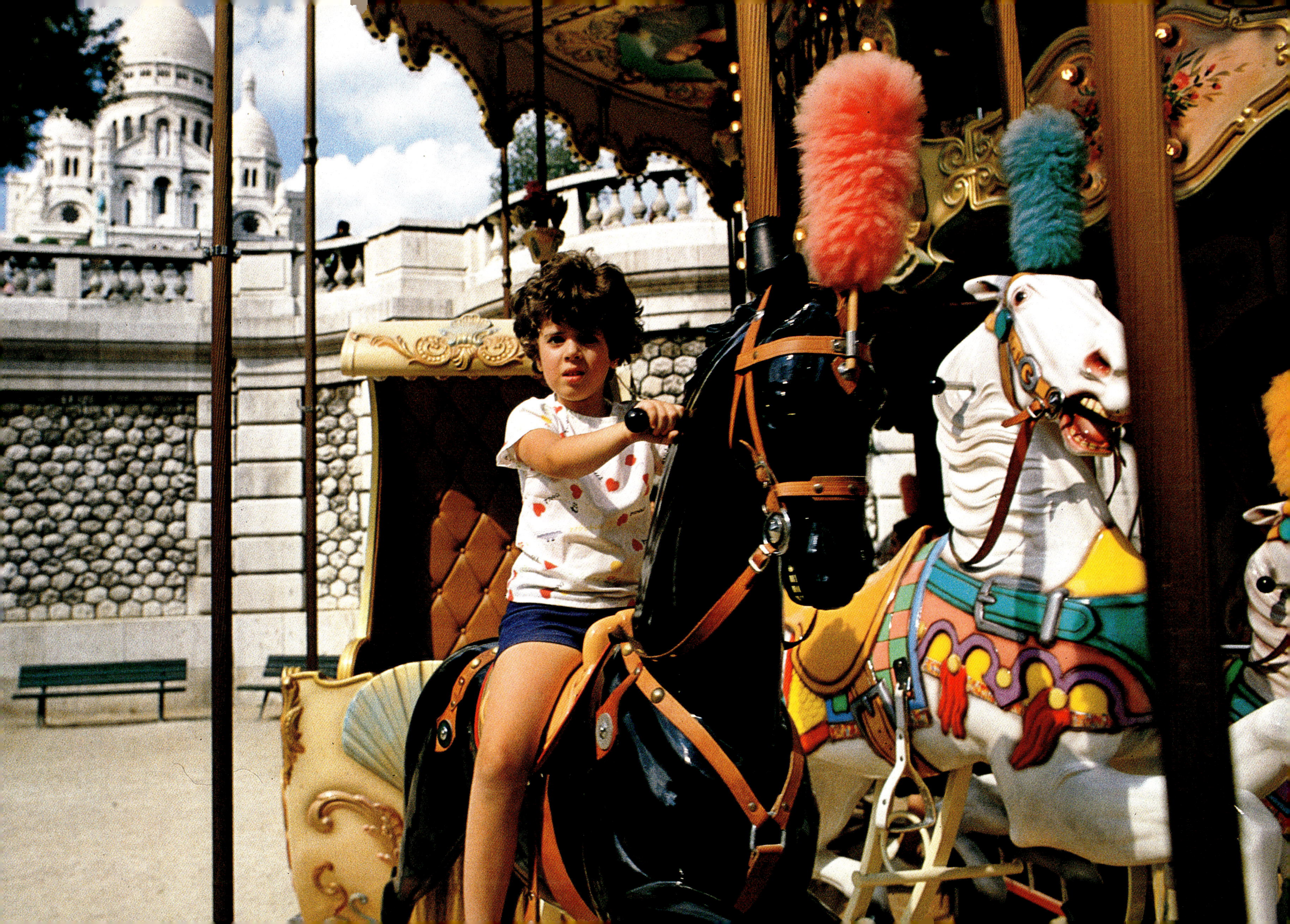

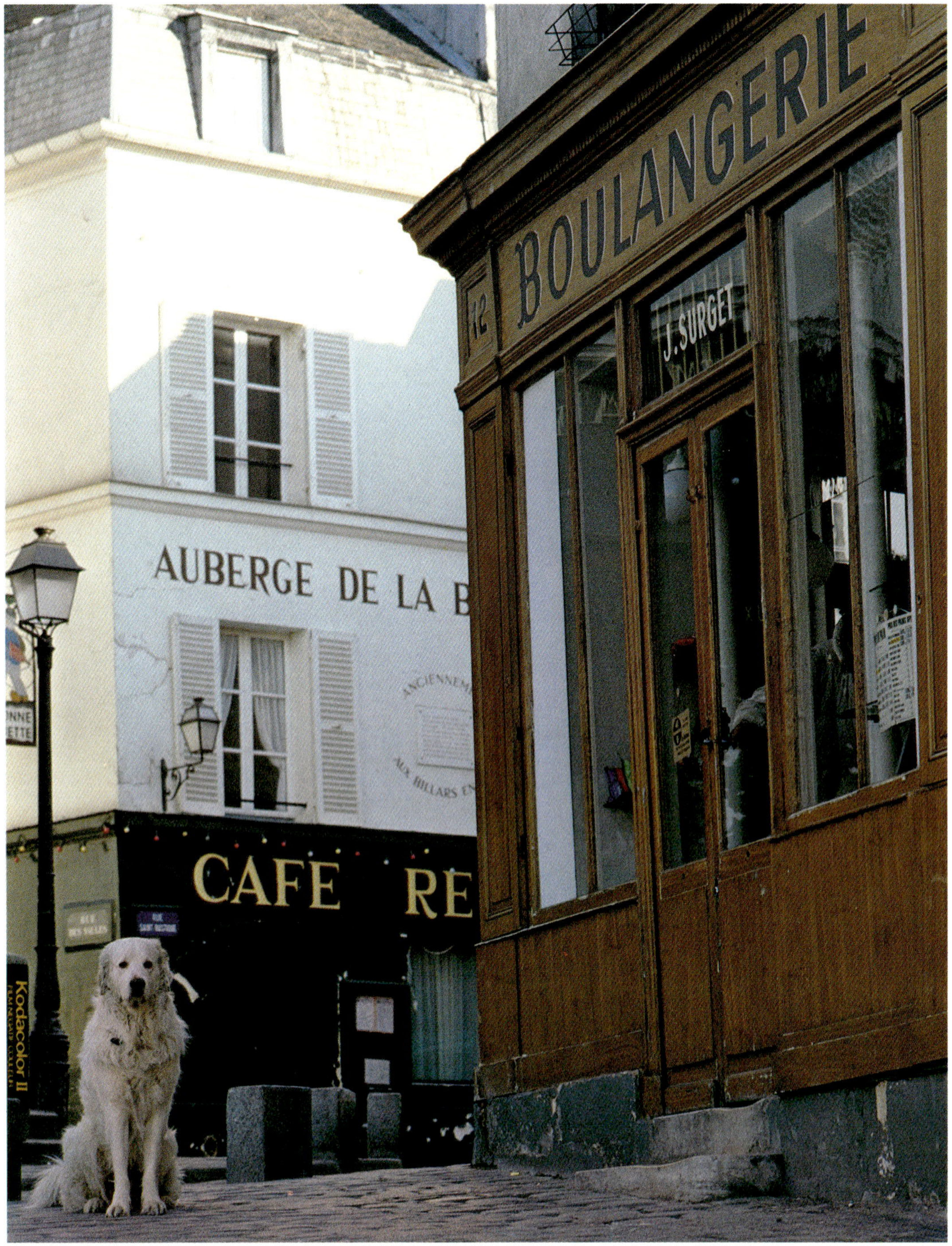

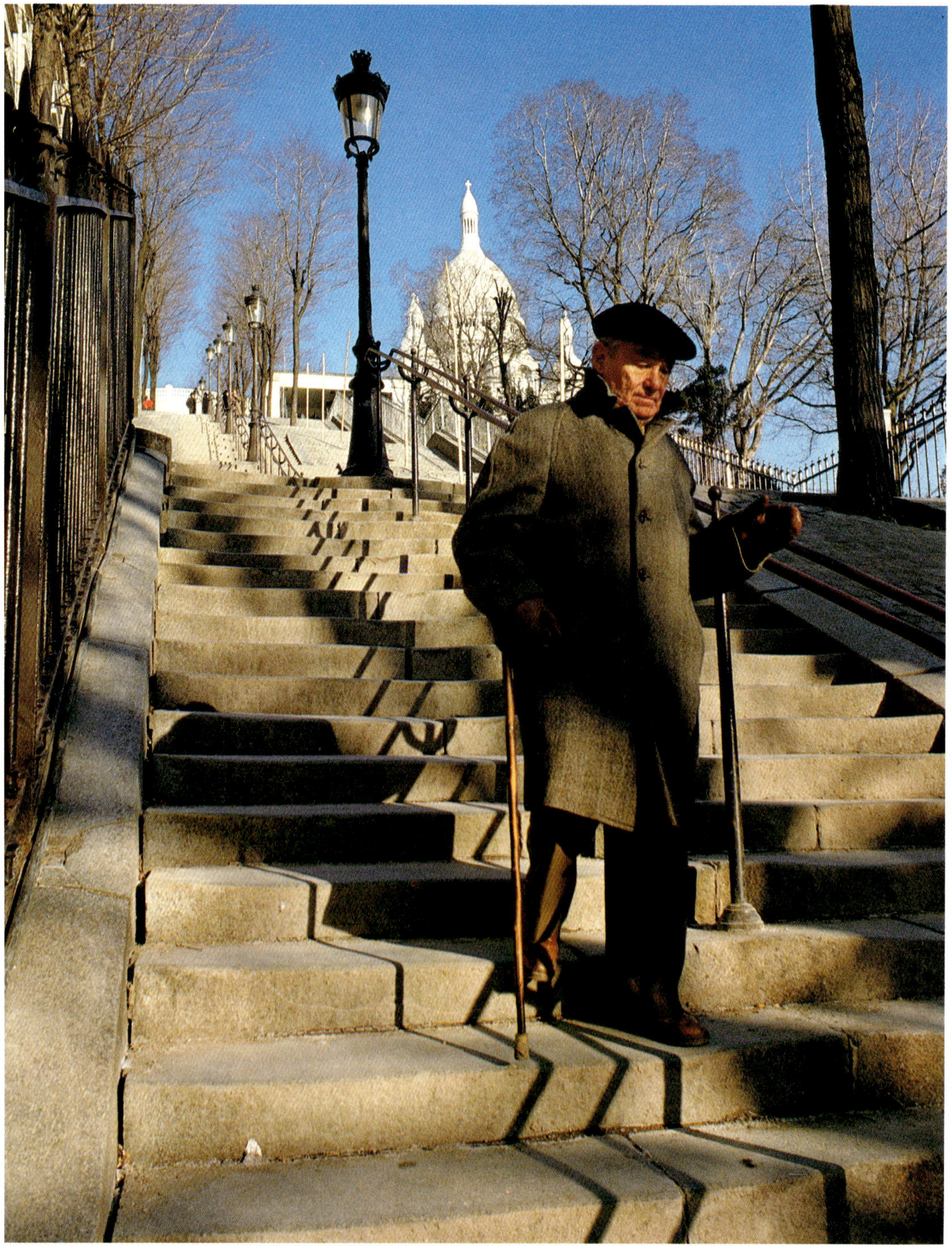

83 84 85

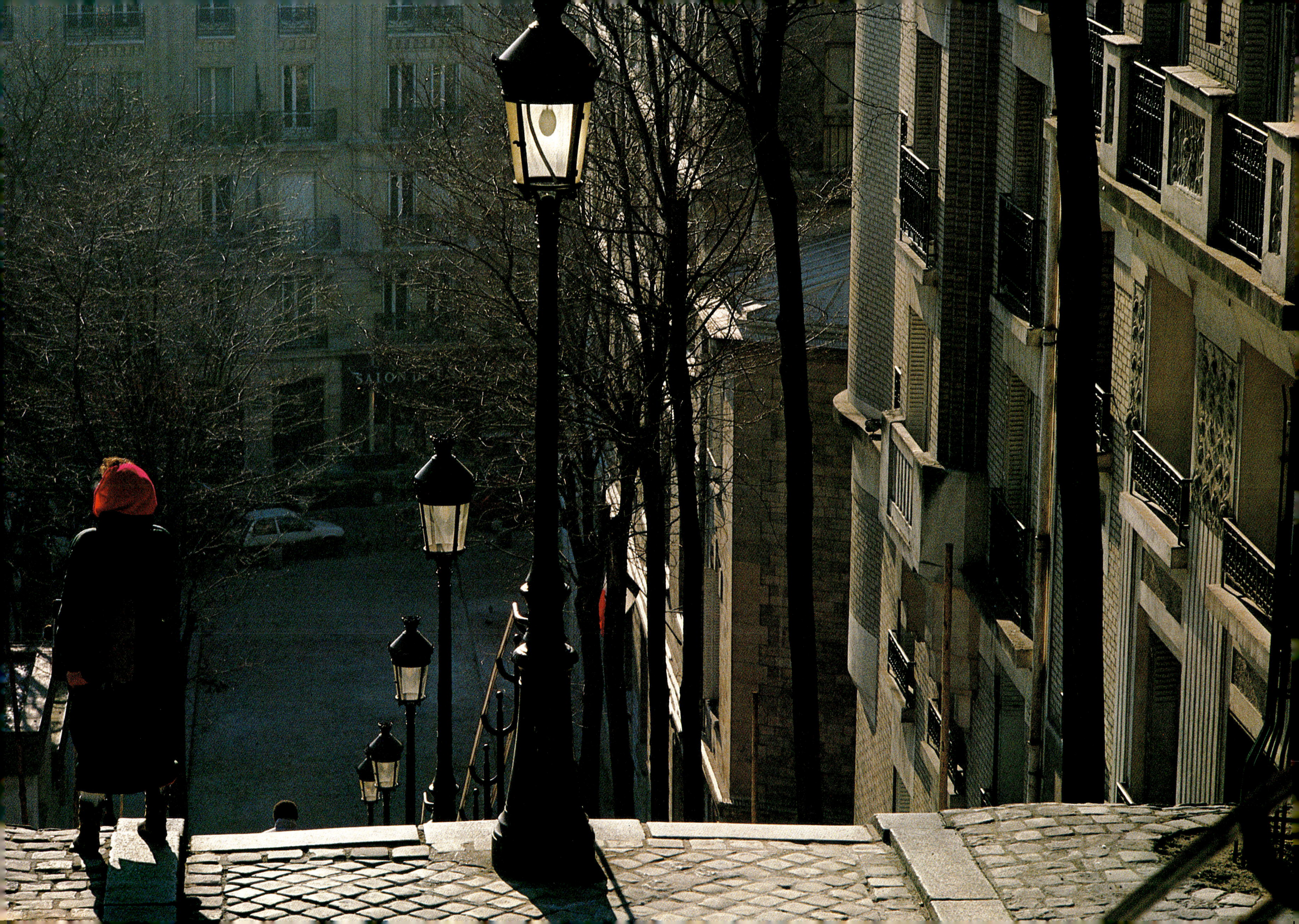

86 87

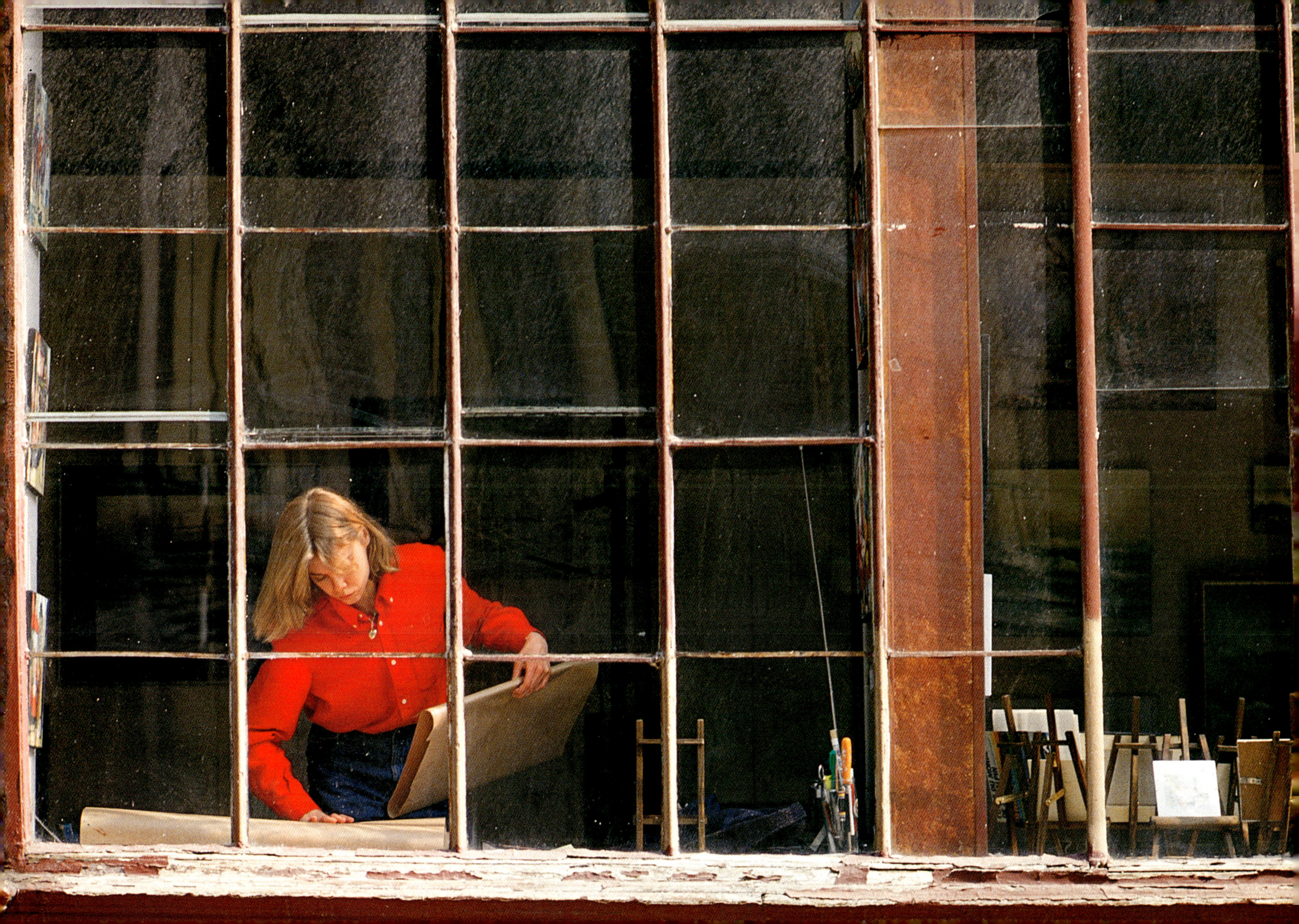

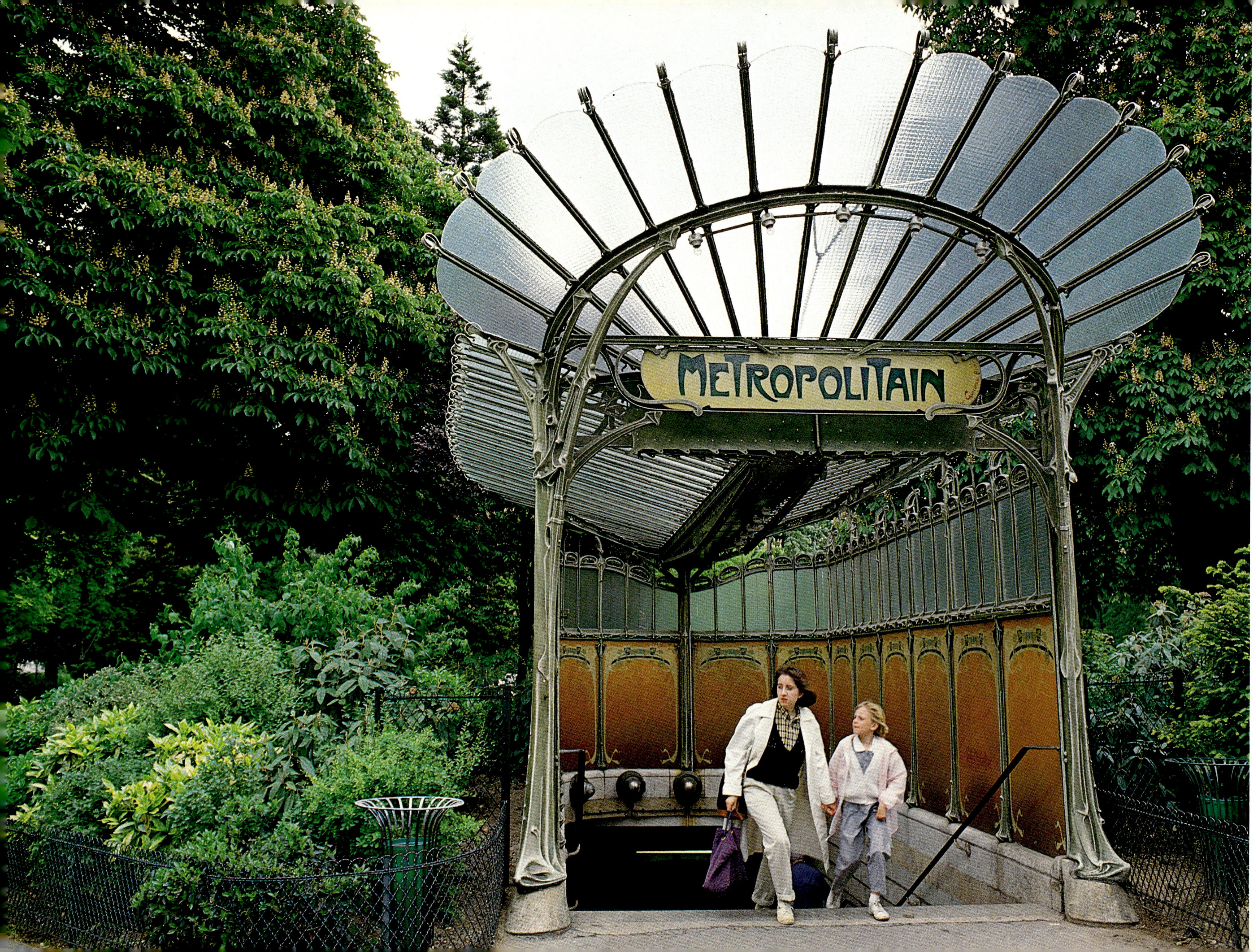
METROPOLITAIN

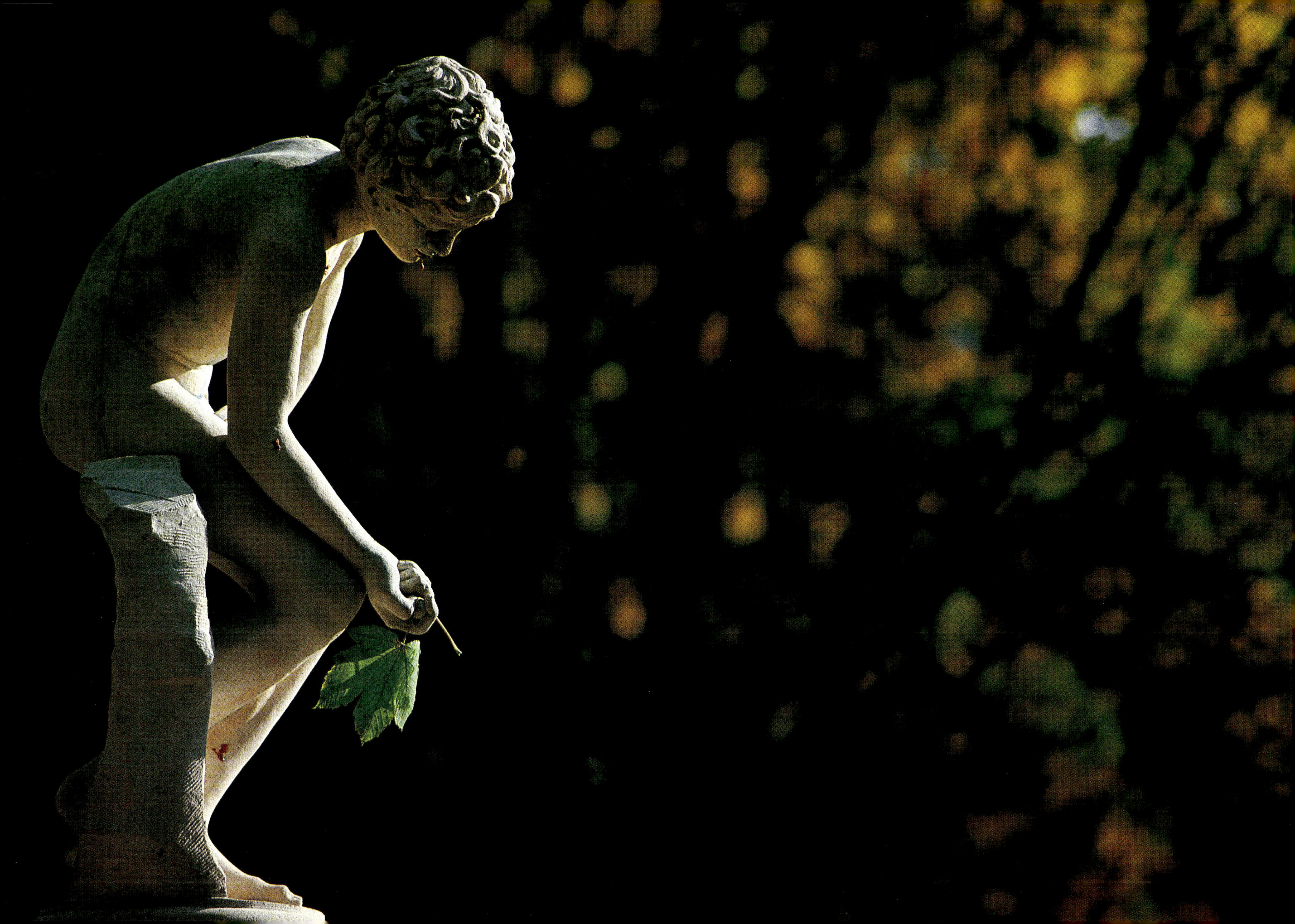

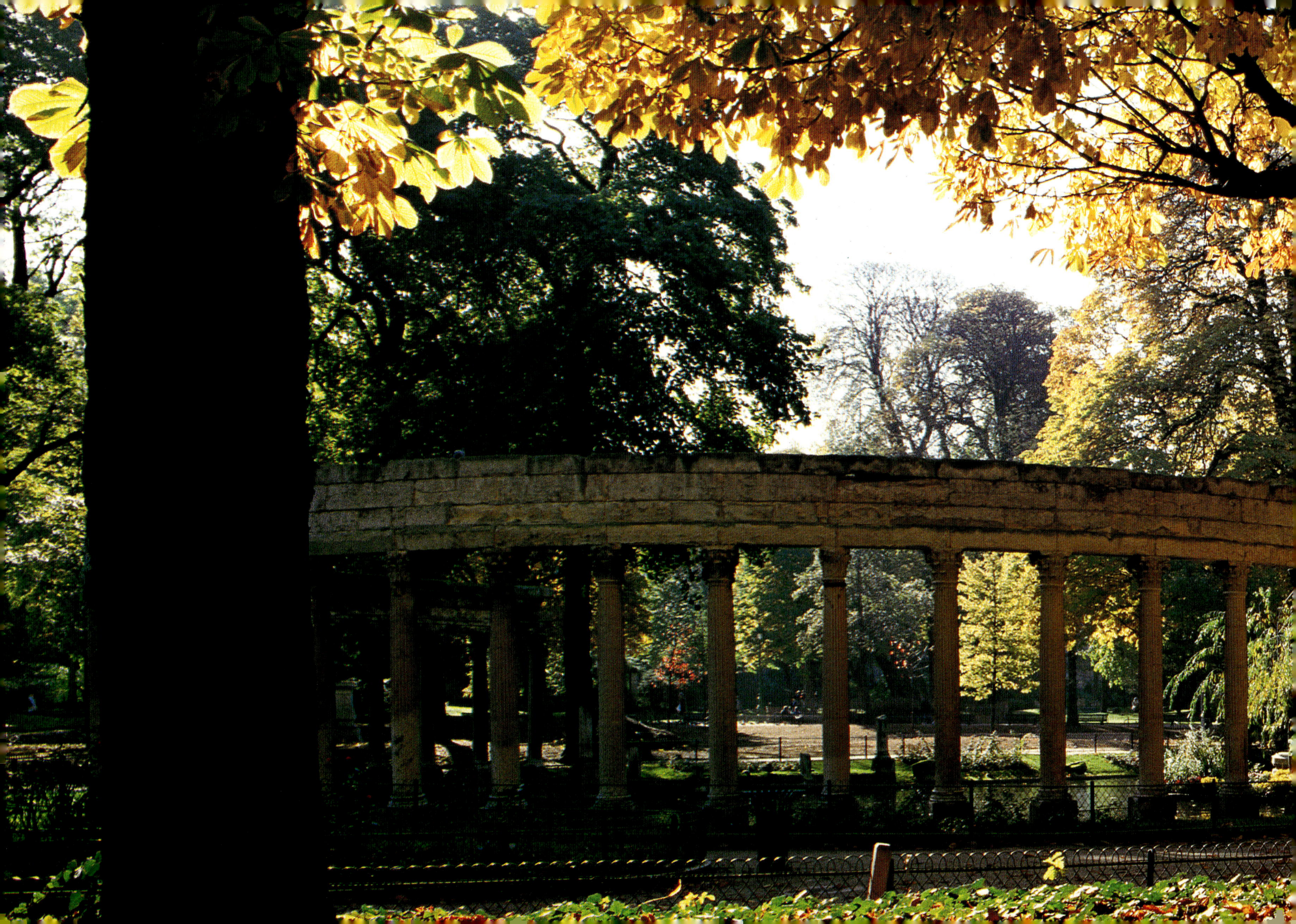

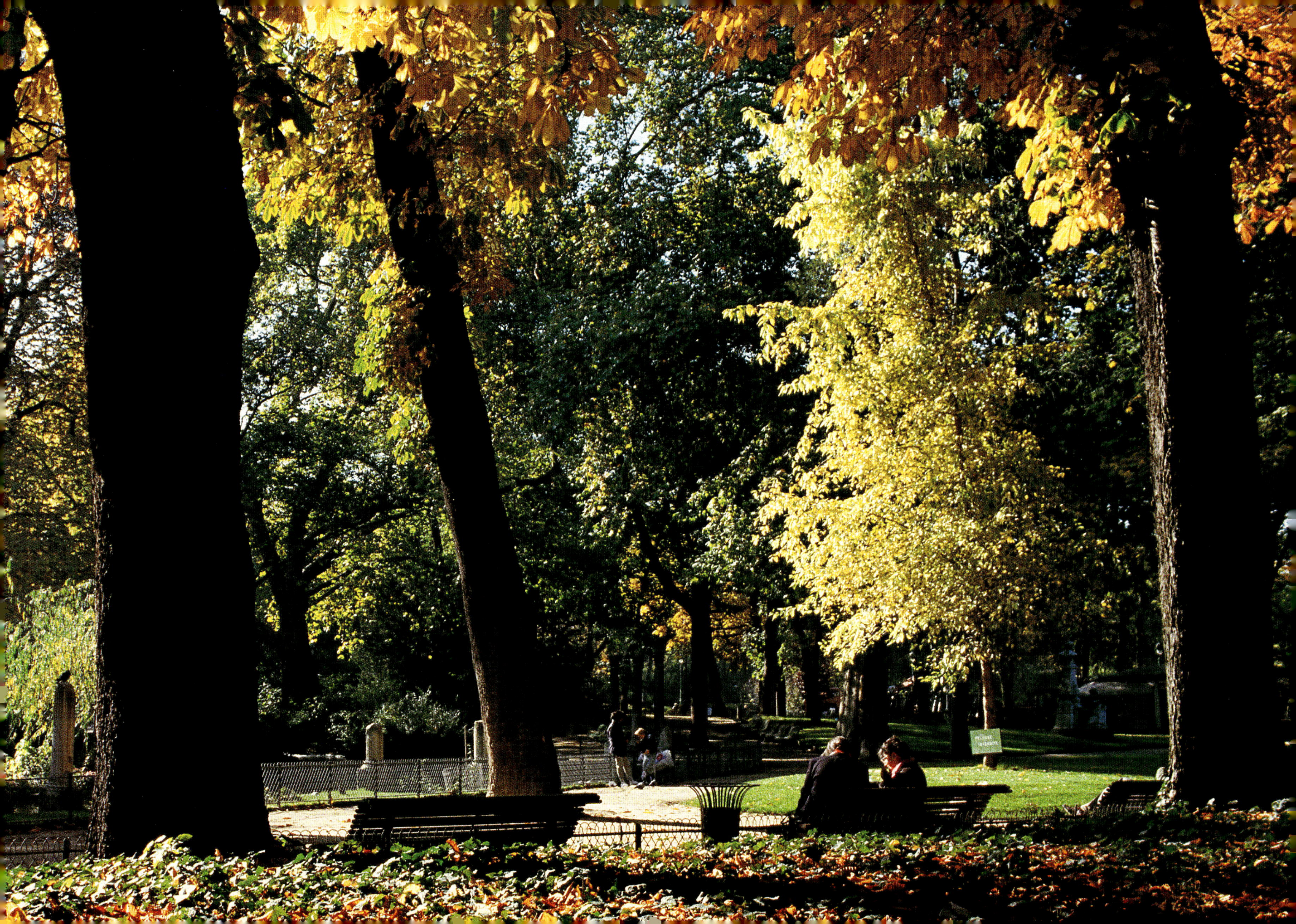

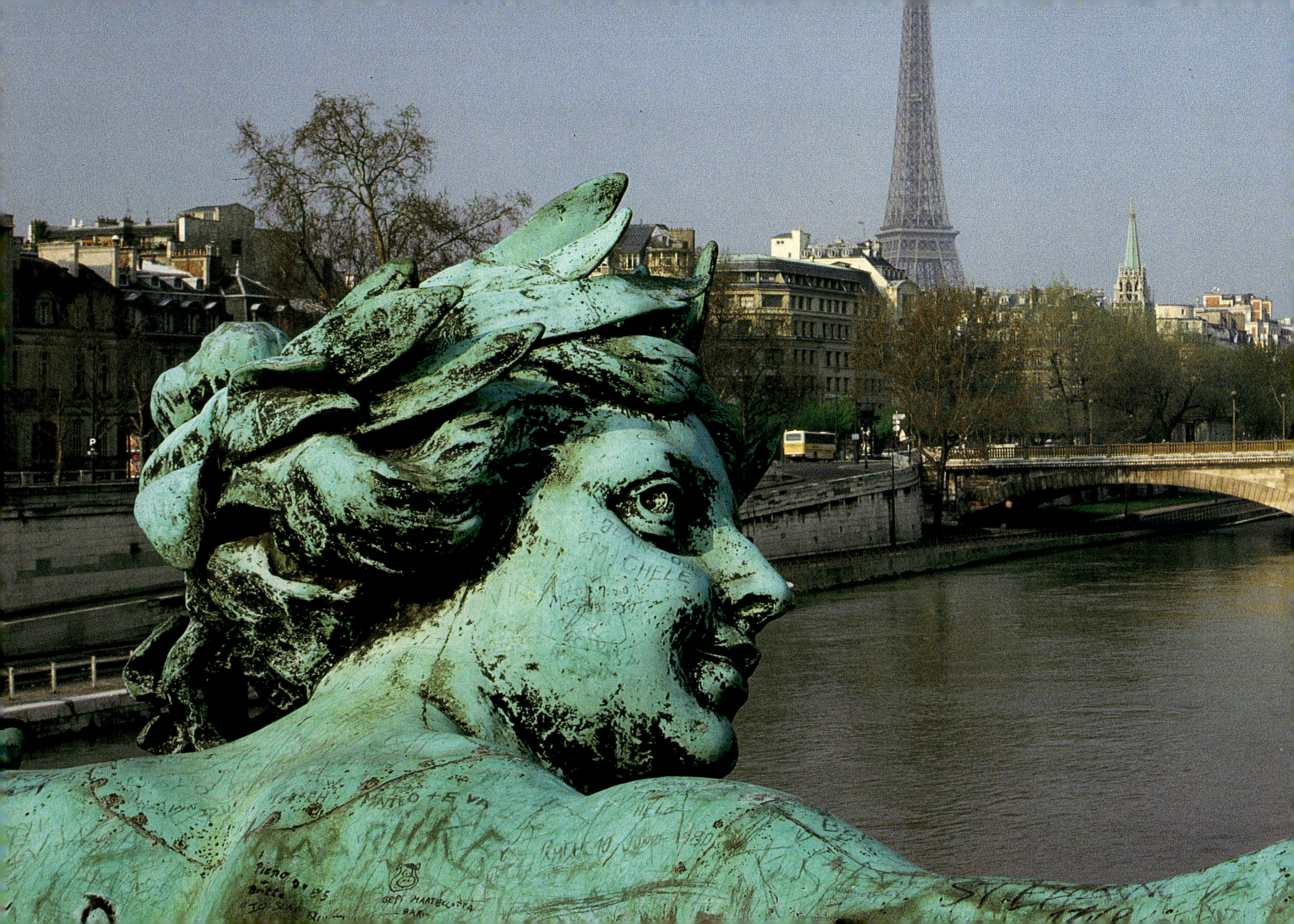
MICHELE

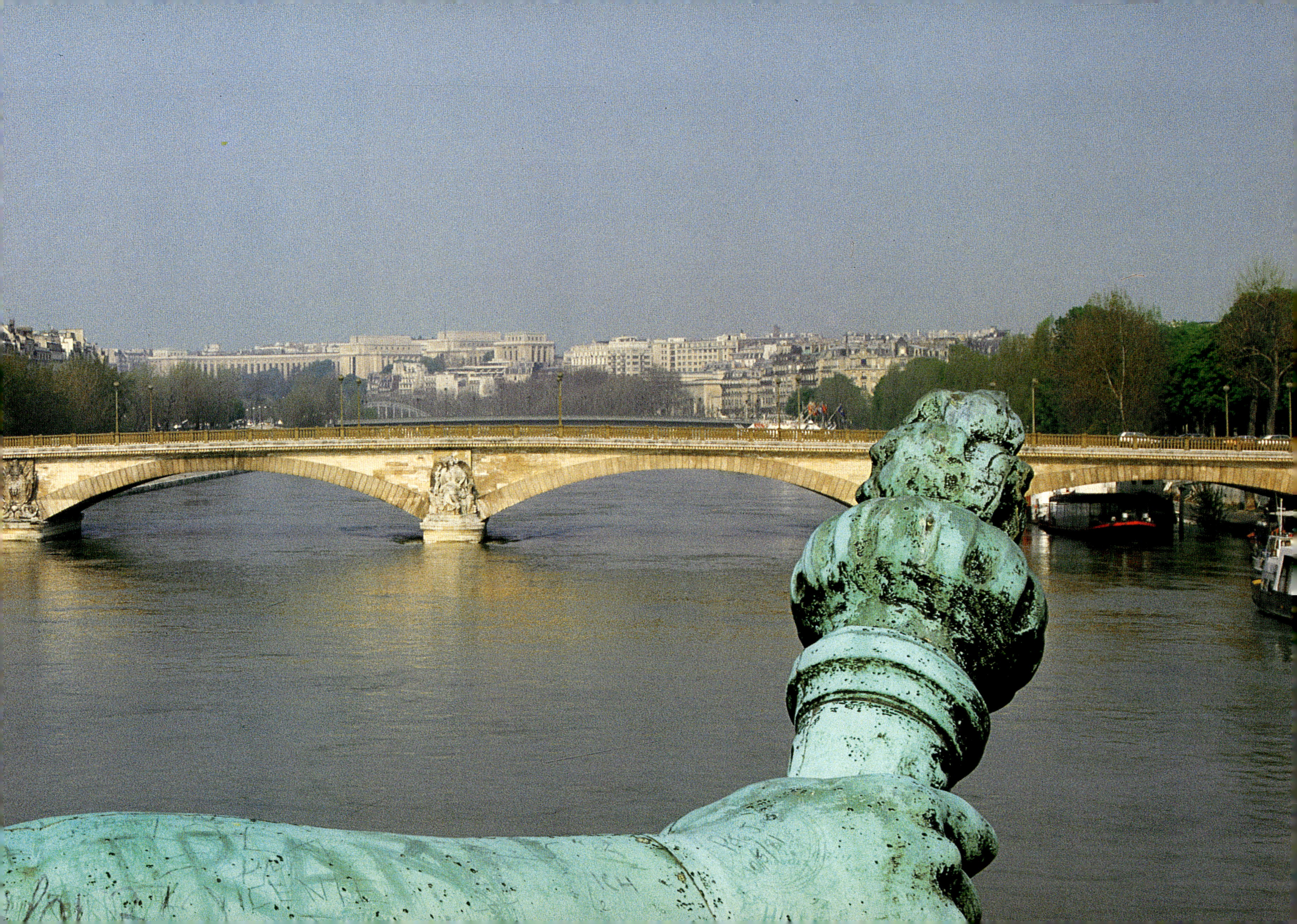

92 93

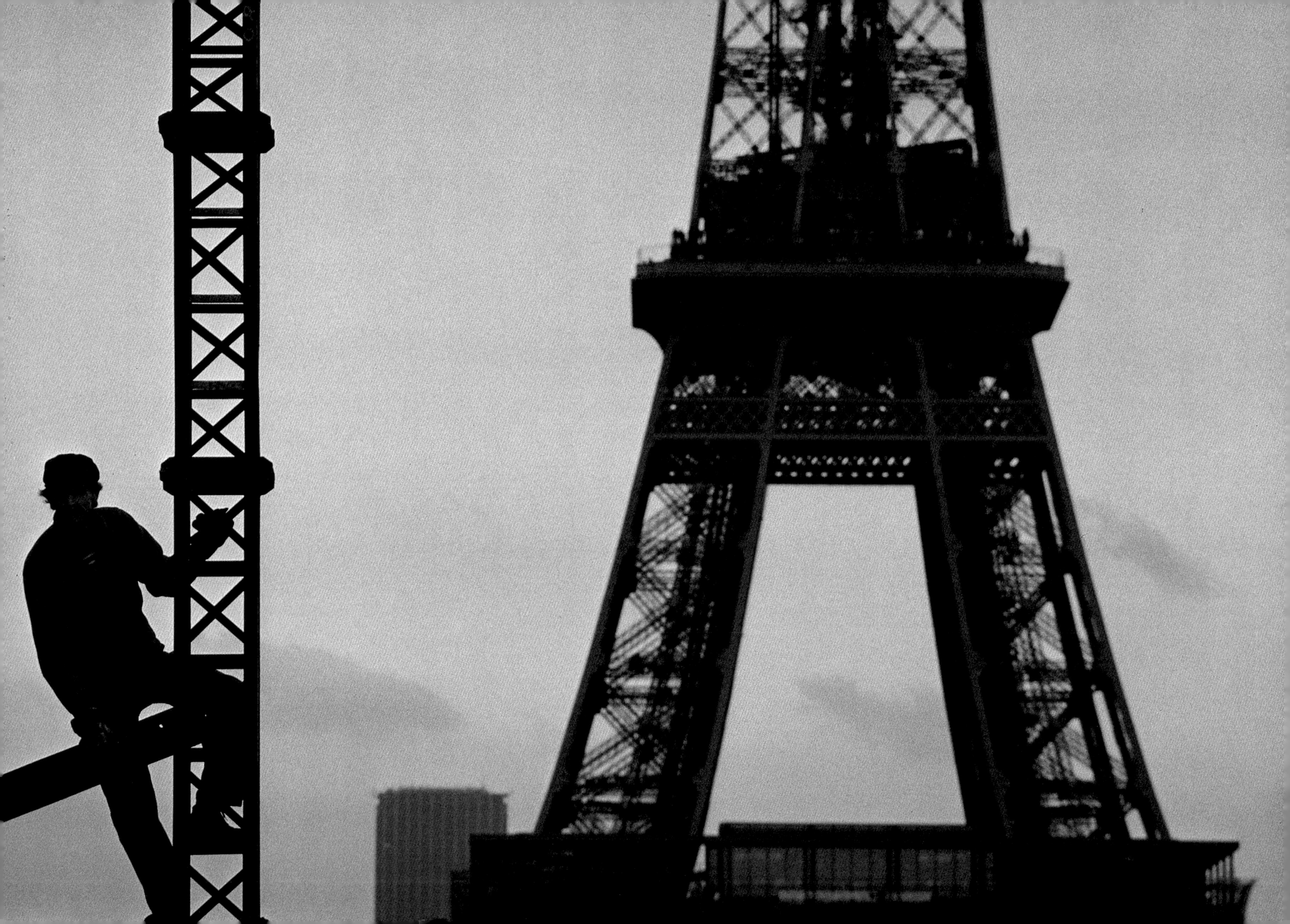

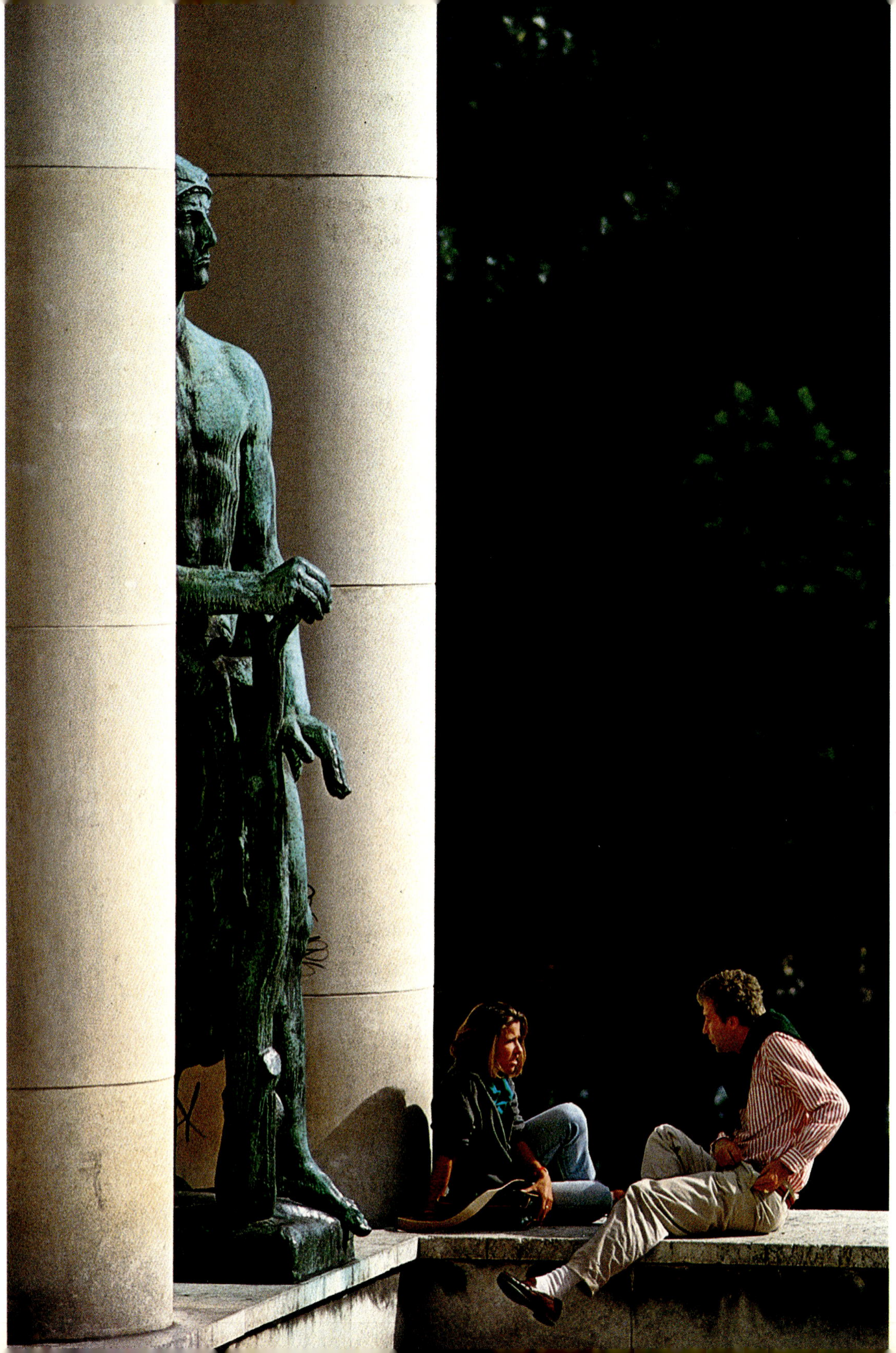

94 95

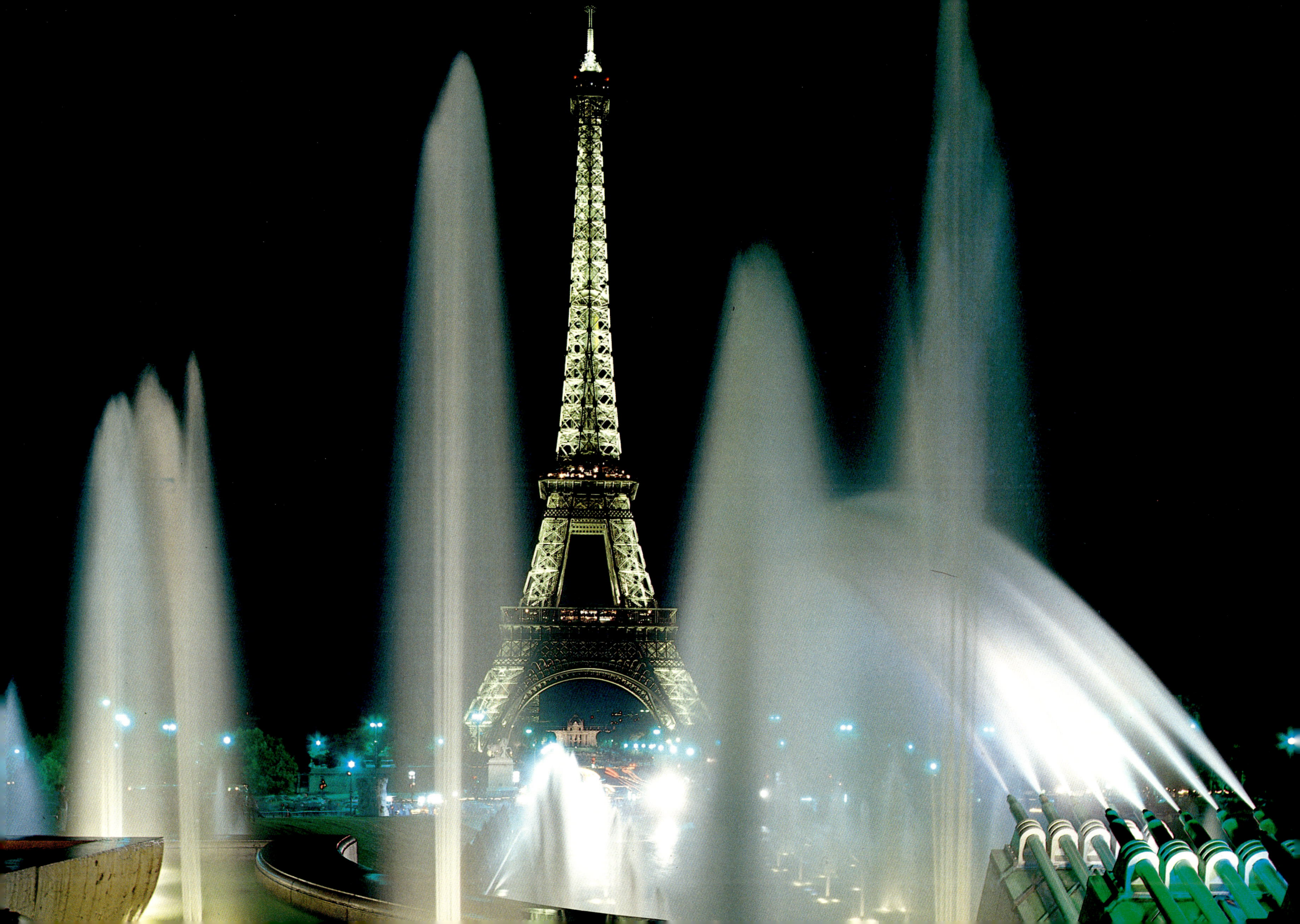

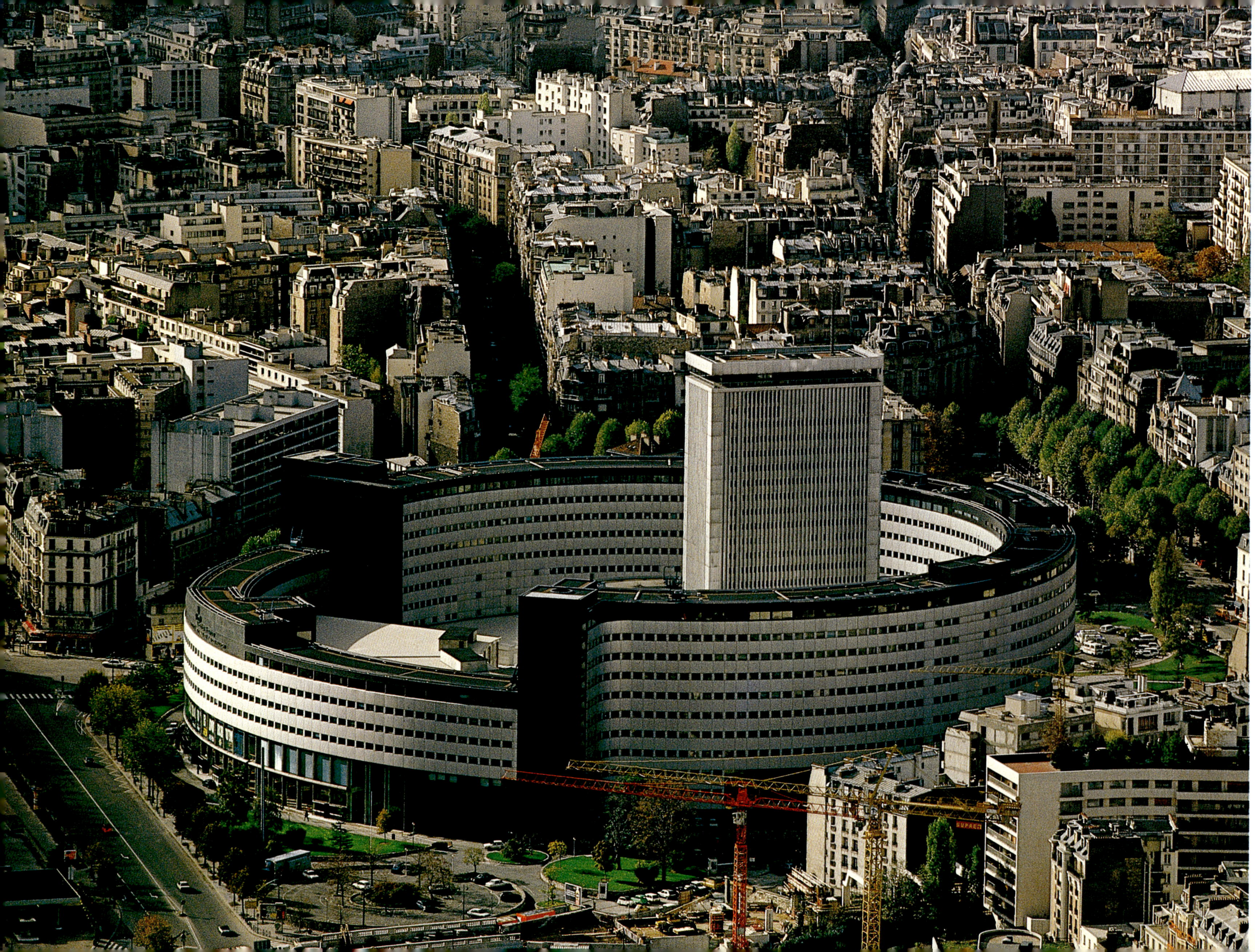

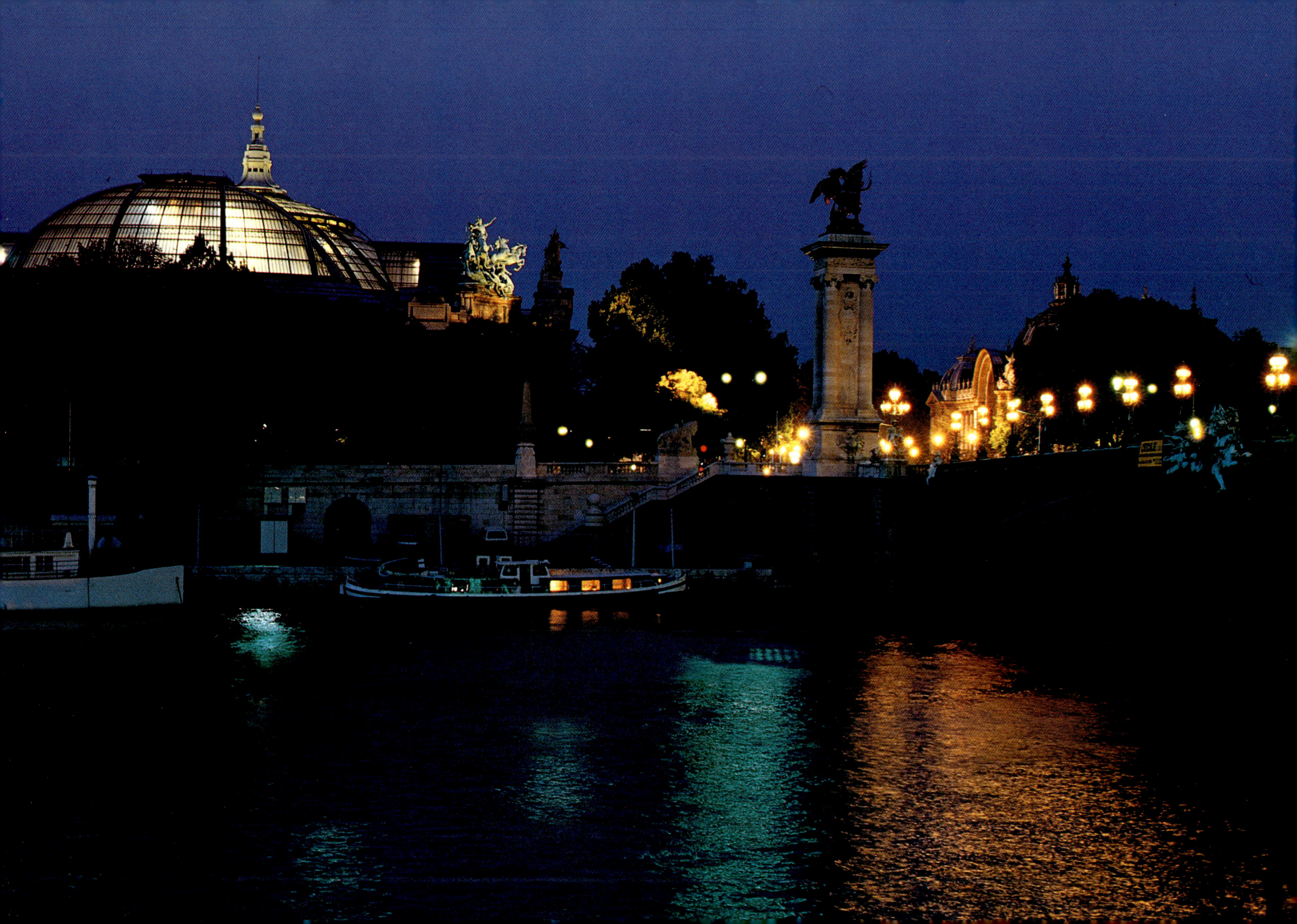

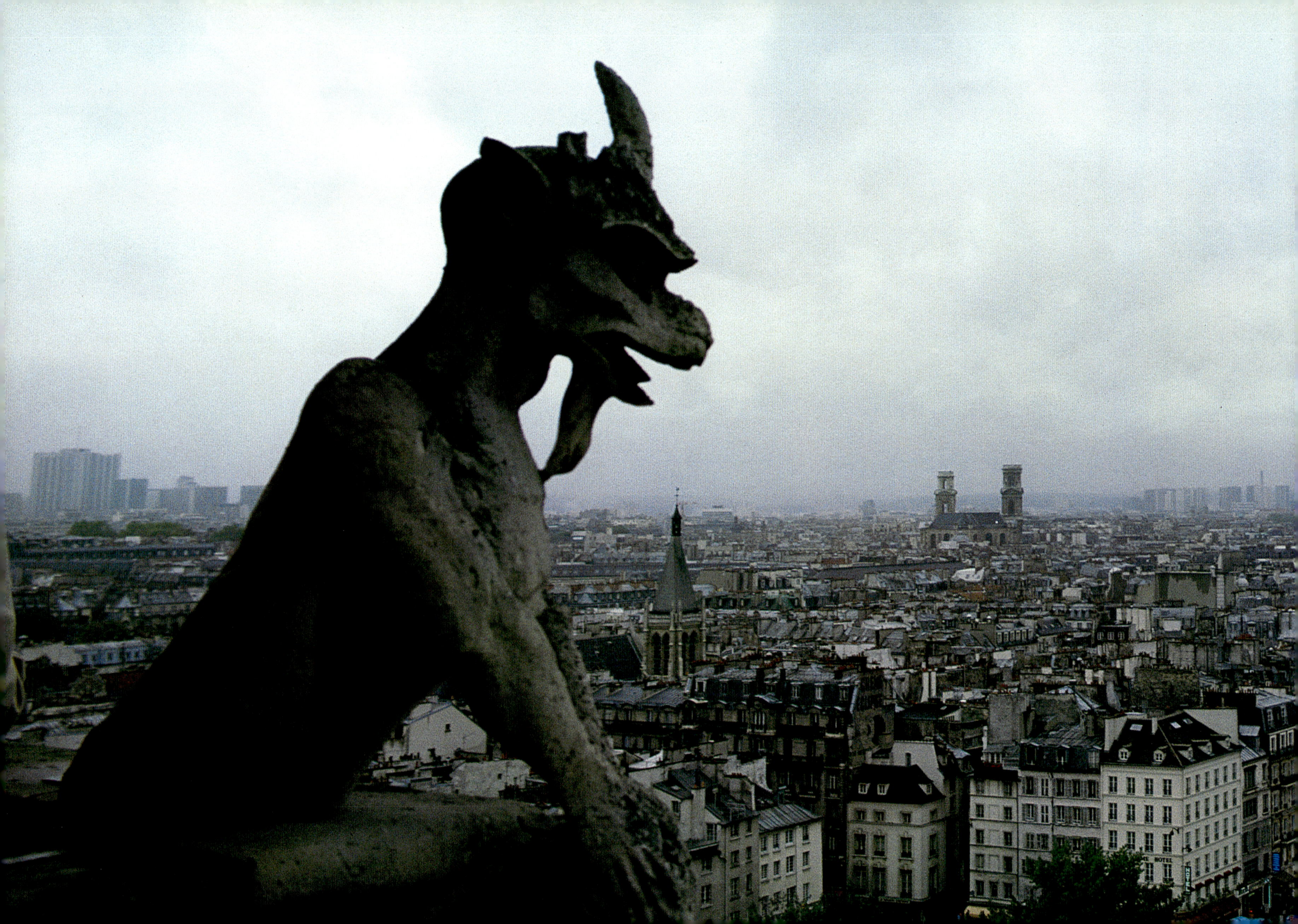

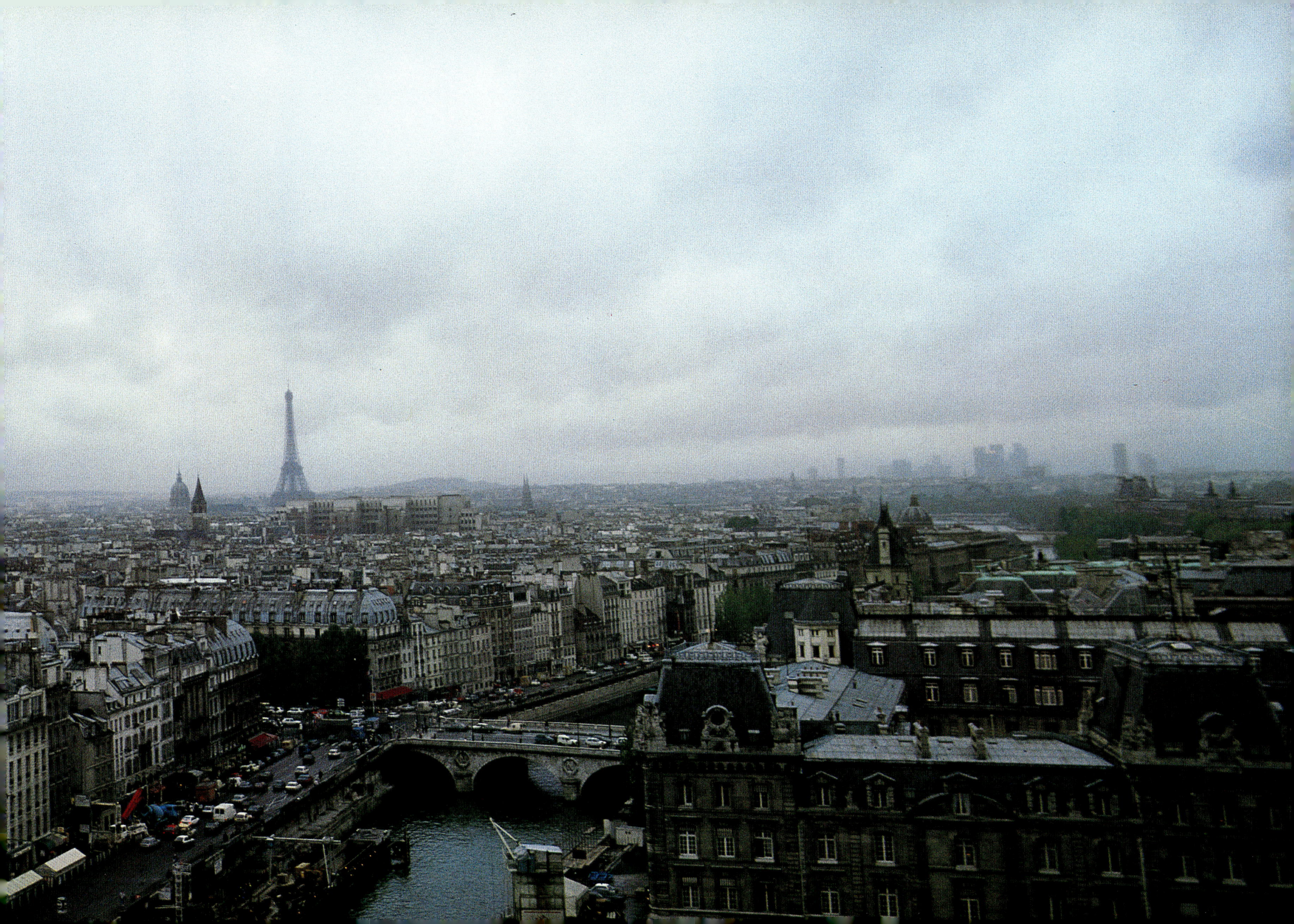

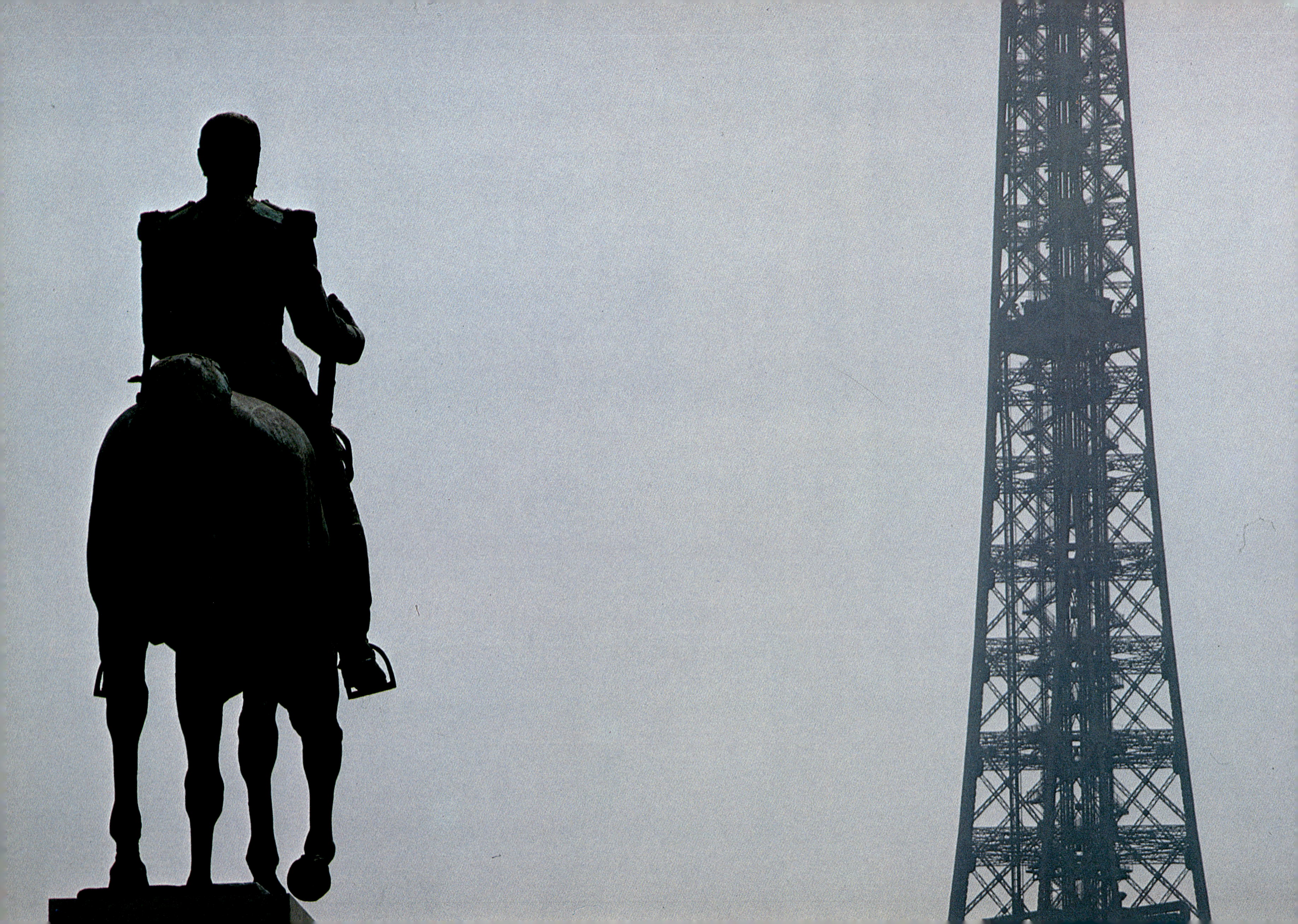

51–53   On the edge of the Marais is the Pompidou Centre, the most controversial and attention-getting building in the world. Since its opening, on 2 February 1977, it has had something like seven and a half million visitors each year – far more than the Eiffel Tower, Versailles, or the Pyramids of Giza. Most frequently likened to an oil refinery, it comes as a shock in the Beaubourg area, which was one of the oldest districts of Paris.

It grew out of the passion for modern art of Georges Pompidou, who succeeded De Gaulle as President of France. It is not a museum with a fixed collection, but a complex where many different sorts of event take place. The Musée National d'Art Moderne, the Centre de Création Industrielle, the Bibliothèque Publique d'Information and the Institut de Recherche et de Coordination Acoustique-Musique (IRCAM) have permanent homes here, but there are also large temporary exhibitions, such as *Paris-Moscow*, *Paris-Berlin* and *Vienna*, which draw crowds of more than five hundred thousand people. Surprisingly, perhaps, half the visitors use the Library. There is also a constant programme of shows, meetings, films and concerts. This 'culture factory' has put Paris back at the centre of the art world, and presents a model for the future.

The vast piazza in front of the building is a permanent fairground, where jugglers, tightrope walkers and acrobats perform as in the Middle Ages, placing their faith in the generosity of their audience.

54   The Galerie Vivienne, which stands on the site of Colbert's house and of the stables of the Duc d'Orléans, was built by a lawyer called Marchoux and until 1825 bore his name. His daughter, the Comtesse de Caen, used her talents as a painter and sculptor to decorate the front facing the Rue des Petits-Champs. The arcade has recently been carefully restored, retaining the antiquarian bookshops where bibliophiles may browse safe from traffic and the weather.

55   This vast dreaming head by Henri de Miller rests on the paving stones in front of Saint-Eustache as on a pillow, inviting visitors to the Forum des Halles to rest on one of the neighbouring benches and to admire the more permanent architecture of that remarkable church.

56, 57   The glass-roofed arcades of Paris, where tiny shopfronts are squeezed together in a dim half-light, retain an air of mystery. Junk shops, antique dealers, booksellers and craftsmen congregate as in an Eastern bazaar. Here the passer-by may find a unique object, a rare book, or perhaps just the buttons from the uniform of a Napoleonic grenadier. The Galerie Véro-Dodat – named after its creators, two *charcutiers* – was famous for its elegant shops in the early nineteenth century. Time has stood still, and in its provincial tranquillity one feels oneself in the past.

58, 59   Is it sensible to bankrupt oneself for one's king? To celebrate the victories of Louis XIV, the Maréchal de la Feuillade laid out a circular *place* and for its centrepiece commissioned from the sculptor Martin Desjardins a statue of the King in his coronation robes, crowned with laurels. When the statue was erected in the middle of the ring of façades by Hardouin Mansart the bill came to 7,000,000 francs. Louis XIV granted a subsidy, but it was only 150,000 francs, and the spendthrift Marshal was forced to economize by gradually reducing the number of lamps in the square, and sacrificing the reliefs below the King's statue. They are now in the Louvre; the effigy of the 'tyrant' was melted down during the Revolution.

The present equestrian statue of Louis XIV, by François-Joseph Bosio, was set up in 1822. The magnificent façades have been excellently restored and cleaned, and the Place des Victoires is once again as elegant as it was in the seventeenth century.

60, 61   The Neo-Renaissance Hôtel de Ville gained greatly in dignity when cars were banished from the square in front. It was built in 1874–82 to replace the old town hall destroyed in the Commune of 1871. The ground here originally sloped down to the river, and the square was known until 1830 as the Place de Grève – 'of the strand'. This was the place for public executions from the Middle Ages right up to the early nineteenth century. Here too the unemployed would gather, giving rise to the expression *faire grève*, which now means to go on strike. The new layout, with its fountains, provides a suitable setting for civic ceremonies.

62   The Hôtel de Sens has had a curious history. It was built between 1475 and 1507, and was until 1622 the Paris residence of the archbishops of Sens. With its three corner turrets, its Gothic portal leading to a passageway covered by a Flamboyant vault, and its handsome inner courtyard it is a rare survival in the city of a medieval mansion.

In the sixteenth century the Hôtel de Sens became the centre of the Cardinal de Guise's plots, when his brother the Duke, leader of the Catholic Ligue, aspired to usurp Henri III's place on the throne; then it witnessed the extravagant life of Henri IV's cast-off wife, Marguerite de Valois, known as 'la reine Margot'. After 1760 it was the headquarters of the mail-coach service to Lyons. It now houses the Bibliothèque Forney, with large holdings of material on the fine and decorative arts as well as a collection of posters.

63   The district around Saint-Merri was populated in the Middle Ages by drapers, tailors and furriers, and was famed throughout Europe for its hats, its perfumes, and its moneylenders. Today the area sees itself as the home of avant-garde art, and the Flamboyant Gothic church has acquired an odd neighbour in the multicoloured moving sculptures of Tinguely and Nicky de Saint-Phalle which decorate a fountain dedicated to Igor Stravinsky. The composer of the *Rite of Spring* is no longer here, alas, to tell us what he thinks of such an aggressive act of homage.

64, 65, 67   The Place des Vosges was created by Henri IV in the Marais on the site of an old mansion that had become a horsemarket. He first intended to build a manufactory there, but decided instead to lay out a square surrounded by thirty-eight houses of brick with stone dressings. Royal whim, or stroke of genius? The King who had promised the common people 'a chicken in the pot every Sunday' wanted to give them a public space for strolling and celebrations. At the same time, he gave the rich fine houses worthy of their rank. Thus by one act of town planning he bound to himself both rich and poor.

From Place Royale in 1607 the square became Place des Fédérés in 1792, then Place de l'Indivisibilité (1793), Place Royale again (1814), Place des Vosges (1831), Place Royale yet again (1852), and then in 1870, once more but finally, Place des Vosges. Why the Vosges? The inhabitants of that region of eastern France were the first to pay their taxes in 1800.

The central garden today has a dismal municipal look to it, but the houses around it have had many famous inhabitants, including Madame de Sévigné, who was born here in 1626, and Victor Hugo, whose house is preserved as a museum. The Pavilions of the King and Queen, taller than the other houses (at the left, in Pl. 64), are differentiated from each other by decorative details. The Queen's is marked by the sun in a medallion, emblem of Marie de Médicis, placed over the central arch. Its front door has carved panels, whereas most of the other doors in the square are decorated only by metal studs, and inside there is a spacious staircase with wrought-iron balustrade (Pl. 65).

66   Libéral Bruant, architect of the Invalides, could afford a handsome house in the fashionable Marais, in the Rue de la Perle. Built in 1685, it is now the Musée de la Serrurerie, where the locksmith's craft is traced from Roman times through the Empire to the latest creations from the Bricard workshops. Among items of special interest are the locks of the Tuileries Palace and Palais Royal, and magnificent Venetian door-knockers.

68   The name of the Hôtel de Carnavalet is a Parisian corruption of the name of its original owner, the Sieur de Kernevenoy, a member of the circle of 'la reine Margot'. François Mansart enlarged it in the seventeenth century, and Madame de Sévigné lived here from 1677 to 1696. A fine statue by Coysevox from the Hôtel de Ville stands in the centre of the courtyard. The galleries of the museum display the history of Paris from the time of François I to the beginning of the twentieth century, by means of shop signs, relief maps of the city, and superb Louis XIV, Régence, Louis XV and Louis XVI furniture.

69   A painting in the Musée Carnavalet by Nicolas and Jean-Baptiste Raguenet shows the *Tournament of the Boatmen between the Pont au Change and the Pont Notre-Dame*; painted in 1752, it is one of a series of pictures in the museum by these artists, who specialized in views of the Seine. The meticulousness of the painting and the documentary accuracy recall views of Venice, and make the series, which covers the river from the Quai de Bercy in the east to the village of Chaillot in the west, an invaluable record of eighteenth-century Paris.

70   The Hôtel de Soubise has its origins in the medieval manor house of Clisson, built in 1375, which was altered and enlarged by the Guise family. It became the seat of the Catholic Ligue during the Wars of Religion, and saw the planning of the St Bartholomew's Day Massacre in 1572.

In 1700 the mansion was acquired by François de Rohan, Prince de Soubise, who with the money that his wife obtained from Louis XIV – for favours of which the complaisant Prince was by no means ignorant – set out to rebuild it completely. He entrusted the work to the otherwise unknown architect Pierre-Alexis Delamair, son of one of the royal builders, who most unusually – and, as it turned out, unwisely – did not belong to the fashionable group surrounding Hardouin Mansart. Delamair created a new façade at the end of a *cour d'honneur* flanked by colonnades with flat roofs topped by openwork balustrades. The centrepiece has only two storeys below a triangular pediment. (It has now lost most of its sculpture.) Delamair's elders in the profession were outraged to find that he had ignored the Classical rule of the superimposition of the orders: instead of Doric, Ionic and Corinthian, here were two tiers of Corinthian columns! Delamair was replaced by Germain Boffrand.

Since 1812 the Hôtel de Soubise has housed the Archives de France. The national archives, established in 1789, have grown to some six million documents and 280 km (174 miles) of shelving, and the nation's collective memory now occupies several other houses in the Marais as well.

71   The façade of the Hôtel de Fieubet, at No. 2 Quai des Celestins, is covered with strange, ornate decoration that contrasts markedly with the garden front, attributed to Hardouin Mansart. Looking in the other direction, you can follow the branches of the Seine as it divides around the Ile Saint-Louis and Ile de la Cité.

72   How many homeless people are there in Paris? Their number is easier to estimate in the winter, when they congregate in hostels or in Metro stations that are left open specially for them. In the summer they are scattered throughout the city. Some prefer to be alone and out-of-doors, where they can drink and forget their sorrows and their destitution in sleep.

73   Who cares, as they down their glass of red wine, whether the word *bistrot* comes from *bistouille* (rough alcohol) or from *bistro* ('quick' in Russian – said to go back to the Russian occupation in 1814)? The bistrot is a Parisian institution. The clientèle vary enormously according to the time of day, from the early customer snatching a quick cup of coffee on his way to factory or office to the idler, drinking at the bar, looking for someone to listen to his rambling talk.

74   They are everywhere, and their droppings desecrate monuments and the statues of great men. They walk more often than they fly. 'All these pigeons', wrote Jules Renard, 'are fun at first, but in the end they're a bore.' The city fathers are aware of the problem, but what can be done?

75   Just downriver from the Quai des Celestins (Pl. 71) is the Quai de l'Hôtel de Ville, seen here from the Ile Saint-Louis. Beyond the Pont Louis-Philippe the tower and early seventeenth-century gable of Saint-Gervais-Saint-Protais rise above the trees that conceal the church's Flamboyant Gothic body. The original church was built in the sixth century and dedicated to two brothers martyred in Rome at the time of the Emperor Nero; the present building was not completed until 1657. Successive generations of the Couperin family served as organists here, from 1656 to 1826. During the First World War, on Good Friday, 29 March 1918, a shell from the great German gun 'Big Bertha' crashed through the vault, killing a hundred people and injuring many more.

To the right along the quai is the Cité des Arts, where French and foreign students with scholarships have a settled home, with access to studios, in the capital.

76   Street demonstrations, whether to support a cause or to air a grievance, are a common sight in Paris. Some are quiet and dignified; others are accompanied by chanted slogans. All can happen in any part of town, and are tolerated by the police. The Place de la Bastille is a favourite venue. Under the column topped by a winged genie are buried victims of the revolutions of 1830 and 1848, whose presence gives demonstrators a sense of the historic justice of their claims.

77   When the light shows green and the red flag is flying there is little hope for the sign declaring 'No Right Turn'.

78   Michel Déon, a Member of the Académie Française, averts his eyes from the Compagnie Républicaine de Sécurité when he is not wearing the

Academicians' green robe and dress sword. Is the lady with him a fan, pursuing him with questions about his current work or the title of his next novel? Fame has its drawbacks as well as its glamour.

79   The Canal Saint-Martin, flowing between picturesque and leafy banks, was the setting for Marcel Carné's famous film *Hôtel du Nord*. The many bargemen who pass through this 4.5 km (3 mile) long link between the Canal de l'Ourcq and the Seine have to be patient as they negotiate its nine locks. In any season but winter you can make the journey in a pleasure boat and imagine for a moment that you are gliding down one of the *grachts* of Amsterdam. Even if you've never seen Carné's film you will respond to the old-fashioned, slightly melancholy atmosphere of the canal.

80, 81, 83–85   It is conventional to say that the Sacré Coeur looks better from a distance. It provides an effective accent on its hilltop, but its Neo-Byzantine style is something of an anomaly in Paris. Like the Eiffel Tower, as the manufacturers of souvenirs well know, it has captured the imagination of tourists. There is also a strong romantic aura about Montmartre itself, and the daubs displayed in the Place du Tertre benefit from their association with Utrillo, Van Dongen, Picasso, and the others who gathered at the Bateau-Lavoir around the turn of the century.

Roland Dorgelès knew Montmartre in its great days, and loved to walk along its cobbled streets to the Lapin Agile – still the same today as when he was a boy of twenty. 'I never vary my route', he wrote in *Au beau temps de la Butte*: 'Moulin de la Galette, Rue Giraudon, Rue de l'Abreuvoir, Rue des Saules and Rue Cortot to the Place du Tertre, then back down again through the Place Ravignan, looking for ghosts at every turn.' The ghosts were those of Apollinaire, Pierre MacOrlan, Francis Carco and Max Jacob, the friends of his youth, before Montmartre was overrun by tourist coaches.

It is nevertheless still possible to find the old village, perhaps on a spring morning when the only denizens of the streets are cats and dogs, or in autumn, late in the day, near the vineyards, just before the vintage, a time of celebration for the tiny community of genuine inhabitants of Montmartre. To climb the many flights of steps and look out through the haze over the roofs of Paris, following in Dorgelès's footsteps, gives one that distinctive pleasure that comes of seeing through the memories of others.

82   In Paris the wooden horses of the carousels are pushed aside by horsepower in the streets. Yet at the foot of the hill of Montmartre there is a fair, where the smack of cartridges hitting the targets in shooting galleries mingles with the whizzing crackle of the roulette wheel and the old-fashioned music of the merry-go-round, slowly running through its perforated cards. The fairground people are keen to maintain their rights in the city. Every year, they take over the Tuileries Gardens and demonstrate to Parisians that the big wheel still goes round, and that the ghost train has lost nothing of its delicious mystery.

86   The dignity of the Gare de Lyon clock tower has suffered somewhat since redevelopment of the surrounding neighbourhood left it marooned among office towers so much higher than its own 64 m (210 ft). The station itself, however, is the home base of the TGV, the fastest train in the world, so that even now the clock tower is a signpost of progress.

87   The fashion for living in an artist's studio when you are not an artist poses a more serious problem in Paris than the conversion of 'lofts' or warehouses does in New York. What are real artists to do, reduced to working in rooms without proper daylight? Montmartre and Montparnasse are still artists' quarters, and the City of Paris is anxious to encourage artists, but how long can this last? Will it be necessary to revive establishments like the Bateau-Lavoir and the Ruche?

88   The canopy of the Porte Dauphine Metro station (in a square now renamed Place du Maréchal de Lattre de Tassigny) is a rare survival of one of the more spectacular types of entrance devised by the Art Nouveau architect Hector Guimard.

89, 90   The Parc Monceau, once known as the Parc des Mousseaux, occupies only part of the land that belonged to the Duc d'Orléans. In 1778 he asked his master of ceremonies, the painter and writer Carmontelle, to lay out a garden there. Carmontelle devised a magical world where the visitor walked as in a dream, from a Roman temple to a Chinese pagoda, and on past a windmill to the ruins of a medieval castle, before coming to a lake laid out as a naumachia, as if for naval battles in the time of the Emperor Hadrian.

In 1882 the shrewd financier Péreire divided the park up into building plots for luxurious private houses, and Haussmann asked the engineer Jean-Charles Alphand to transform what open space remained into an 'English garden'.

The circular pavilion at the entrance to the park is one of Claude-Nicolas Ledoux's toll gates, constructed in the late eighteenth century as part of the excise barrier thrown up around the city by the Farmers-General. Beyond it, a host of statues are dotted about on the grass in typical late nineteenth-century fashion. At the head of the oval pool of the naumachia is a colonnade made up of sixteenth-century fragments from the unfinished mausoleum of Henri II at Saint-Denis.

The Parc Monceau witnessed the first parachute jump in the world, when André-Jacques Garnerin leapt from his balloon at an altitude of 1,000 m (3,280 ft) on 22 October 1797.

91   Lovers in Paris are no respecters of art. Statues exist to provide strong backs and long arms on which their loves can be recorded. Does Susana still love Piero? In 'Le Pont Mirabeau' Apollinaire observed that love is no more permanent than the flowing water of the river; but their linked names will survive as long as does the Pont Alexandre III.

92   More than a hundred sculptors worked on the complex of the Palais de Chaillot (see Pl. 6). Among the more famous were Pyras, Gimond, Couturier, Niclausse and Yencesse, who were responsible for the gilt bronze figures that line the vista between the Palais de Chaillot and the Eiffel Tower, with the Champ de Mars in the distance.

93, 95   Parisians greeted the Eiffel Tower with derision. Their reaction was due to a misunderstanding: they thought that Eiffel meant his structure to be taken as a work of architecture, whereas his intention was entirely technical – to demonstrate that in little more than two years, with a lot of iron and a lot of guts, it was possible to erect a daring challenge to the laws of statics.

Since its inauguration at the Universal Exposition of 1889 time has been kind to the Tower. Not only is Paris unimaginable without it: it has actually become the symbol of the city. Forgetful of its 70,000 tons it soars into the night sky, slender, glowing, envied by the ethereal but so much more earthbound fountains of the Palais de Chaillot.

94   On the Quai de Tokyo beside the river two museums were erected, like the Palais de Chaillot, for the 1937 Exposition. One held the picture collection of the City of Paris, the other the collection of the State. Since the Musée National d'Art Moderne moved out (to be divided between the Pompidou Centre and the Musée d'Orsay), the complex has gradually decayed. But it is surely worthy of preservation: the colonnade that links the two buildings, the reflecting pool, and the statues, which include Bourdelle's *France*, are all interesting works characteristic of the years immediately before the Second World War.

Away from the quai and its ceaseless roar of traffic, all is peaceful. The setting looks like an antique theatre, and the couples who meet there might be actors rehearsing their lines.

96   This vast circular building, 500 m (more than 1,600 ft) in circumference is the headquarters of Radio France. The original design had a taller tower, but height restrictions prevented its construction. Parisians instantly seized on the shape, with a hole in the middle, and christened the building the 'Palais Gruyère'. All the radio stations were grouped here so that they might enjoy better working conditions and the latest technology: inside there are sixty studios and a large auditorium, used by France Culture, France Musique, France Inter, Radio France International and FIP 514.

97   A glimpse of the magic of Paris in 1900: beyond the Pont Alexandre III, with its rows of lamps, are the Grand Palais and Petit Palais, all built for the Universal Exposition that welcomed the twentieth century. The exhibition halls were sneered at when they were new, but they have gradually become a feature of the city. Nestling between the trees of the riverbank and those of the Champs Elysées, their glass domes gleam at night like giant glowworms in a garden. Part of this vast complex is now the home of the Palais de la Découverte, where science and technology are presented in popular form. The rest of the Grand Palais and the Petit Palais are given over to permanent collections and temporary exhibitions which attract thousands of visitors each year.

98   Paris turns blue at dusk; here and there from the sea of grey roofs church steeples stand out. Off in the distance tower blocks ring the horizon, but the Eiffel Tower asserts its empire over them. In a moment the lights will come on all over the city and bring to an end this soft, indistinct, melancholy afternoon.

99   Surely there can be no such thing as a marshal on horseback without a hat? The poet Jacques Prévert would have said so; but he would have been proved wrong by Robert Wlerick and Raymond Martin, whose statue of Foch erected in the Place du Trocadéro in 1951 outraged soldiers and horsemen alike. It took a second world war for Foch, the allied commander in 1918, to receive his monument opposite that of Joffre, who led the French Army at the beginning of the First World War. They are separated, as befits military men, by the Champ de Mars.

River and islands

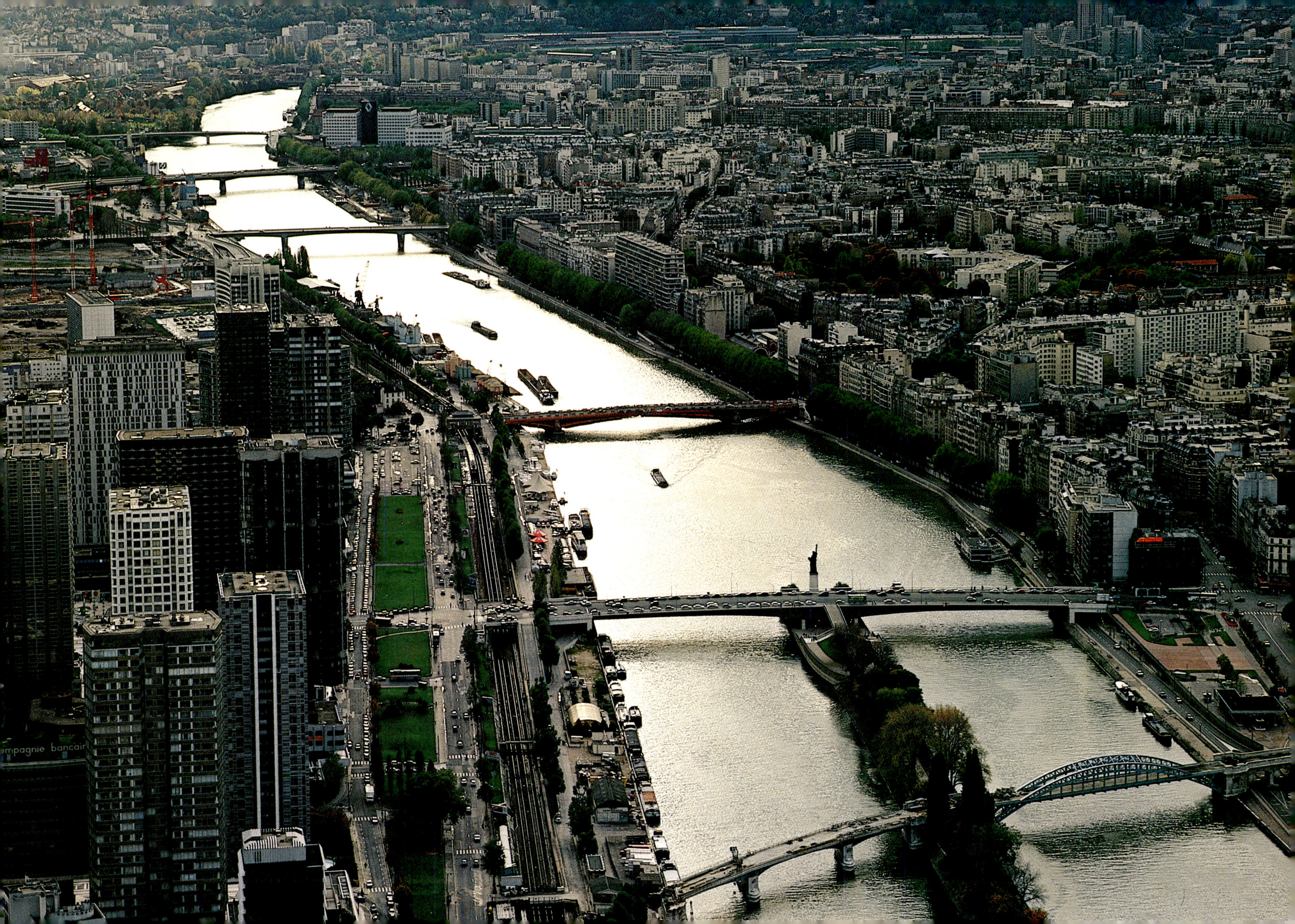

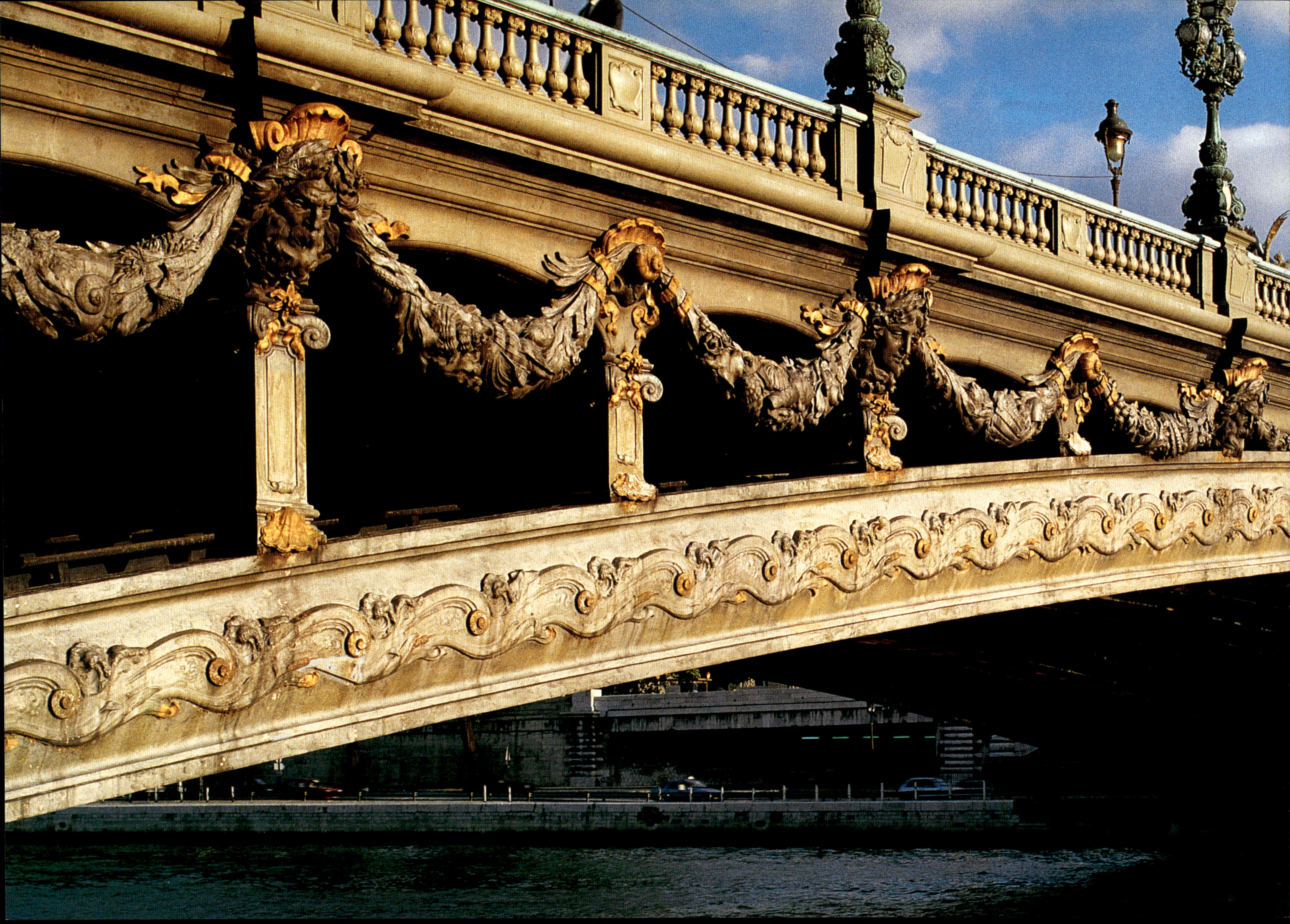

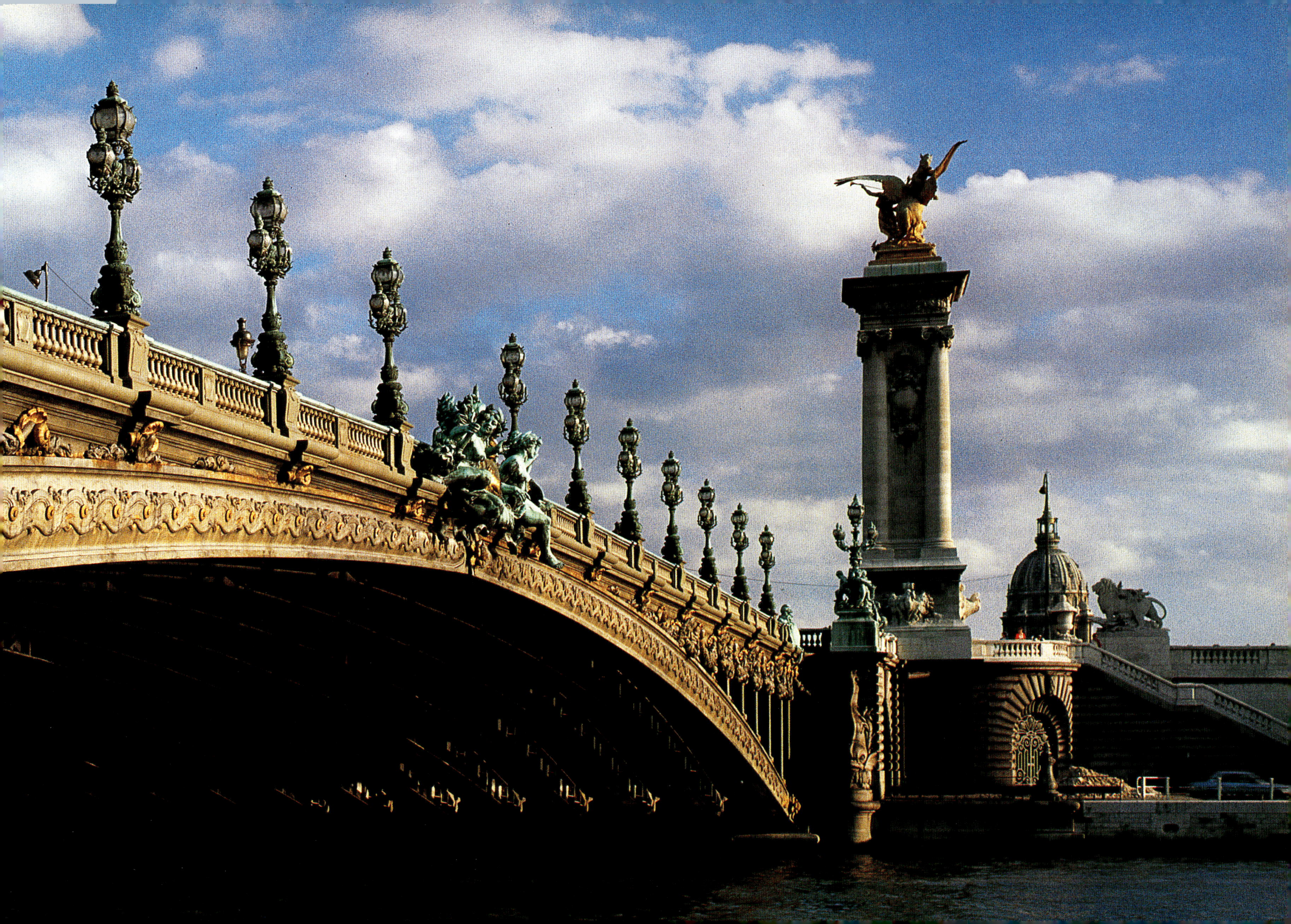

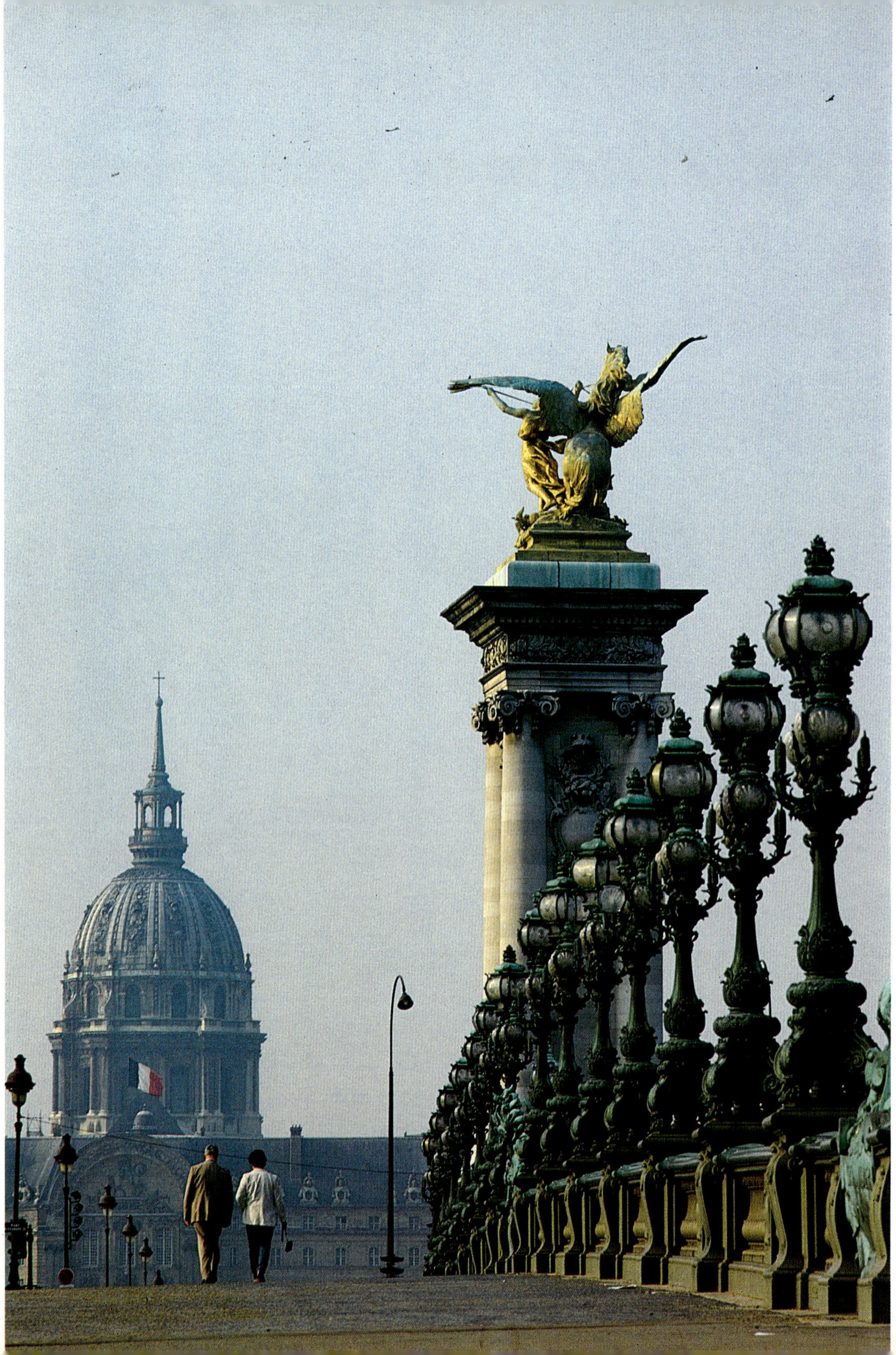

104 105

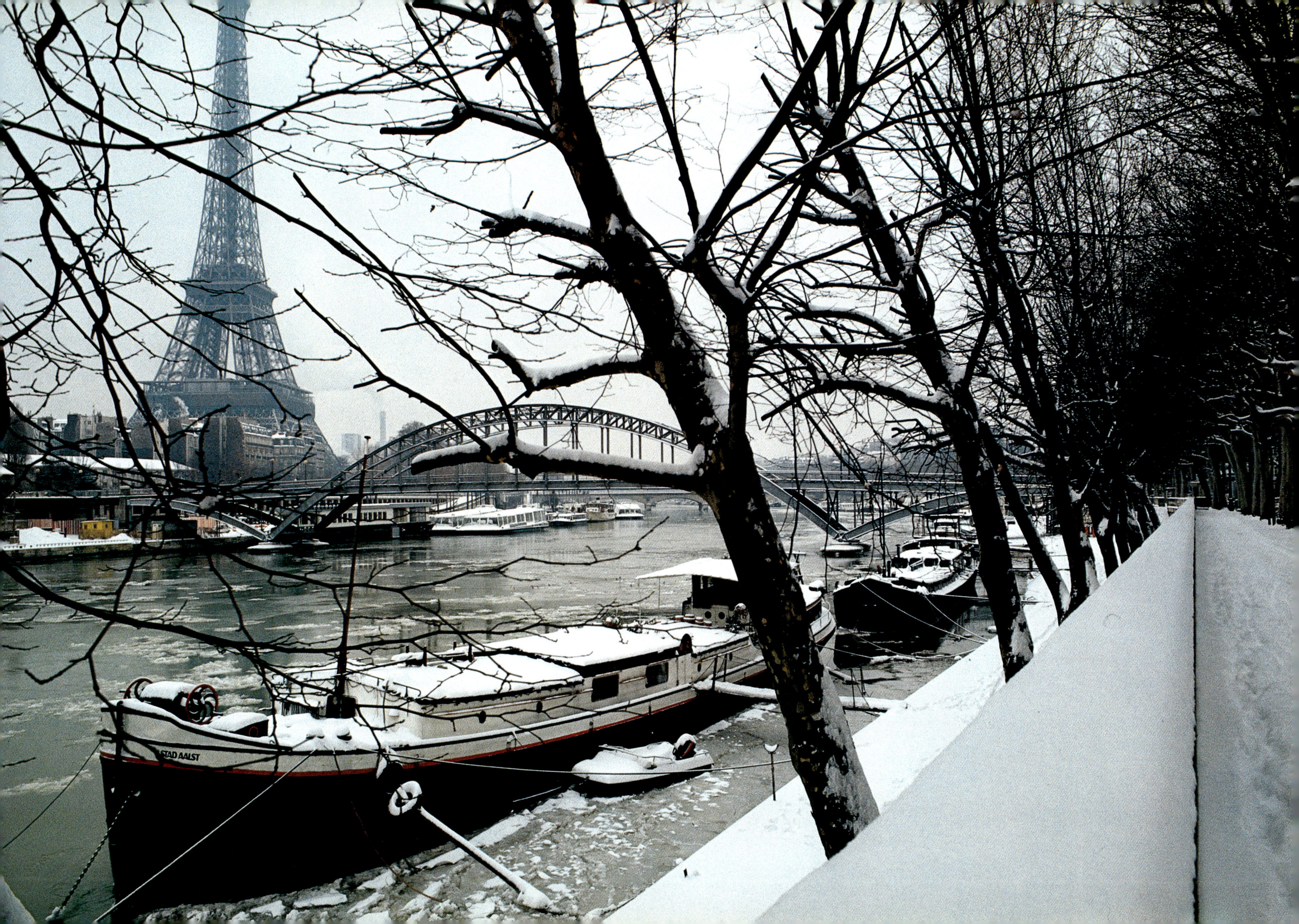
STAD AALST

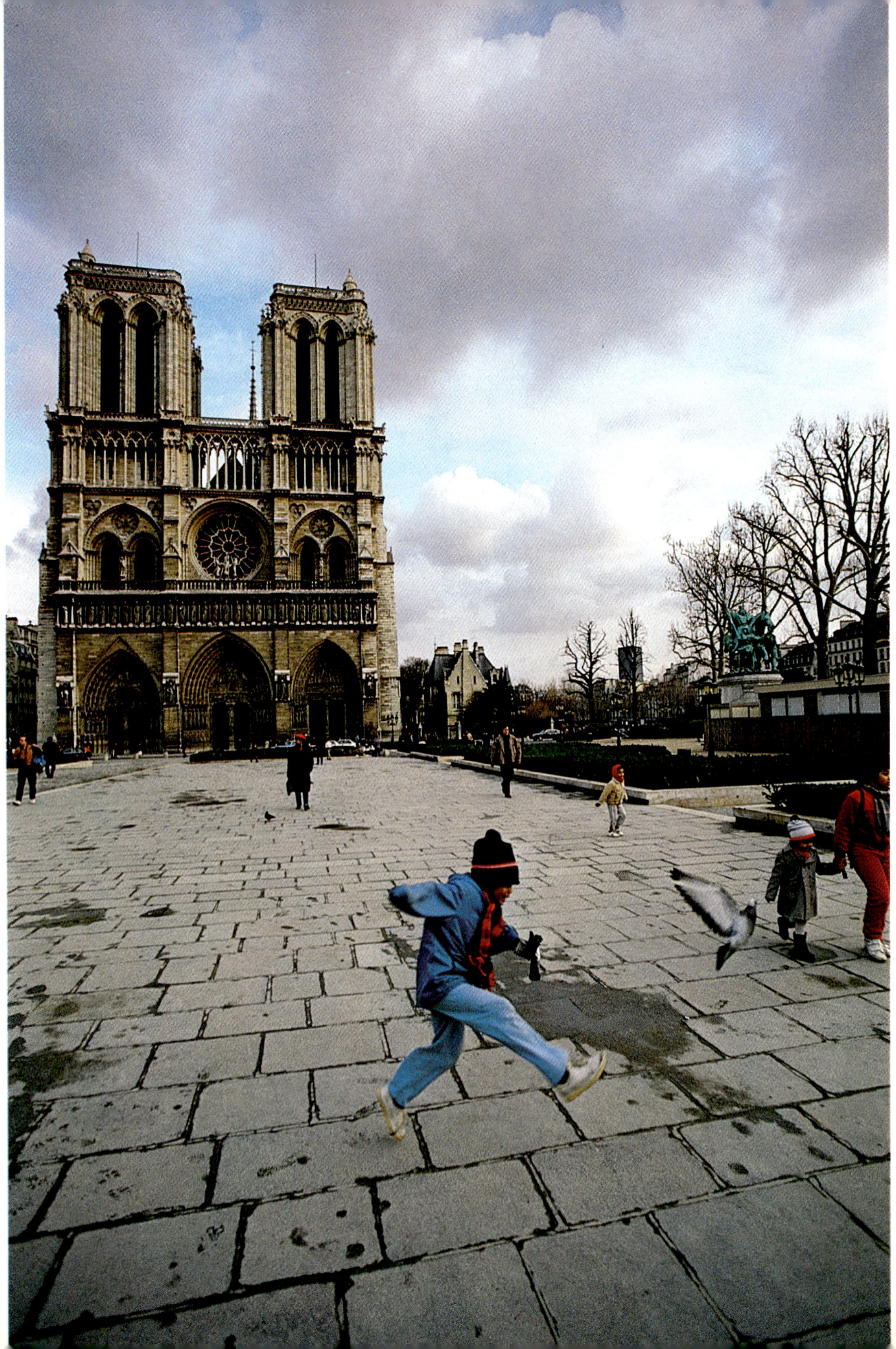

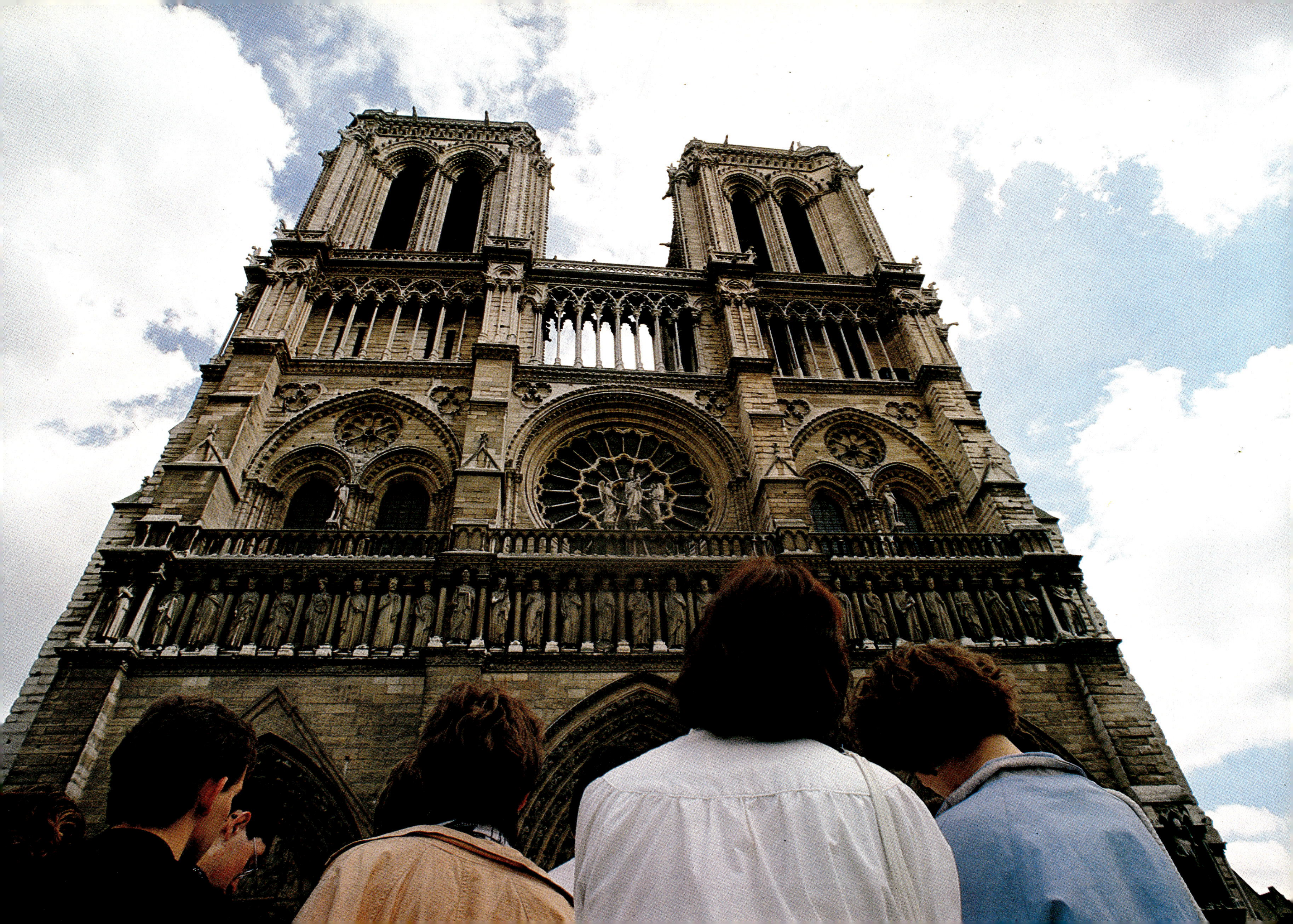

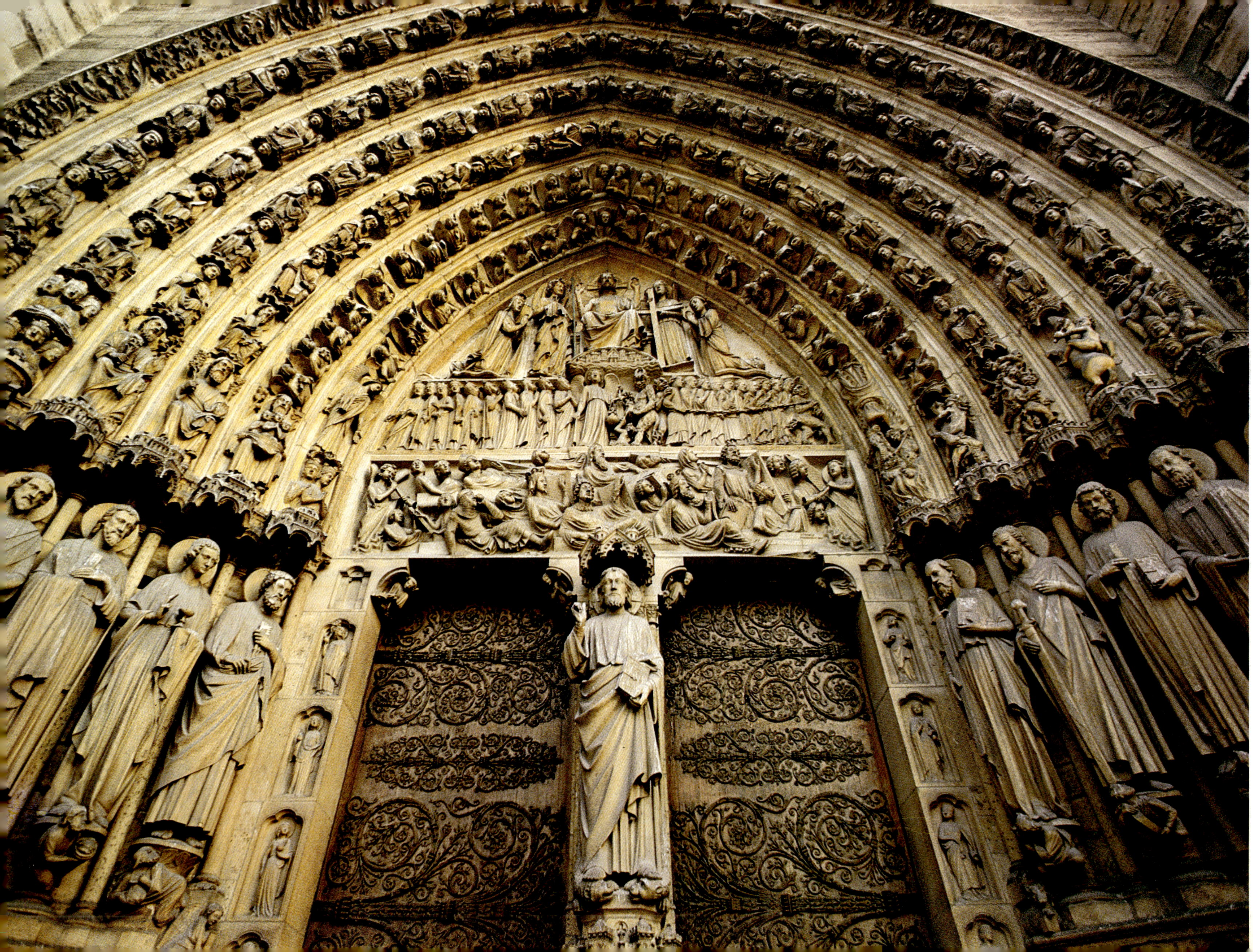

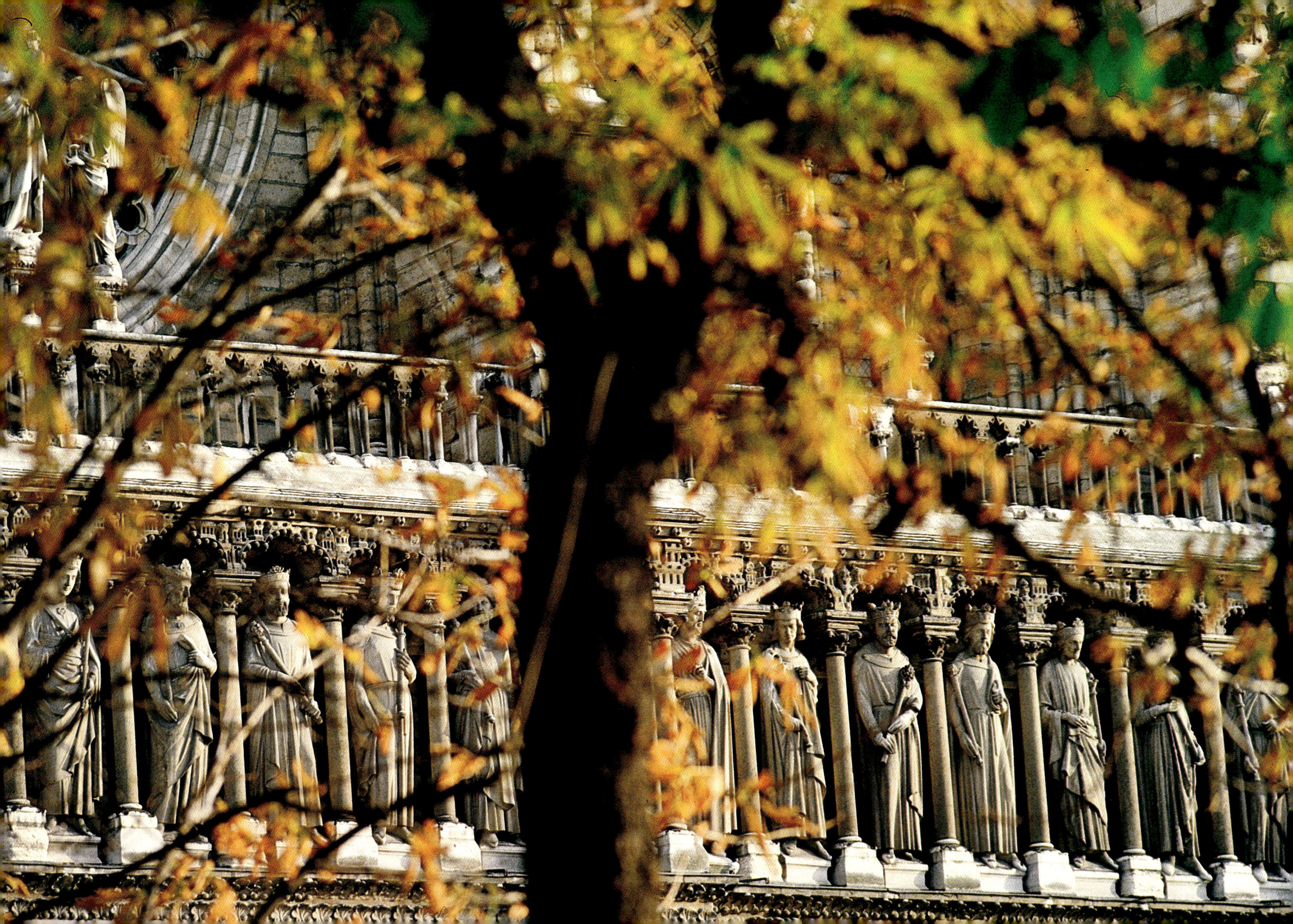

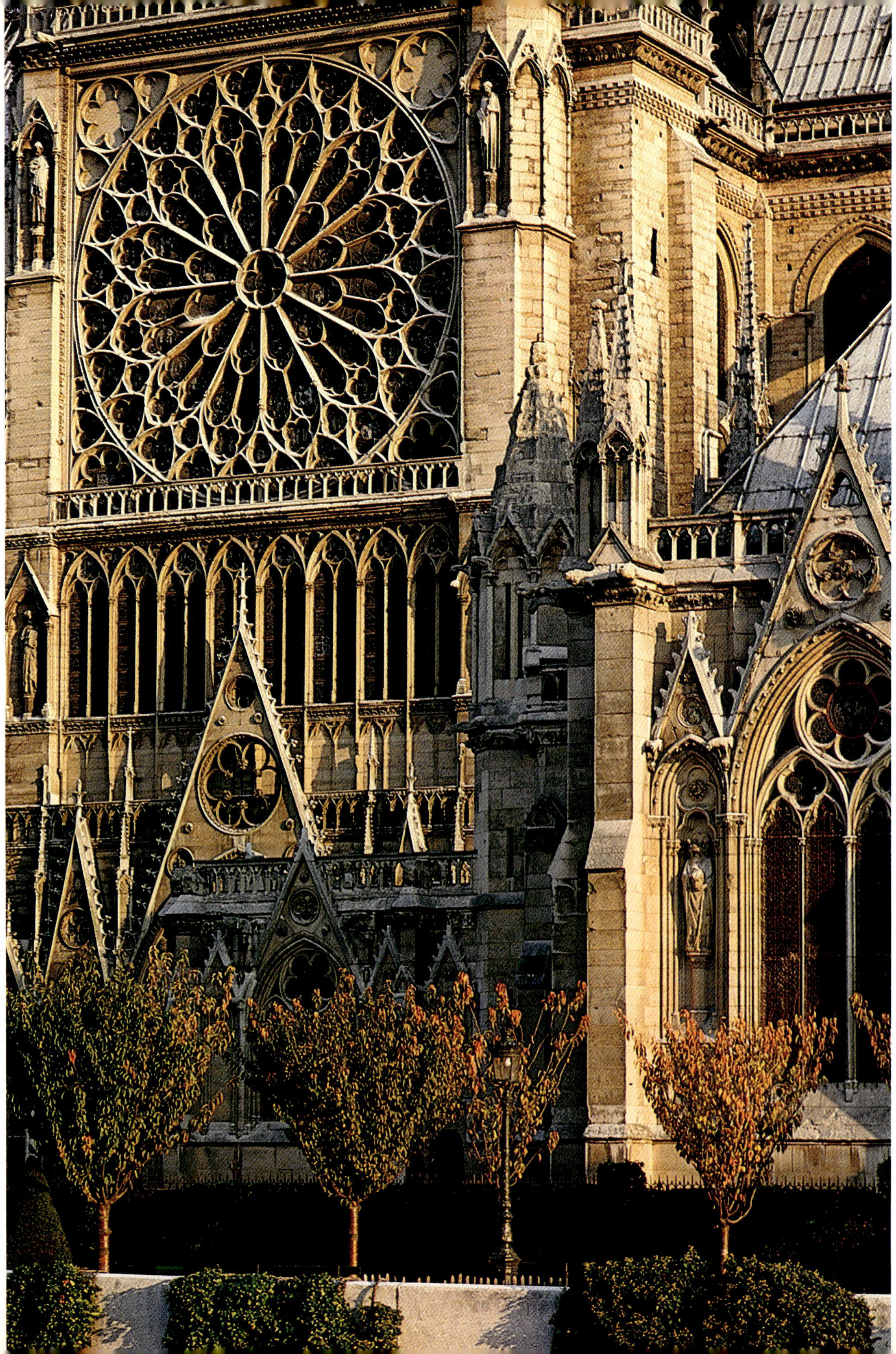

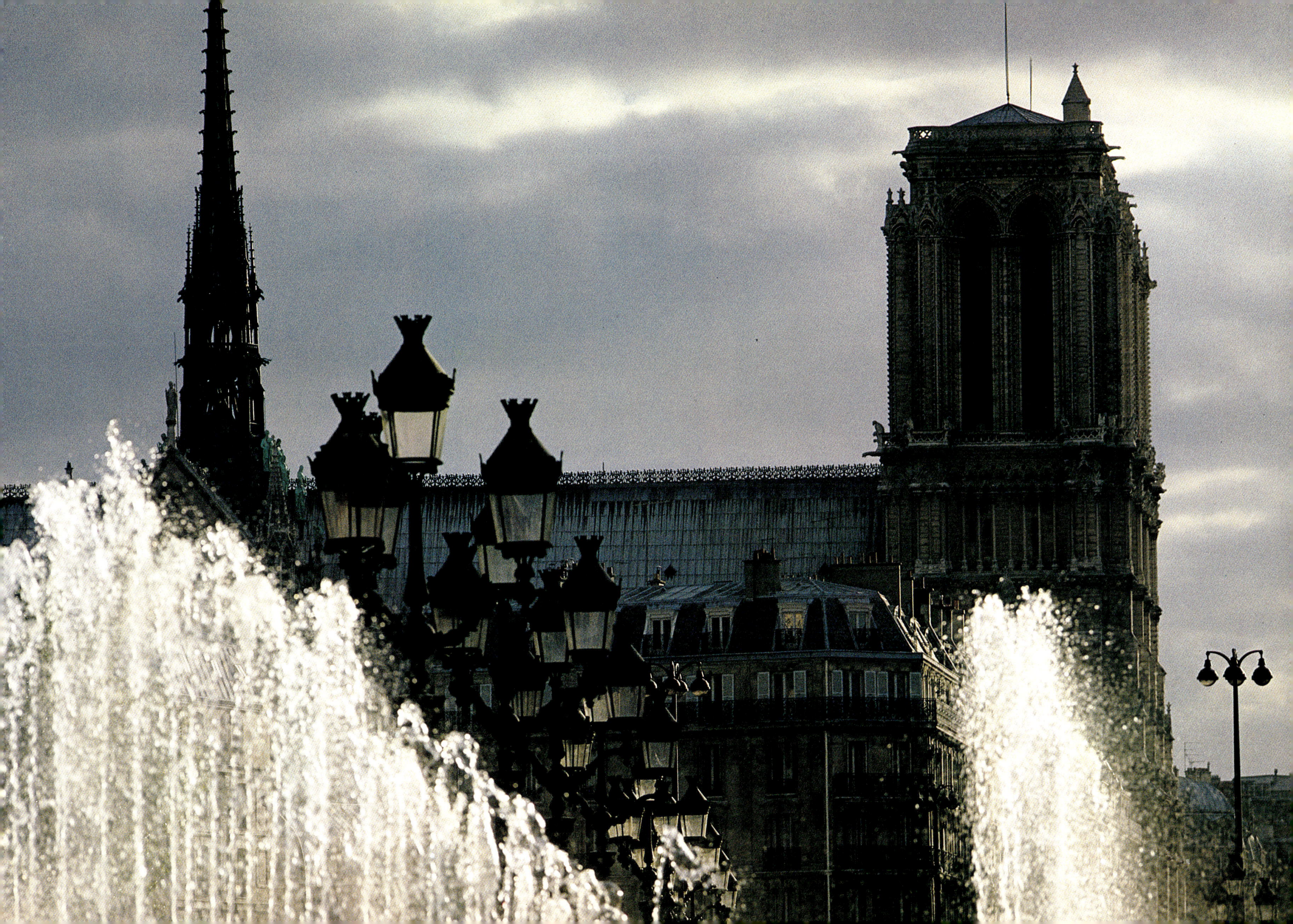

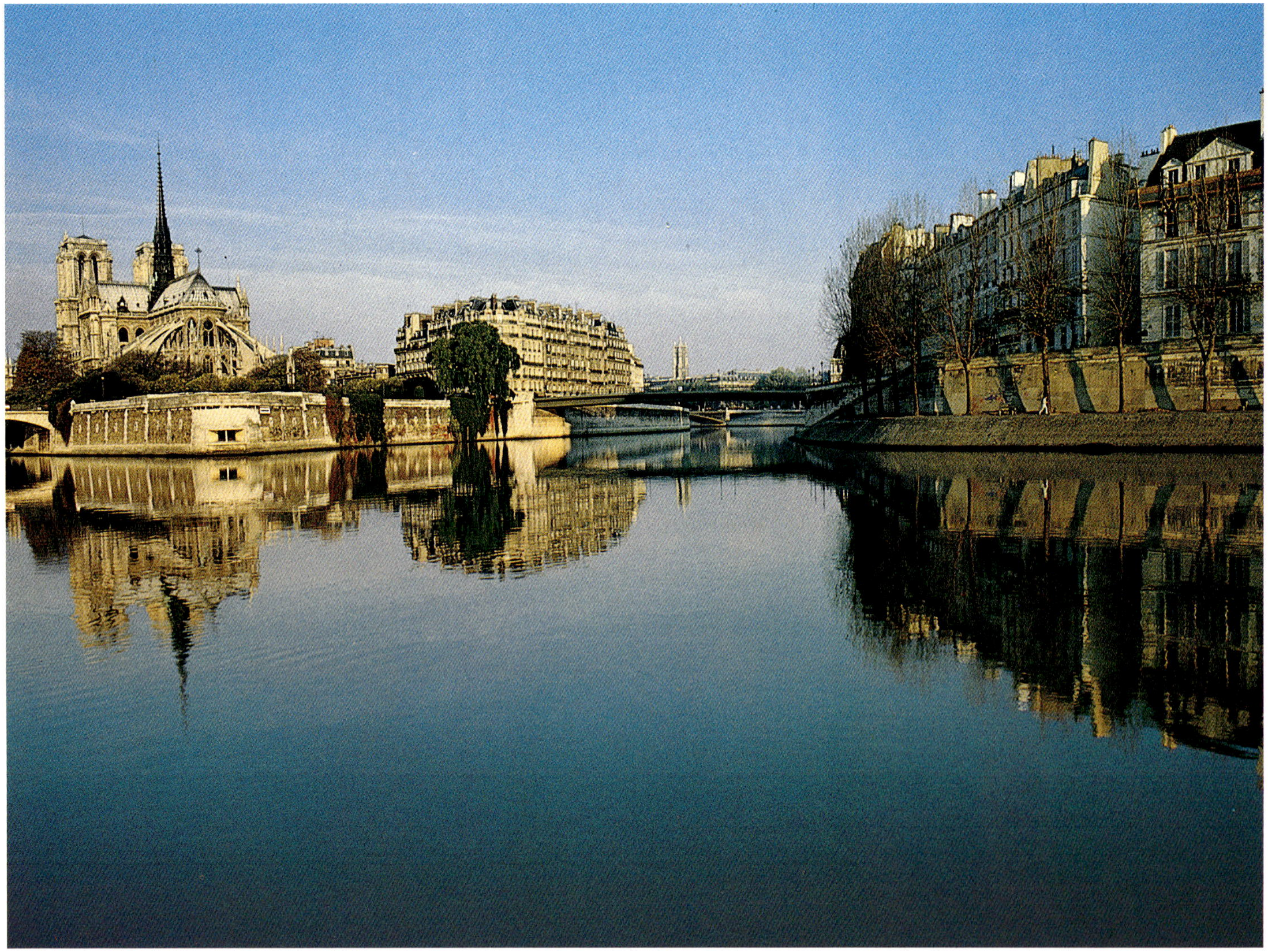

112 113

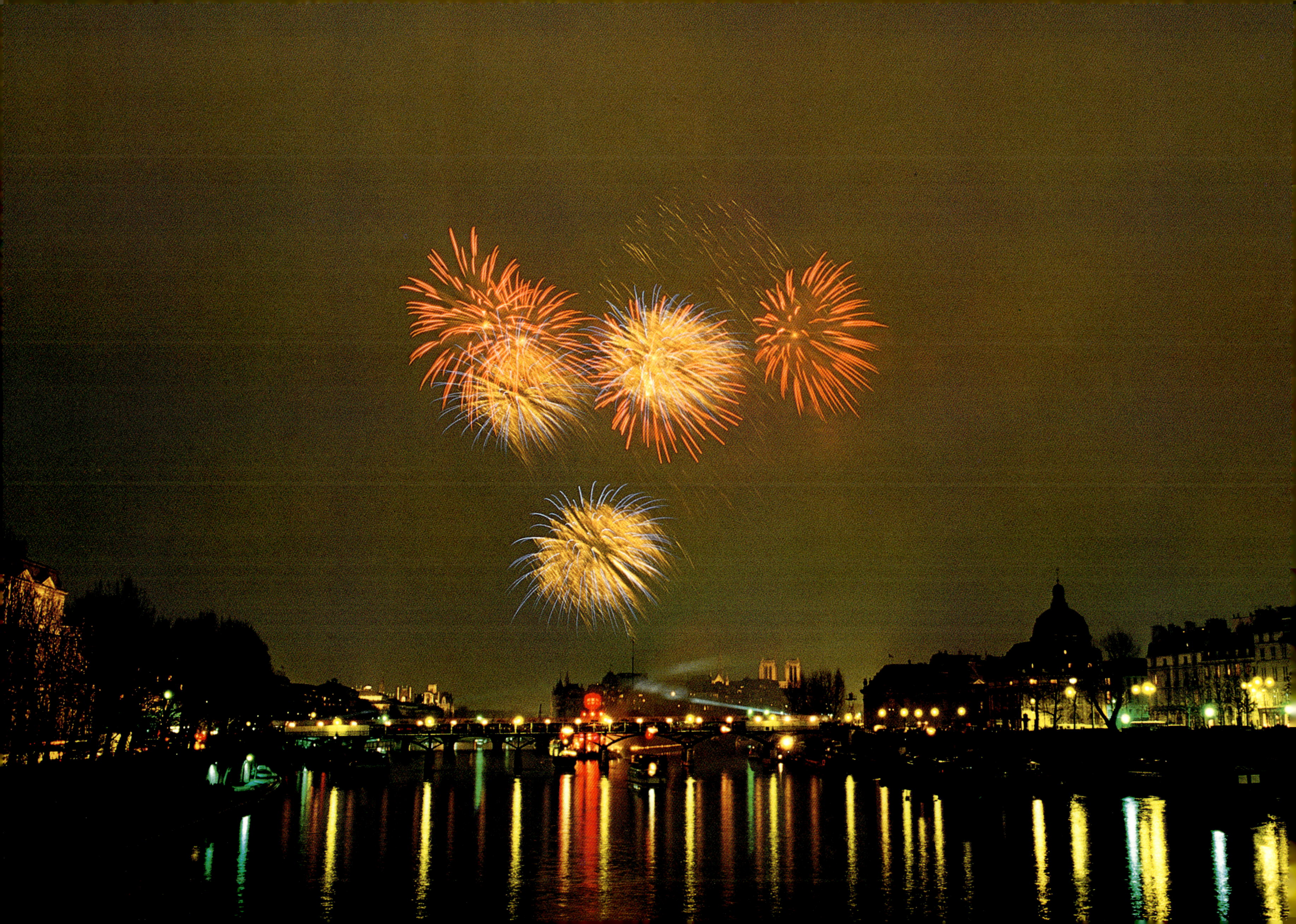

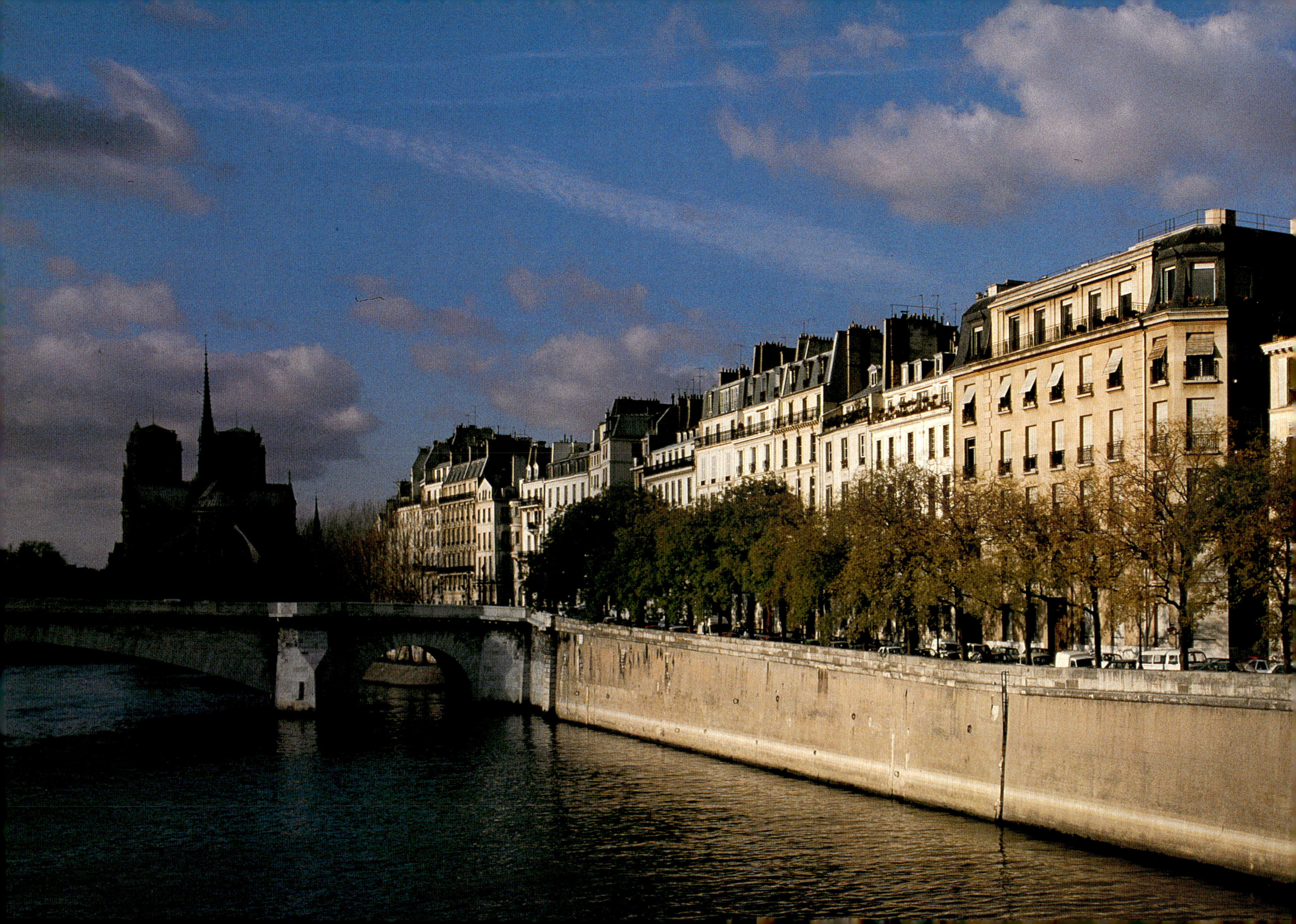

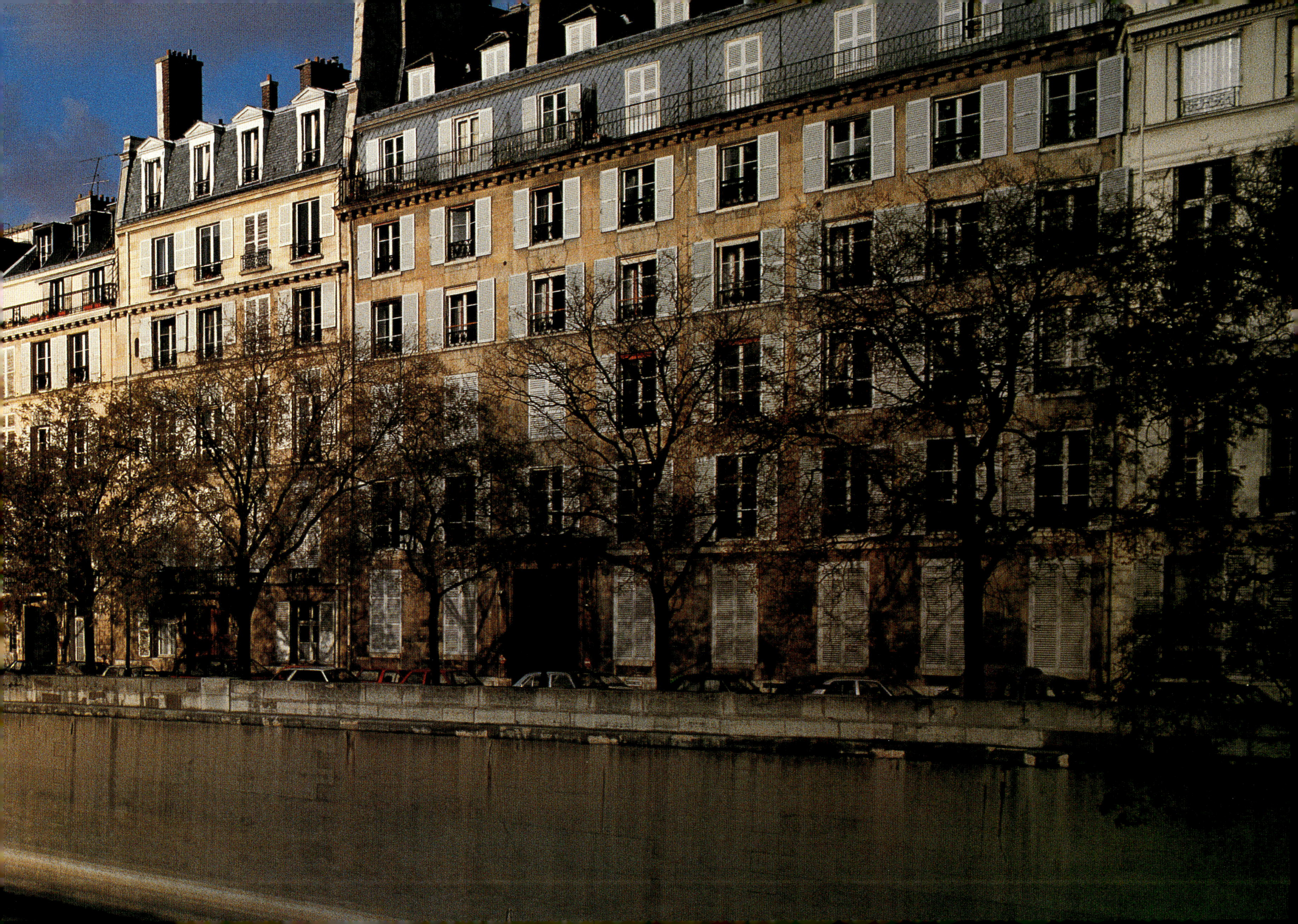

115 116

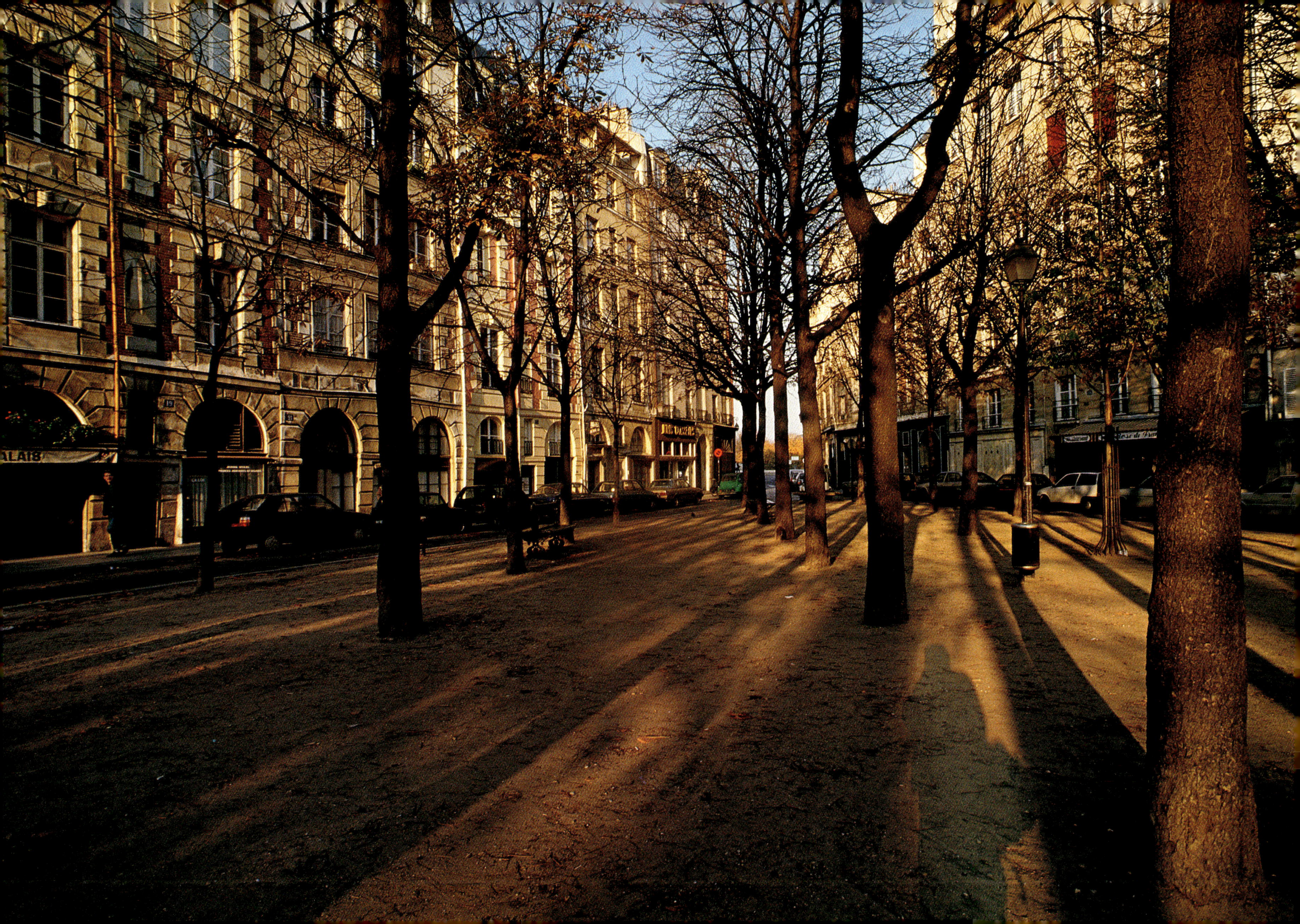

117 118

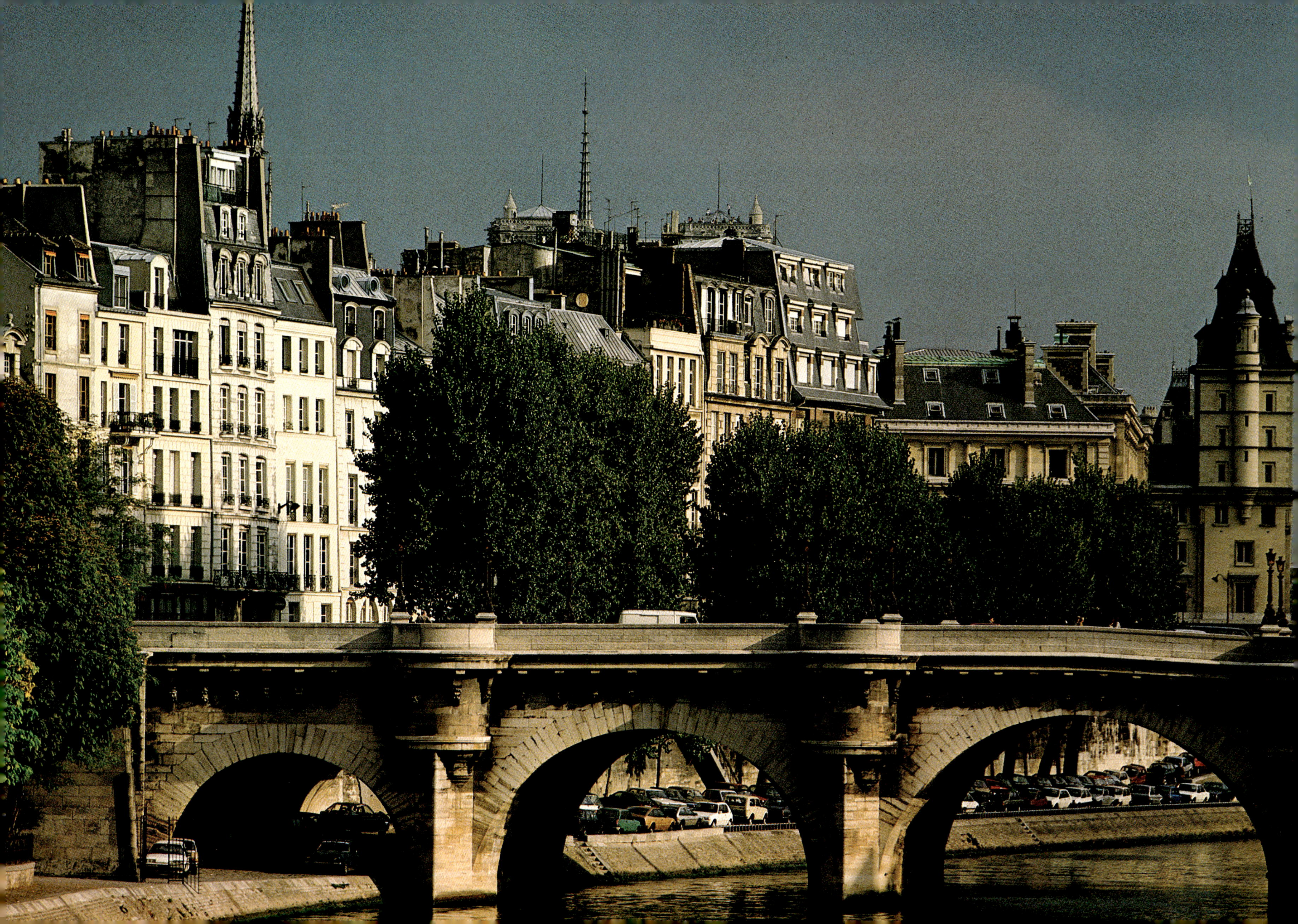

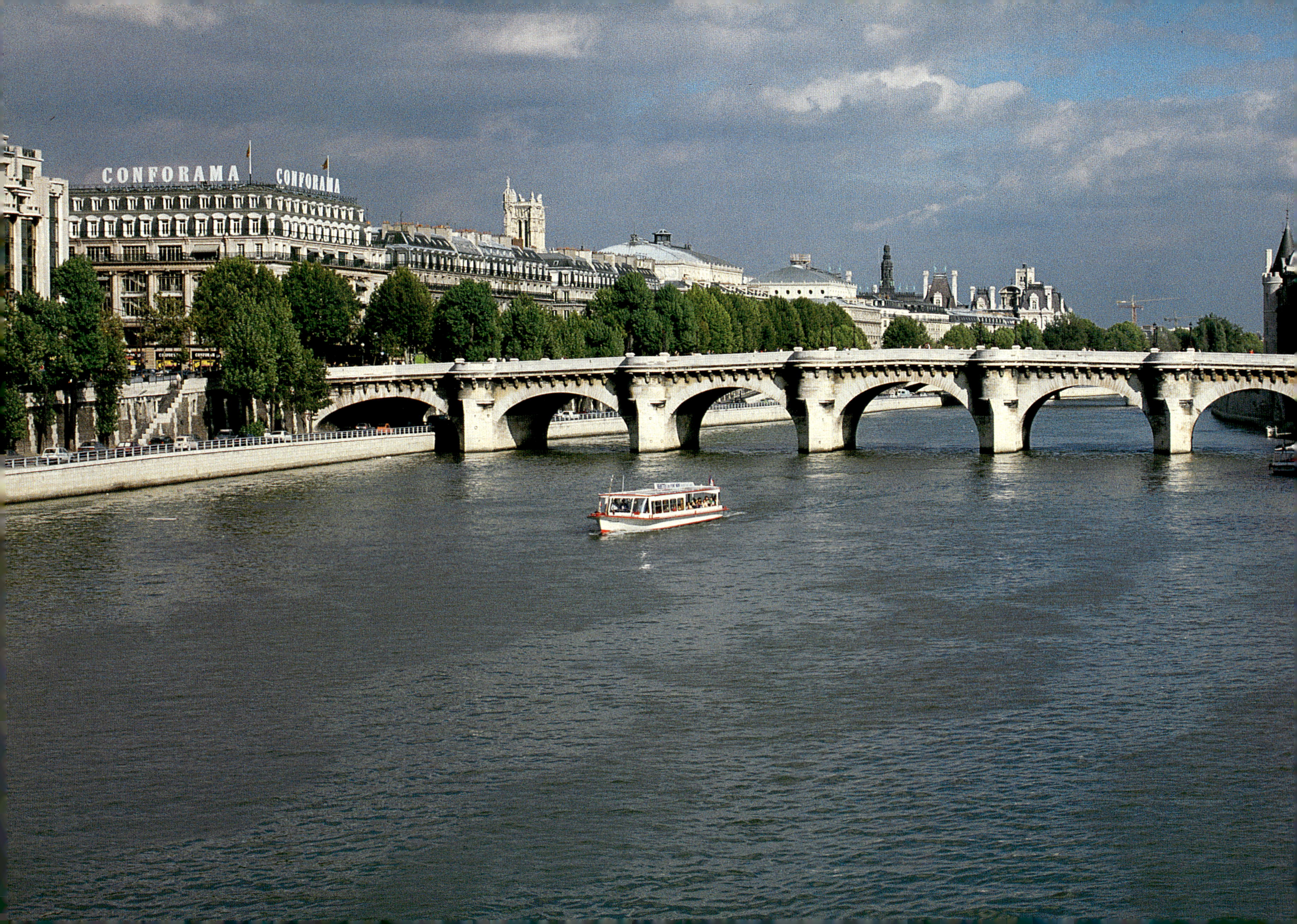
CONFORAMA
CONFORAMA

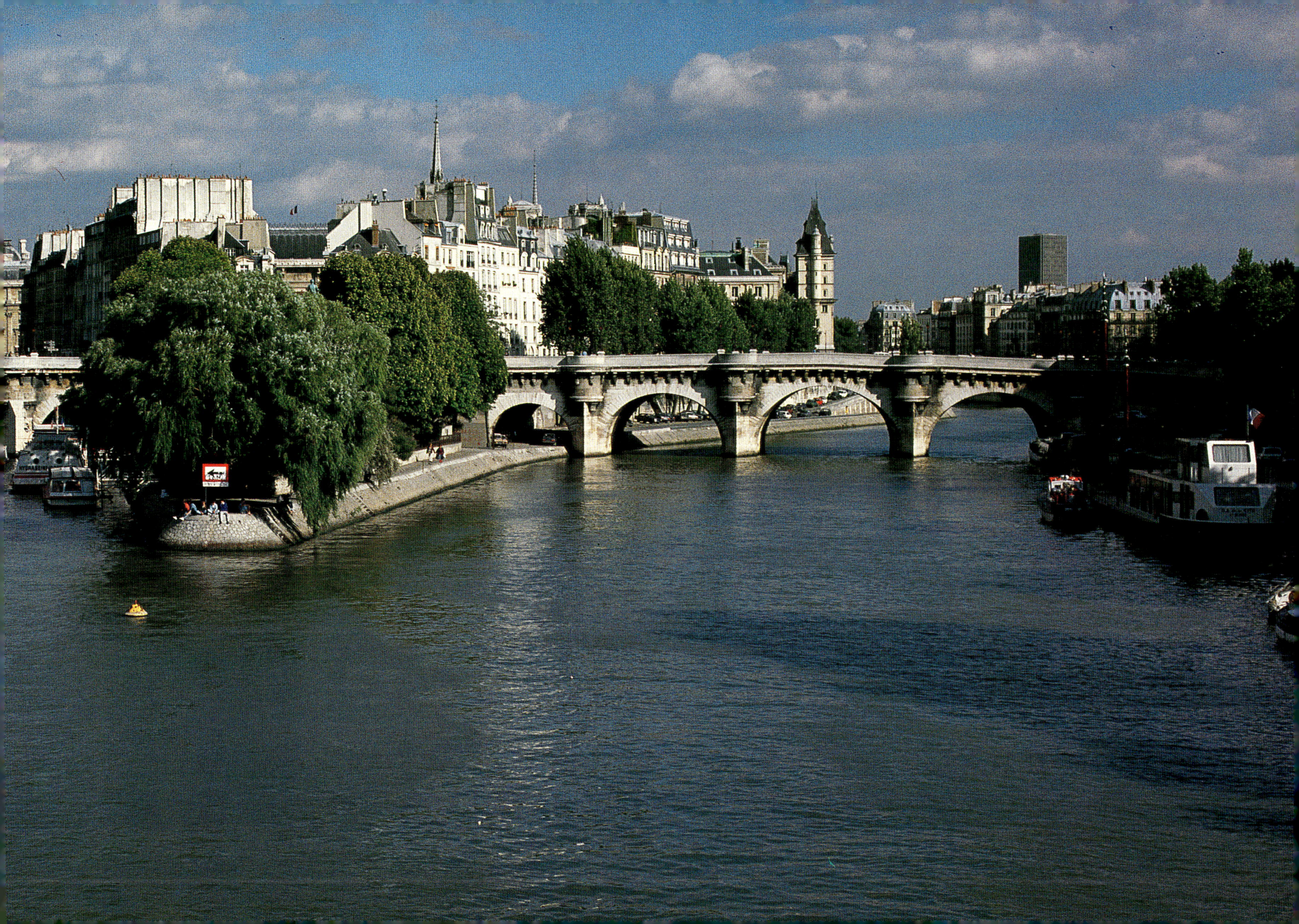

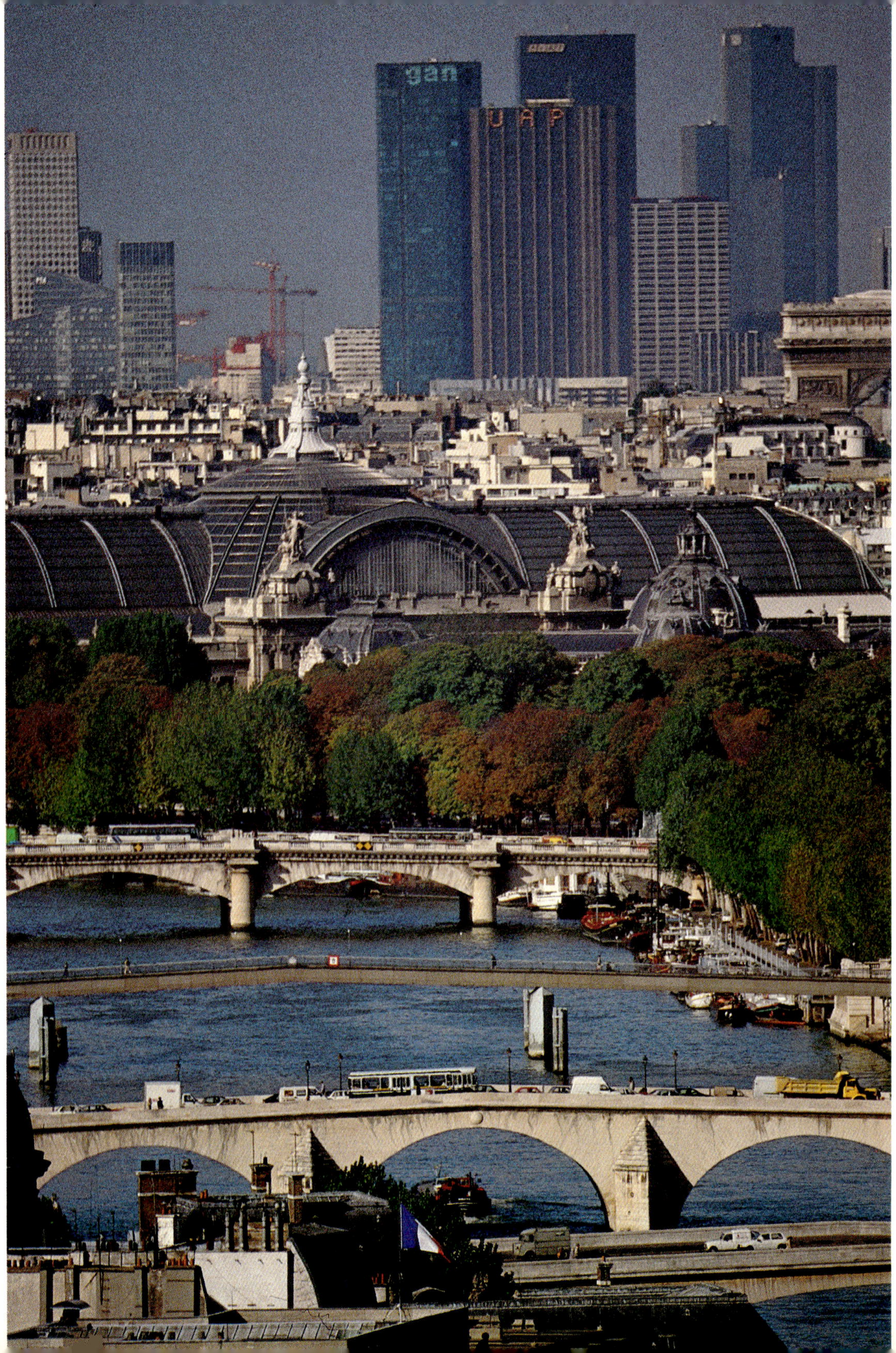
gan
UAP

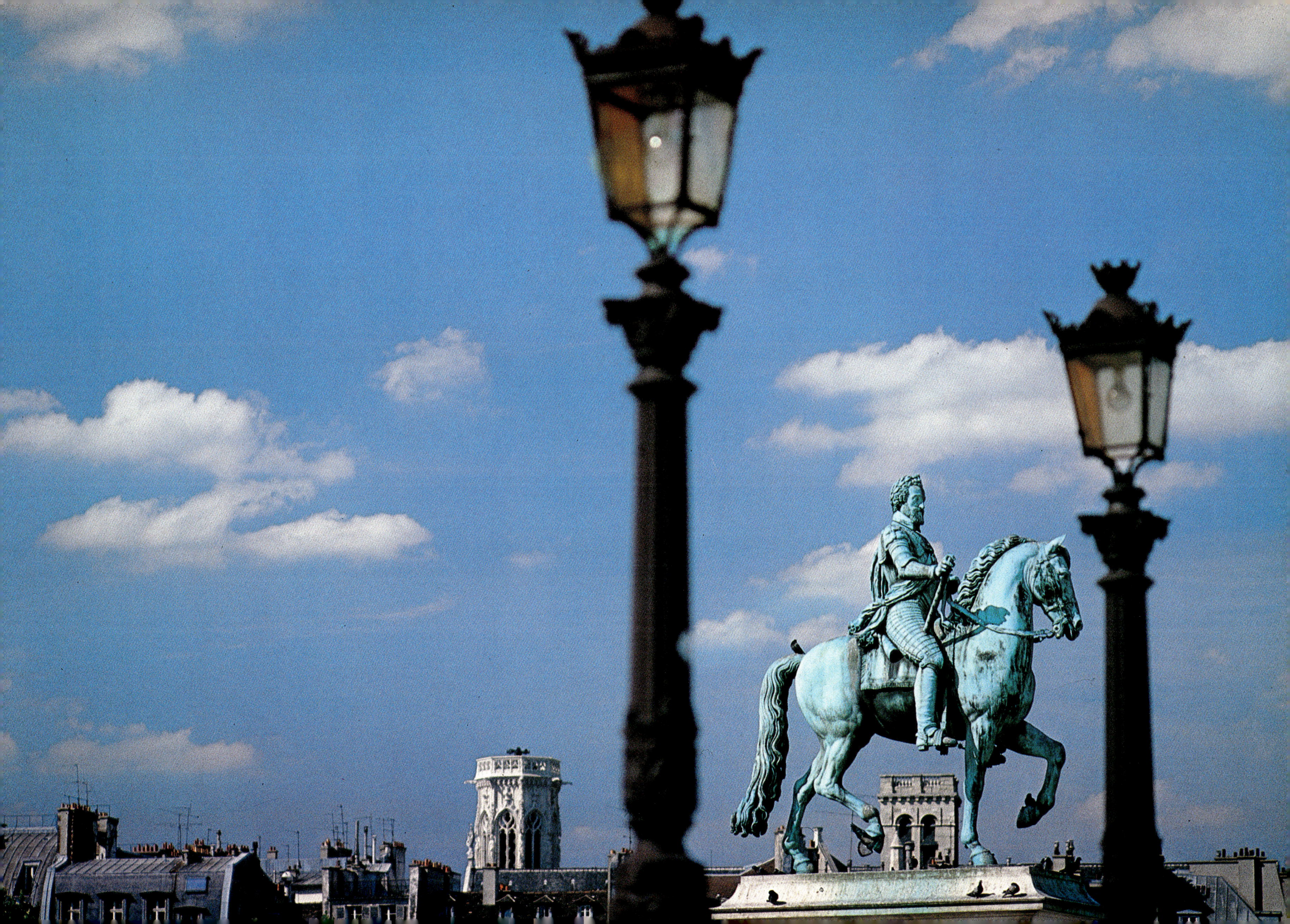

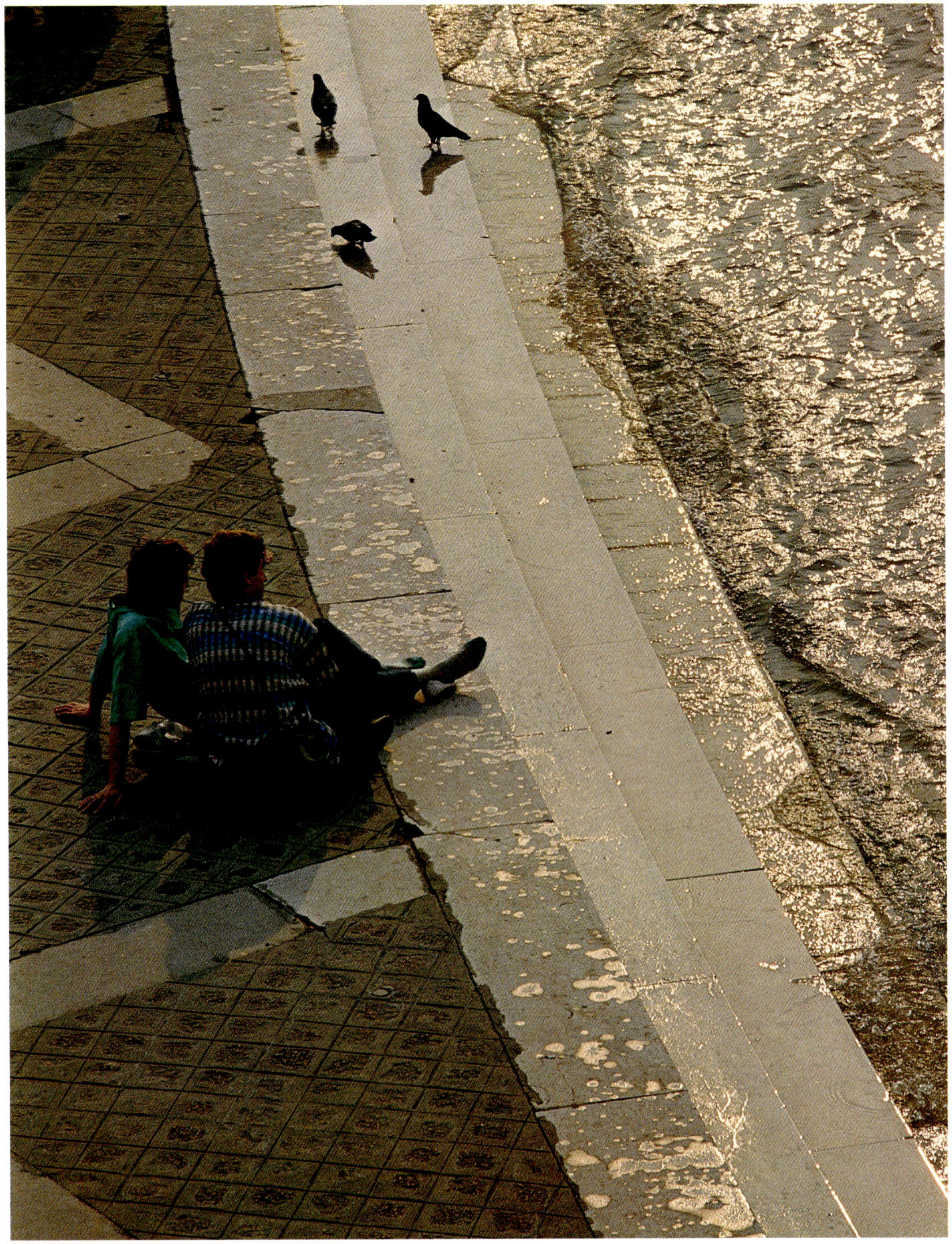

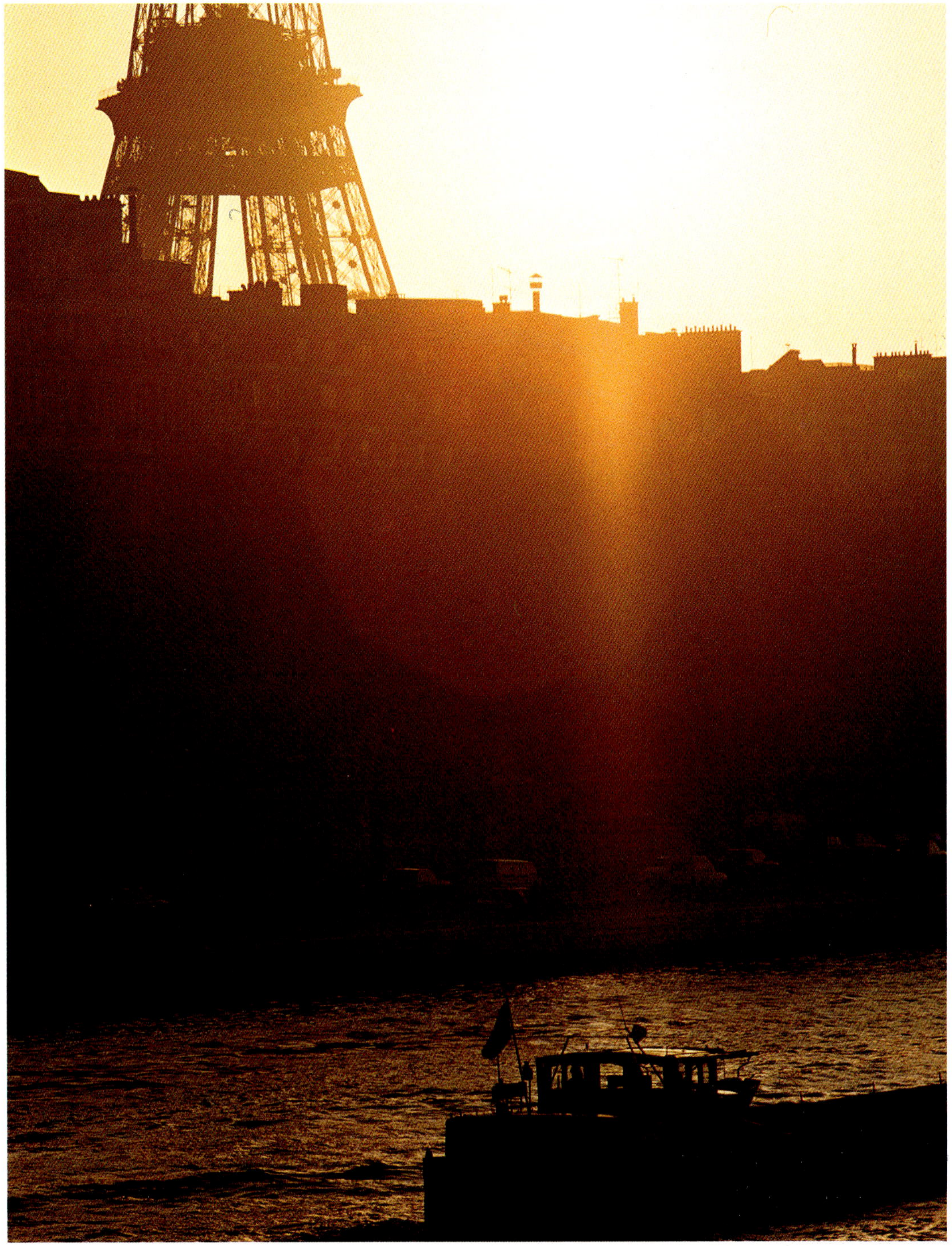

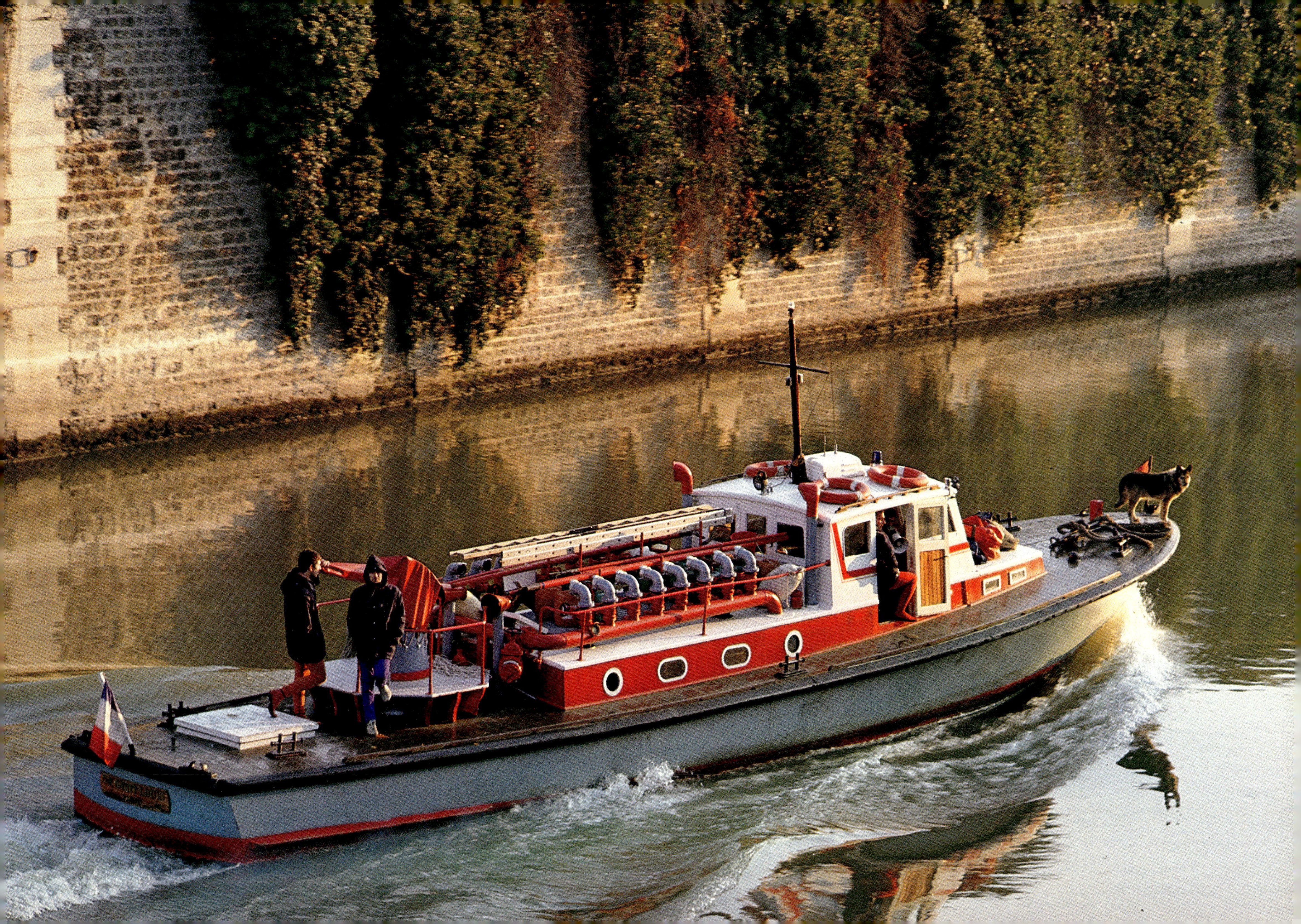

125 126

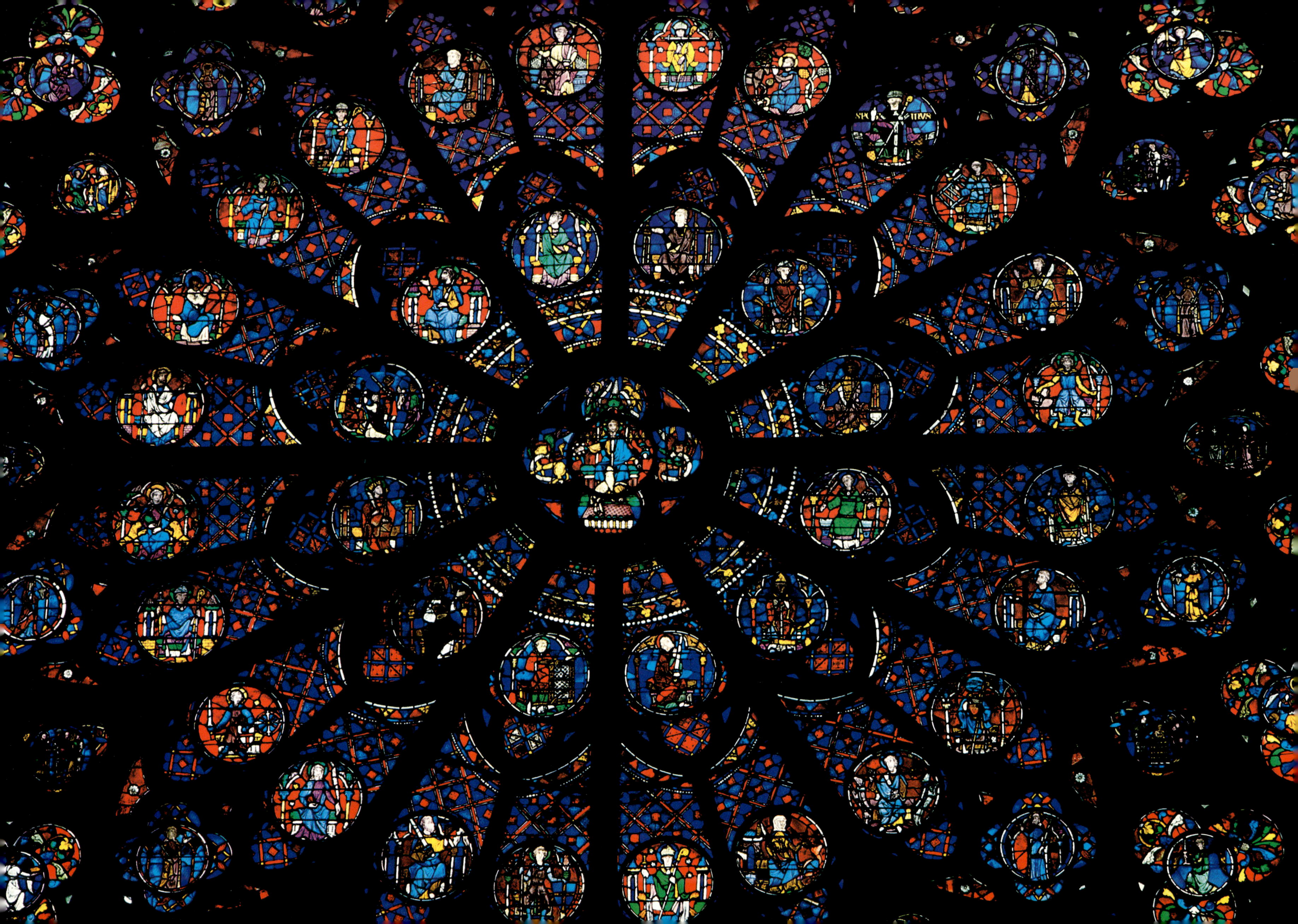

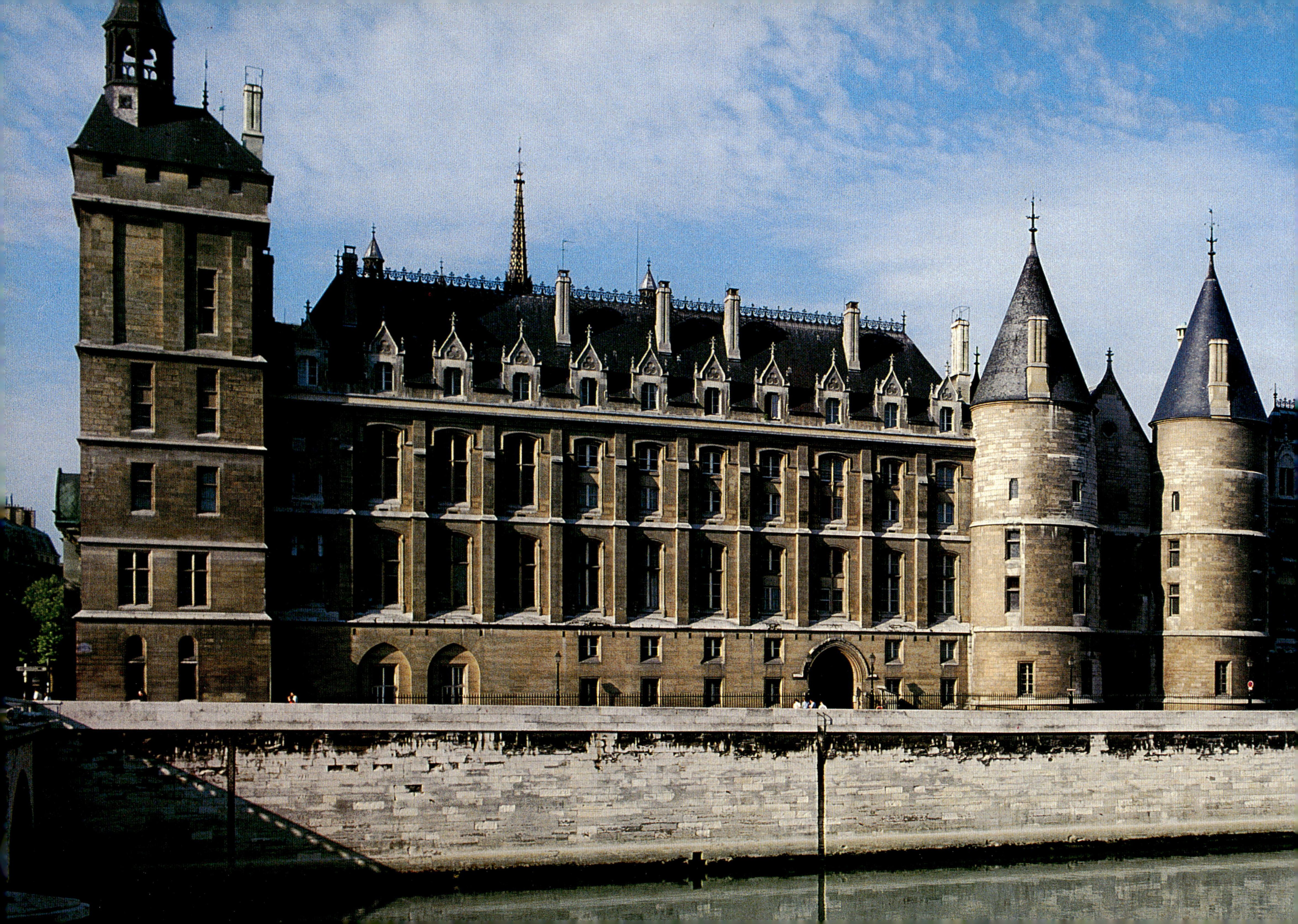

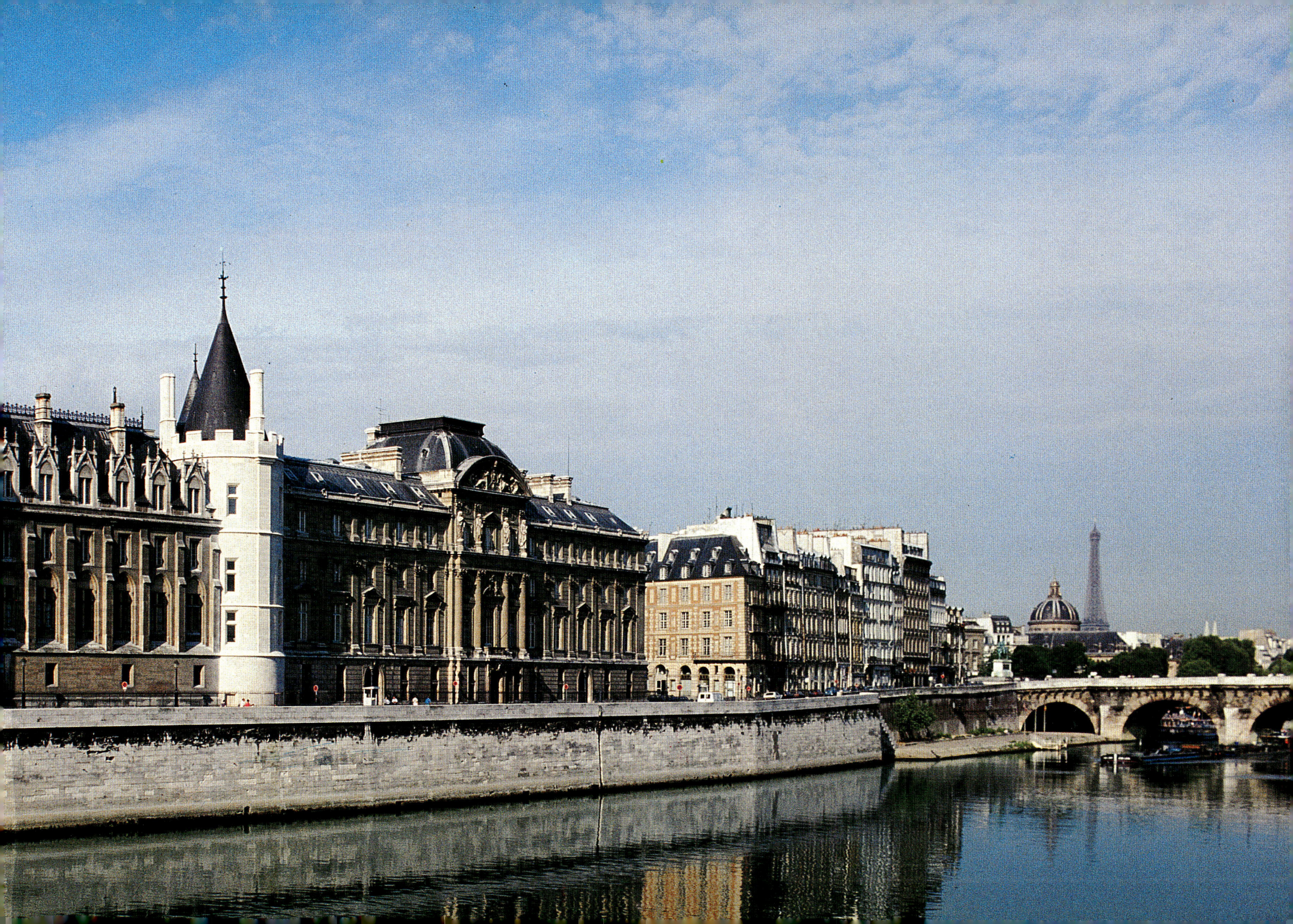

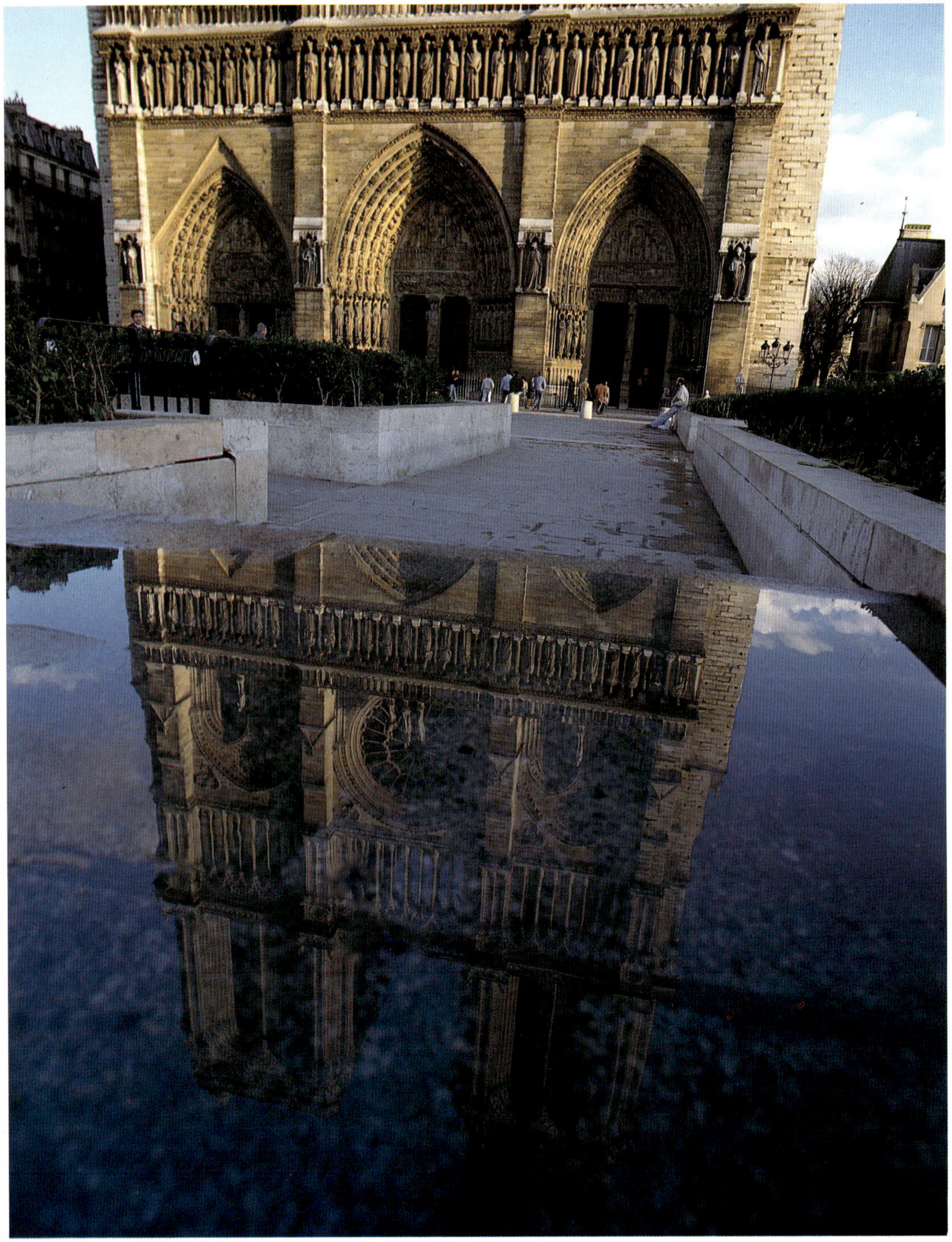

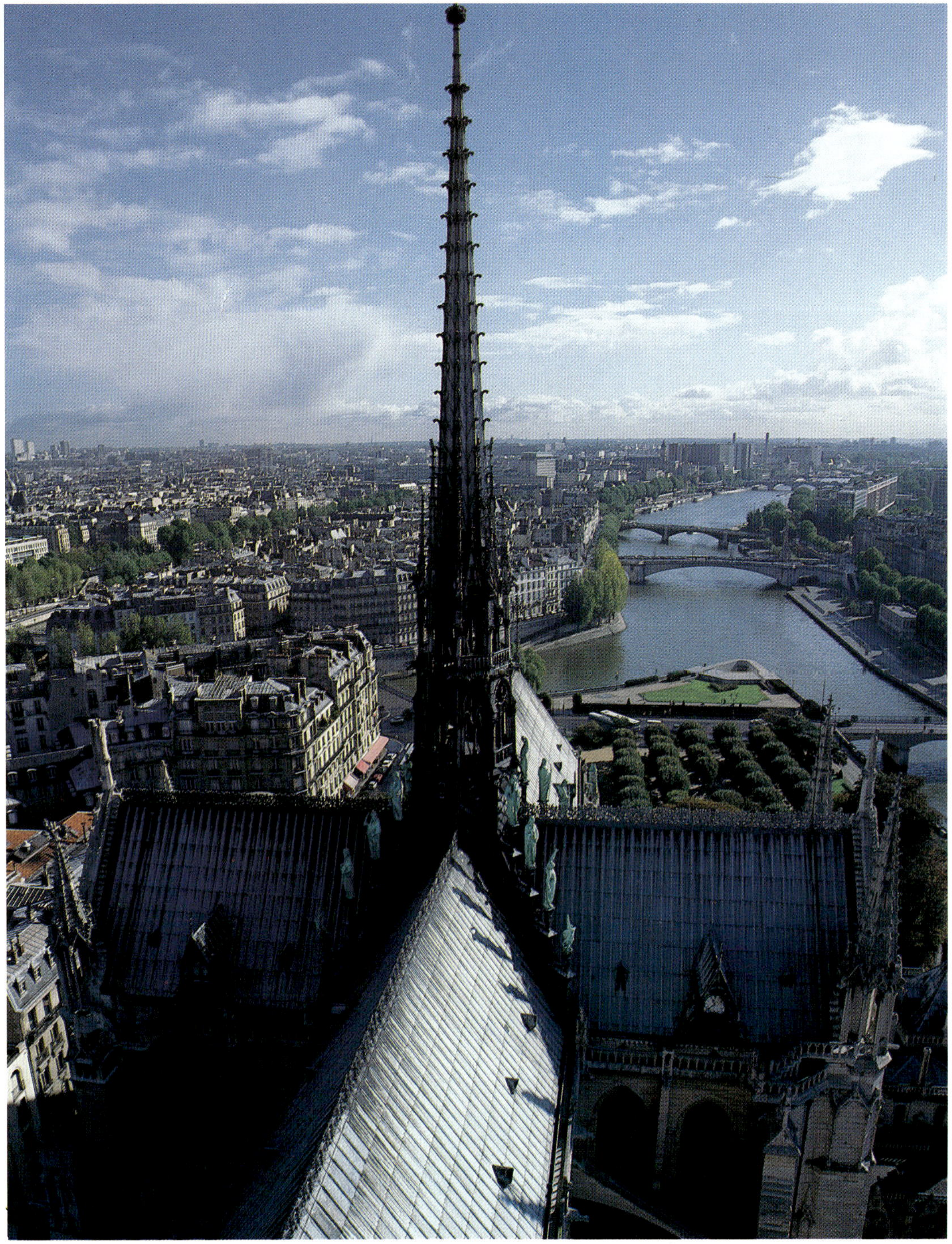

100   The Seine runs gleaming through Paris, reflecting the last glow of the evening sky which transforms it into a golden flow of lava, crossed by dark, delicate bridges.

101, 102   The foundation stone of the Pont Alexandre III was laid by Nicholas II, the last of the tsars, on 6 October 1896 during a visit to Paris. The bridge commemorated his father and symbolized the growing friendship between France and Russia: the Emperor and Empress were escorted to the ceremony by Félix Faure, President of the Republic, through cheering crowds of Parisians. It was opened in 1900.

With its single span of more than 107 m (350 ft), manufactured in the workshops of Le Creusot in eastern France, the bridge was a remarkable technical achievement in its day. Its generous width carried the line of the Esplanade des Invalides (whose dome is seen in the background here) across the river to the Grand Palais and Petit Palais, newly built for the Exposition of 1900 (see Pl. 97). The elegant arch was designed by the architects Rosal and Alby; and while the rich sculptural decoration by Frémiet, Jules Dalou and Alfred Lenoir has occasionally been criticized, in its festive free Baroque the bridge is a splendid example of the style of the turn of the century.

103   *Liberty giving light to the People* is a smaller version of the great Statue of Liberty by Auguste Bartholdi which was given by France to the United States in 1886. It was presented in thanks by the American people in 1889, and stands on an artificial island upriver from the Allée des Cygnes, near the Pont de Bir-Hakeim. Here, as the Seine divides into two streams, *Liberty* greets the tugs that make their way against the current.

104   Paris in the snow seems curiously reversed, like a photographic negative, as the blanket of white eliminates colour and relief and transforms each scene into a simplified version of itself.

105   The Seine is a large-scale indicator of the city's weather: if the giant figure of a zouave attached to one of the cutwaters of the Pont de l'Alma has wet feet, then the season has been unusually rainy. If there are ice floes on the river, then it has been exceptionally cold for weeks, and all shipping comes to a stop.

106–111   Notre Dame stands on a site which for two thousand years or more has been a place of prayer. A Gallo-Roman temple was succeeded by an Early Christian basilica, then a Romanesque church, and finally by the present cathedral, founded by Bishop Maurice de Sully and begun in 1163. Under the direction of the master masons Jean de Chelles and Pierre de Montreuil, workers from the different guilds – stonemasons, sculptors, carpenters, smiths and glaziers – worked together to produce this miracle of Gothic art. Many great ceremonies have taken place here, from St Louis's return to Paris with the Crown of Thorns in the thirteenth century to the mass celebrated by Pope John Paul II in 1980. At the Revolution the Cathedral was transformed into a Temple of Reason and then a shrine dedicated to the Supreme Being. On 2 December 1802 Pope Pius VII officiated at the coronation of Napoleon as emperor. The publication in 1831 of Victor Hugo's novel *Notre-Dame de Paris* led to a great surge of popular interest which culminated in calls for the building's restoration. Viollet-le-Duc's ensuing work has been widely criticized, but it is certain that much of what he did was essential if the ailing structure was to survive.

Seen from the river (Pl. 104), Notre Dame rises from the Ile de la Cité like a tall ship. To the square in front of it, the *parvis*, it presents its façade (Pls. 106, 107, 128). The three great portals – of the Virgin, the Last Judgment, and St Anne – have tympana carved with scenes from the Bible and Christian legend. Above is the Galerie des Rois (Pl. 109), filled with twenty-eight statues of the kings of Judah and Israel. Higher still rise the towers, whose height is accentuated by their tall narrow bell-openings. The vast rose windows in the transepts (Pls. 110, 126), together with the other windows filled with stained glass, bathe the interior in a calm, filtered light.

112 The two islands of Paris are linked by the little Pont Saint-Louis. The Ile de la Cité (on the left) is the cradle of the city; the Ile Saint-Louis (on the right) was created by the fusion of two smaller uninhabited islands (see Pls. 154, 155). The Ile de la Cité is a religious and administrative centre, housing as it does not only the Cathedral, the Bishop's Palace and the Sainte-Chapelle but the Prefecture of Police, the Palais de Justice and the Tribunal de Commerce. The Ile Saint-Louis, on the other hand, is residential, and contains many fine seventeenth-century houses including the famous Hôtel Lauzun and Hôtel Lambert.

113 Major festivals and holidays in the summer always end with a display of fireworks, guaranteed to please the crowds. This one, above the Pont des Arts, is unusually fine. Below its multicoloured rockets lie the Louvre, Notre Dame, and the domed Institut de France.

114 The Quai d'Orléans may not have the finest houses in the Ile Saint-Louis, but it forms a splendid composition with Notre Dame. Where the quay meets the Rue Budé is a little museum devoted to the Polish poet and patriot Adam Mickiewicz. At the far end, the Ile Saint-Louis is like the prow of a ship pointing towards the Ile de la Cité.

115, 116 The Place Dauphine, named in honour of the future Louis XIII, fills the tip of the Ile de la Cité between the Pont Neuf and the Palais de Justice. The houses were all of brick and stone (similar to those of the Place des Vosges: see Pl. 67), but the overall effect has suffered from alteration and demolition, including the destruction of one whole side of the triangle. The two handsome houses that flank the entrance from the Pont Neuf give a good idea of its original appearance. It has now been made traffic-free, so that it is a good place to read or to sit and dream.

117, 118 'Pont Neuf' may mean 'new bridge', but it is new only in name, for its original construction in the sixteenth century makes it basically the oldest bridge in Paris. The openings above the piers, where the roadway widens, were formerly populated by showmen, tooth-pullers and quacks, and crowds flocked there to laugh at Tabarin or Pantaloon. The bridge has survived all the great floods unscathed, and indeed 'to be as fit as the Pont Neuf' became a byword for rugged good health. The areas above the piers, which also held tradesmen's stalls, now provide a refuge where weary tourists may rest on their crossing of the river.

119 The Ile de la Cité. Here two centuries before the birth of Christ the Parisii, a small Gaulish tribe, came to settle and to live off the fish they caught in the river. Thus were born the Roman Lutetia and the city of Paris. Like a ship, secured to the banks by bridges, the island has its stem to the Louvre and its stern to the Ile Saint-Louis. Its cargo of

architectural treasures includes the Sainte-Chapelle, the Conciergerie, Notre Dame, the Palais de Justice and the Hôtel Dieu, and a flower market is laid out on its starboard deck.

120 The view from the towers of Notre Dame is amazingly foreshortened by the telephoto lens. The bridges on the river appear like a flight of steps leading to the Grand Palais. Beyond on the right is the Arc de Triomphe; in the distance, closing the view like a slammed door, are the high-rise blocks of the district known as La Défense.

121 If the statue of Henri IV by the Pont Neuf, which replaces the original 'Vert Galant' destroyed at the Revolution, has something of an imperial air, that would not be surprising: its bronze comes from the figure of Napoleon removed from the Vendôme Column in 1818 and from the monument to Napoleon's general, Desaix, which had stood for a time in the Place des Victoires. It is said that the bronze-founder was a fervent Bonapartist and that he hid within Henri IV a statuette of Napoleon and manuscripts praising the Emperor.

122 The Quai Saint-Bernard, in front of the Jardin des Plantes, provides plenty of space for sunbathing in the summer. The river itself, alas, is far too polluted for a swim.

123 The mood of the Eiffel Tower as it watches over Paris and the flowing river is at one with that of Apollinaire's refrain:
Vienne la nuit, sonne l'heure
Les jours s'en vont, je demeure.
(Let night fall, the hour strike. The days go by. I remain.)

124 To enable them to cope with all emergencies, the fire department maintain light vessels on the river with extremely powerful pumps.

125 The Saint-Chapelle, built by St Louis to house precious relics, has the finest stained glass in Paris. Through its dazzling colours it filters the light of the city to create a mystical atmosphere. The windows filling the walls of the upper chapel contain 134 scenes from the Bible.

126 The rose window in the south transept of Notre Dame dates from around 1270 (see also Pl. 110). It was restored in the eighteenth century and again by Viollet-le-Duc in the nineteenth century, but some of its original glass survives.

127 Since the creation of a new road at low level along the right bank of the river, barges are no longer the only vehicles to pass underneath the bridges. The Voie Georges Pompidou has been much criticized; but it does offer new views of the city. Here we are looking across at the Palais de Justice and the Conciergerie, with the latter's newly restored Tour Bonbec. Beyond is a corner of the Place Dauphine (see Pl. 116), then the Pont Neuf with the statue of Henri IV (Pls. 118, 121). Further still are the dome of the Institut de France, the Eiffel Tower, and the white twin spires of Sainte-Clotilde.

128, 129 When the old houses surrounding Notre Dame were demolished in the nineteenth century the building was fully revealed to west and east. Looking east from the towers, beyond the *flèche* is the Ile Saint-Louis and, in the far distance, the new development around the sports centre at Bercy.

The Left Bank

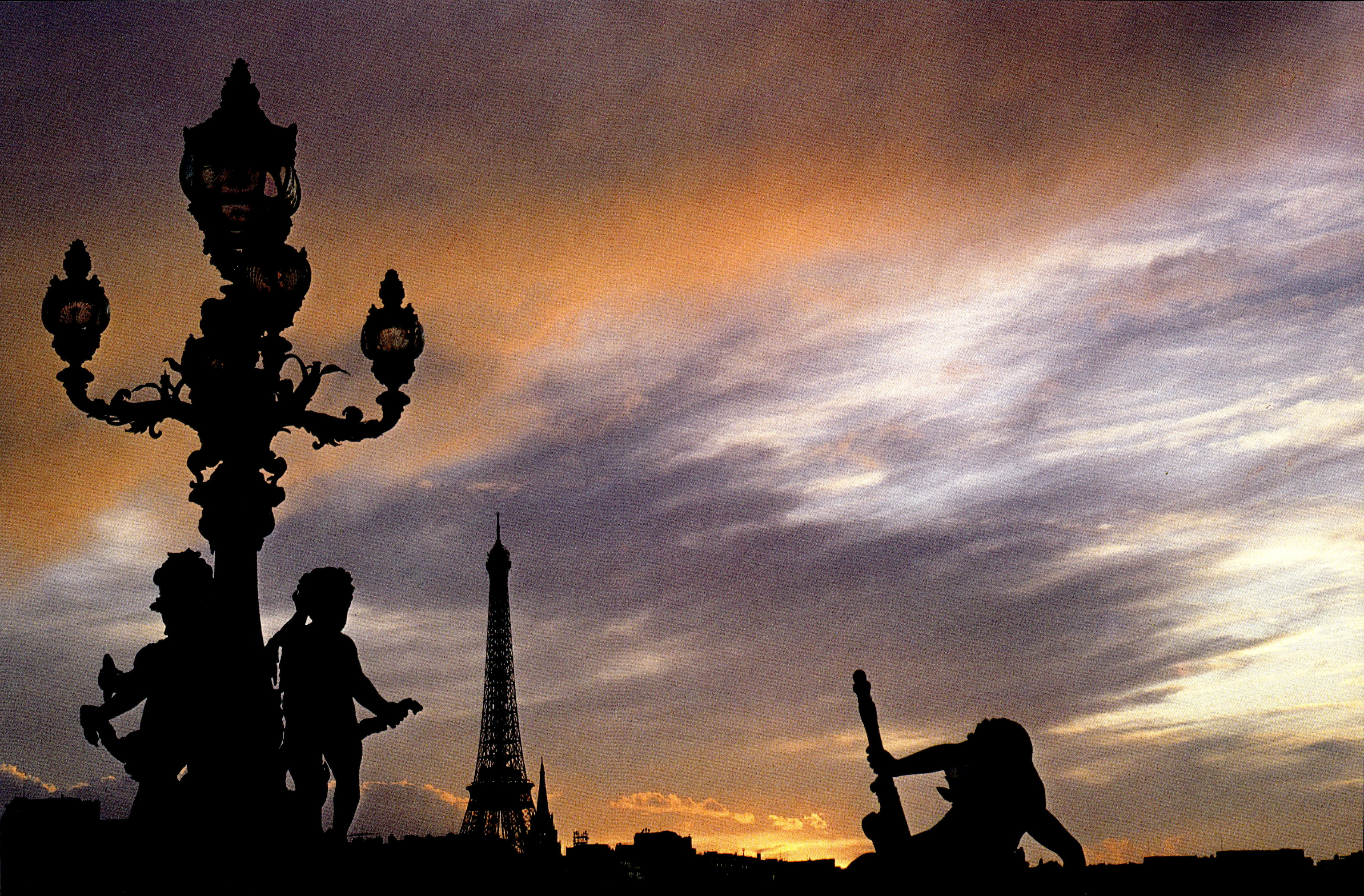

131 132

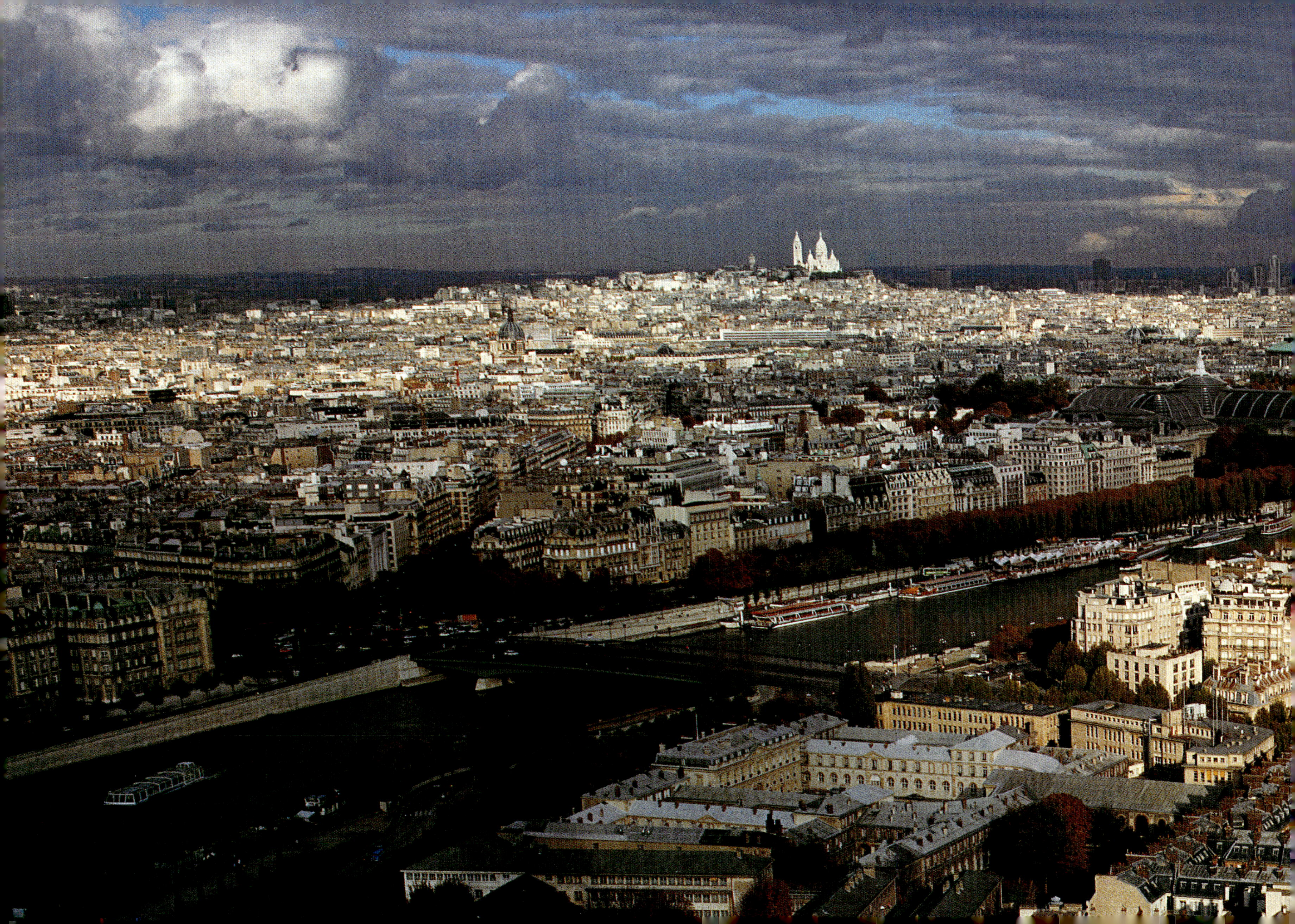

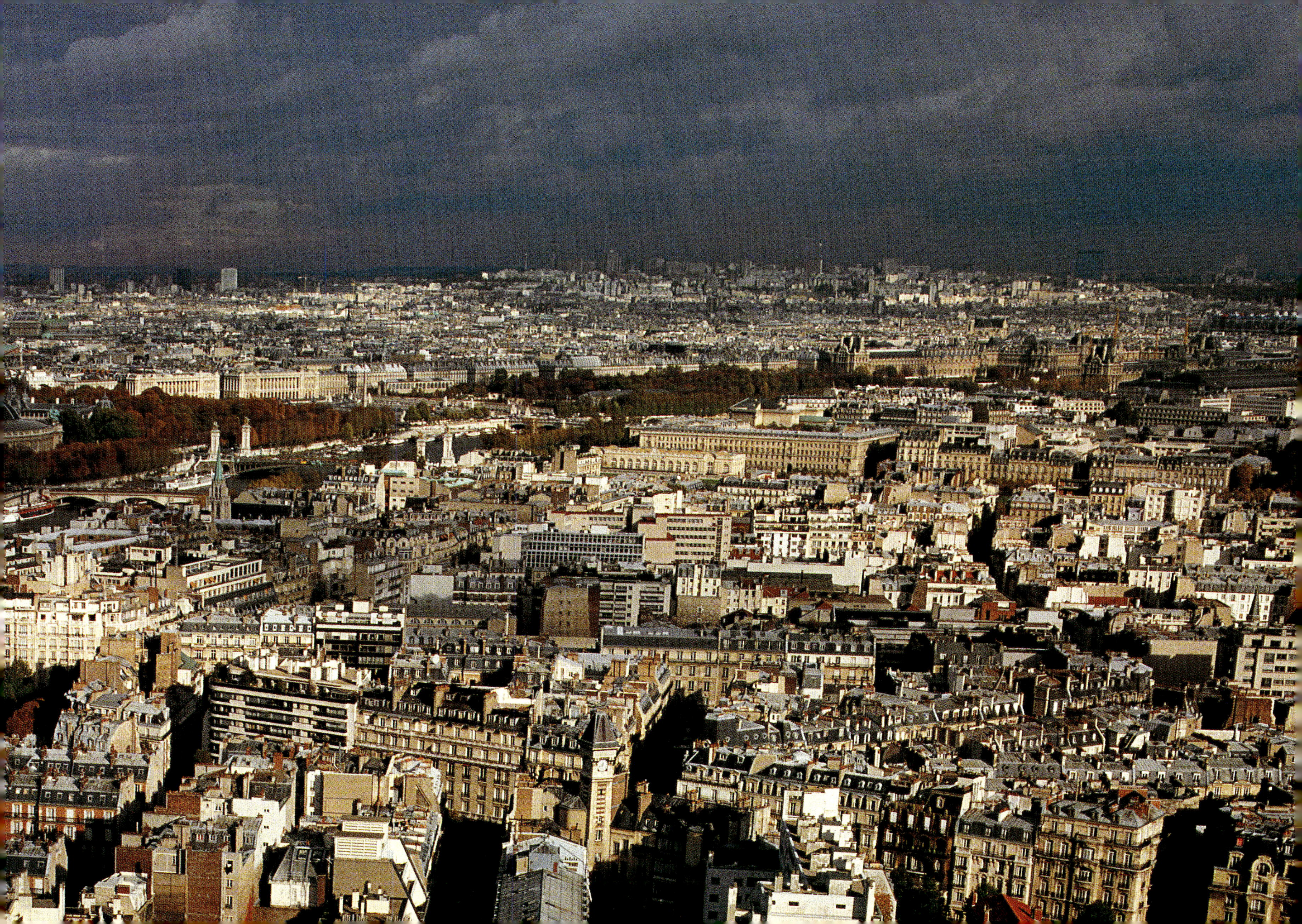

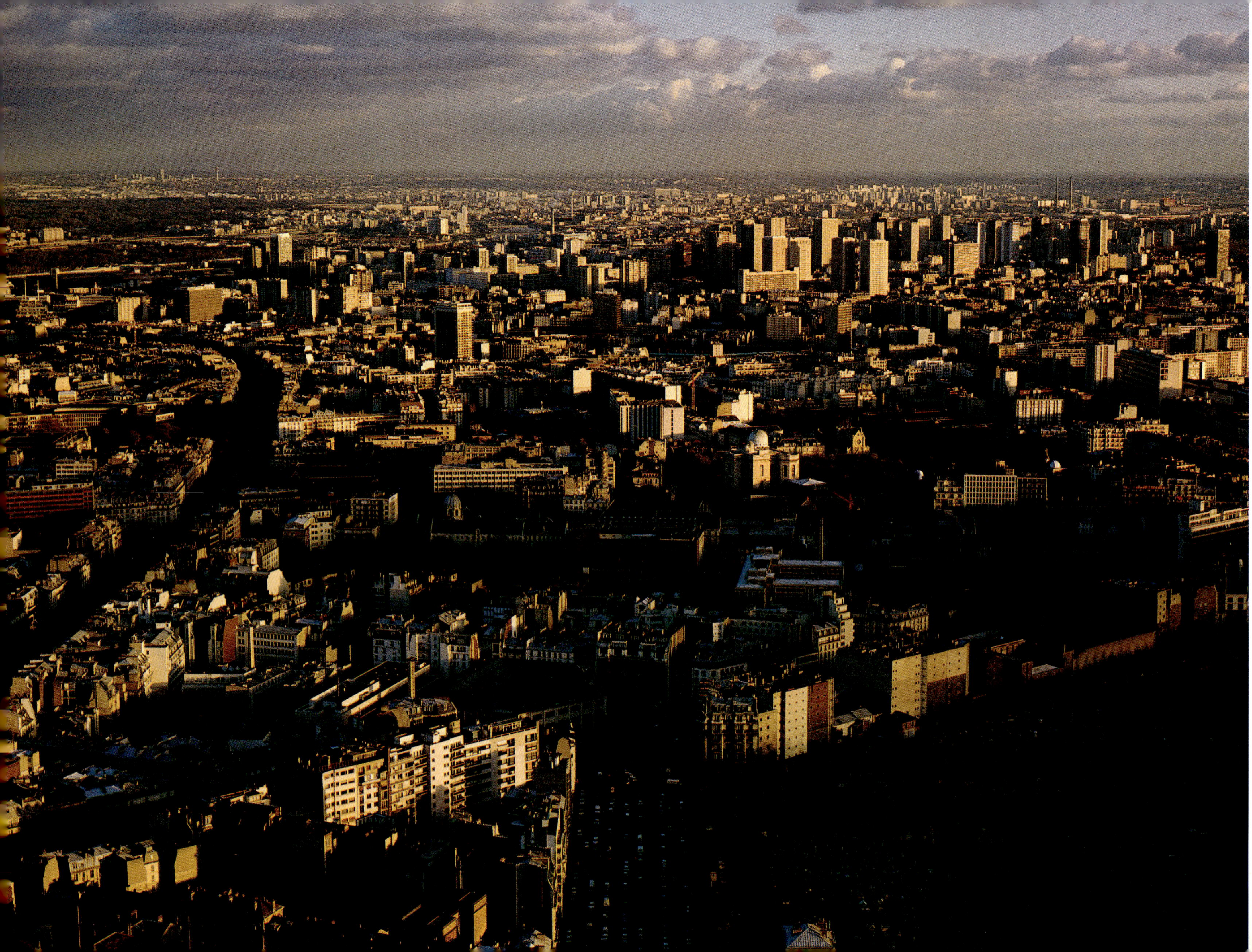

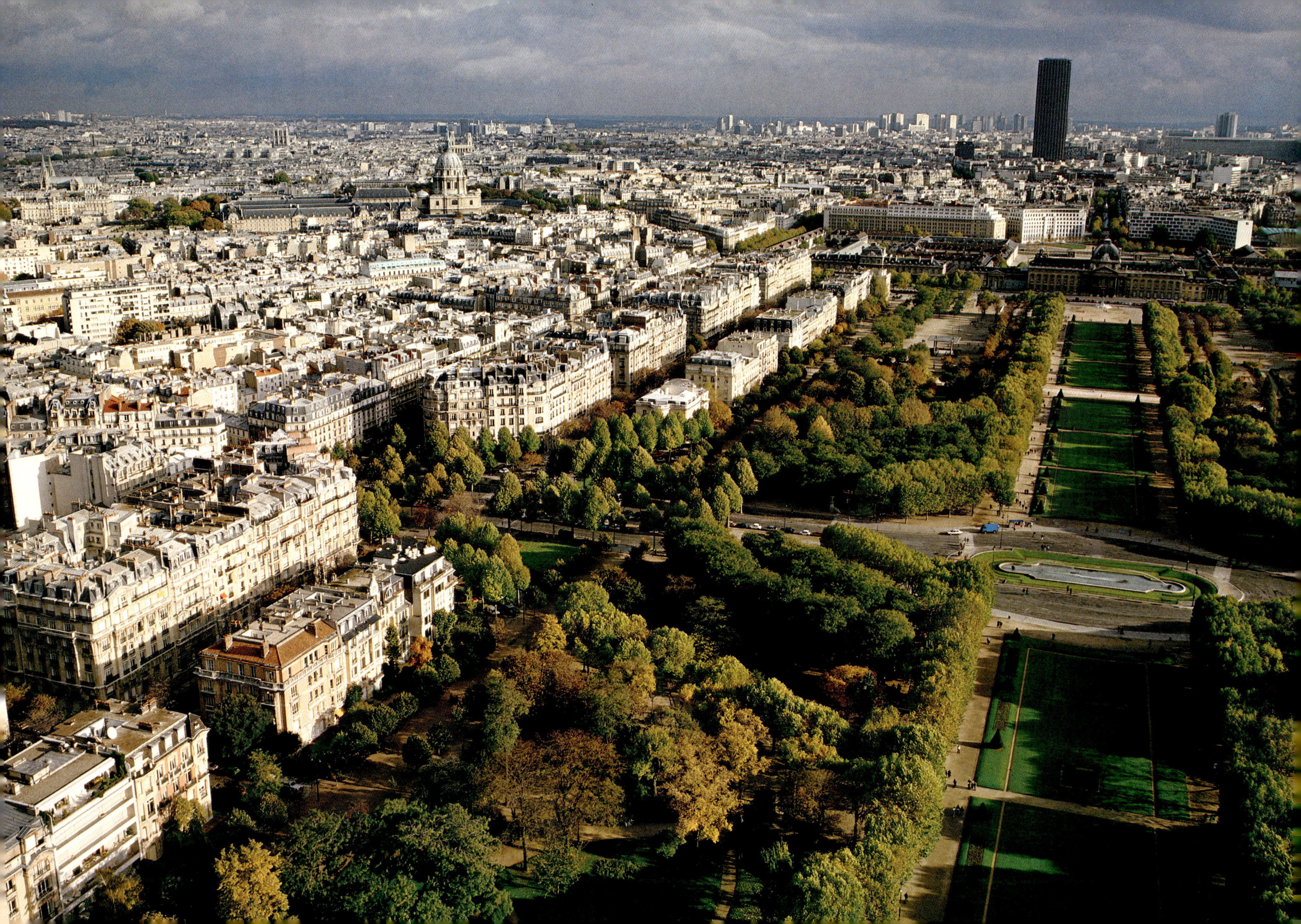

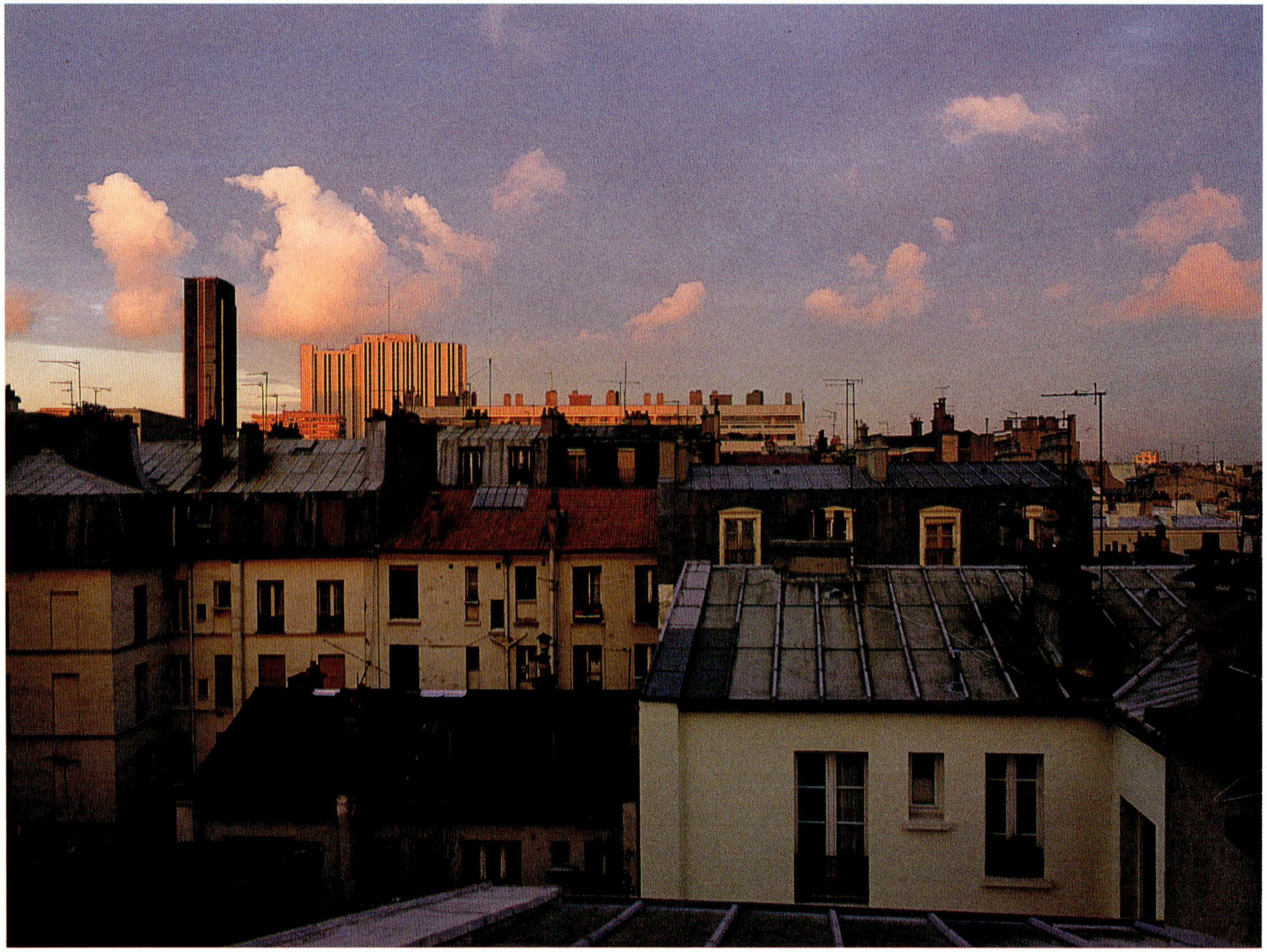

136 137

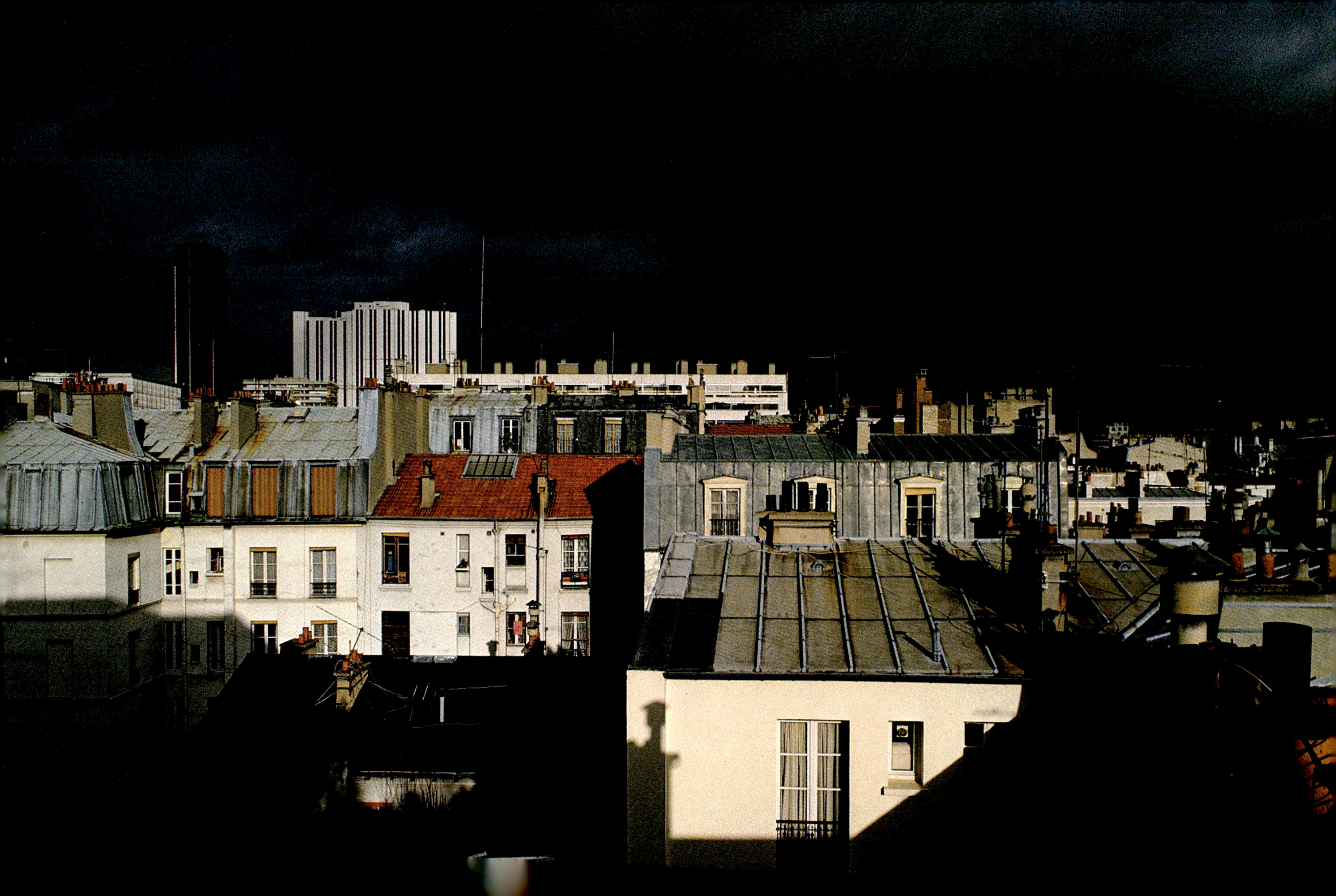

138 139

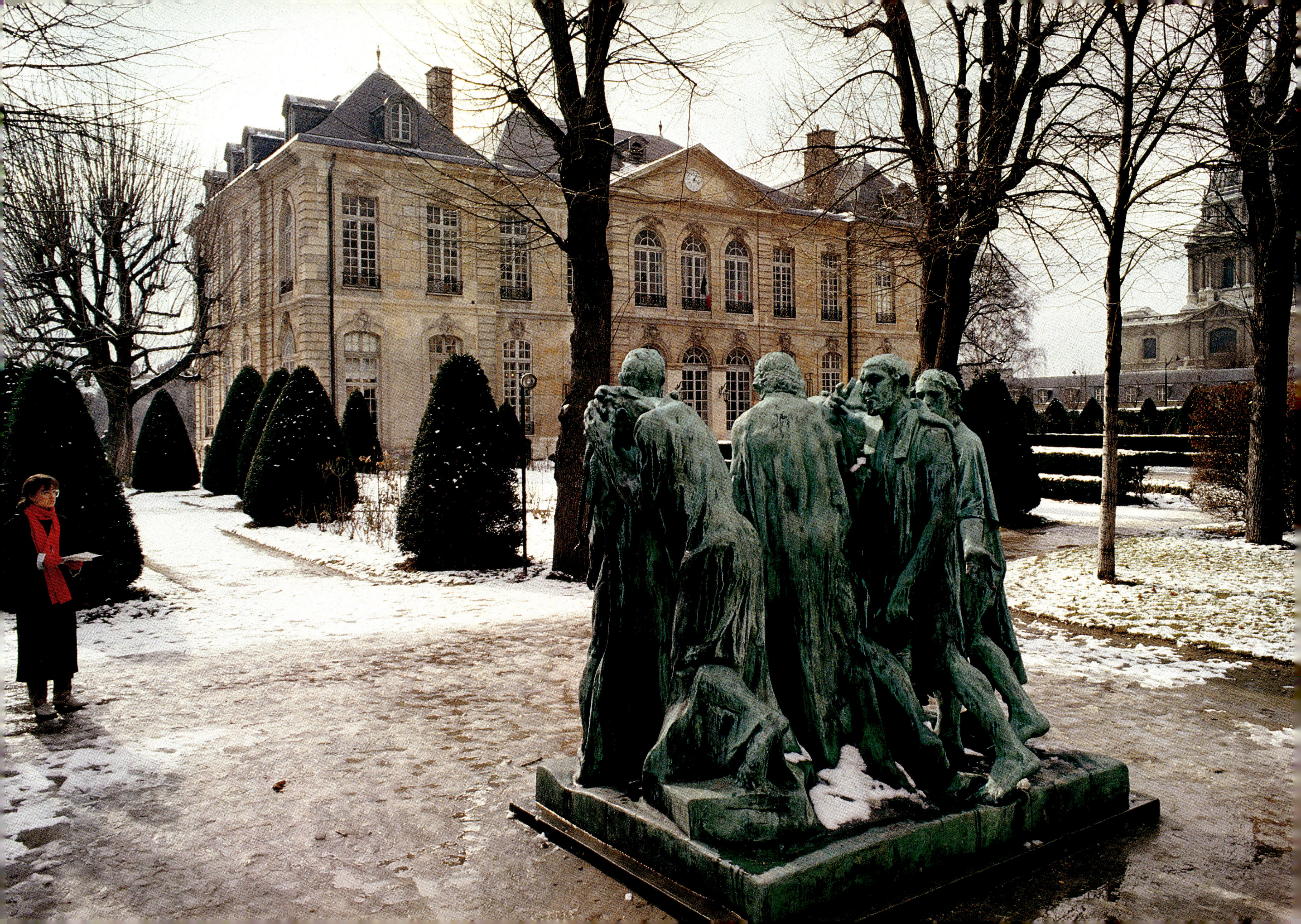

140 141

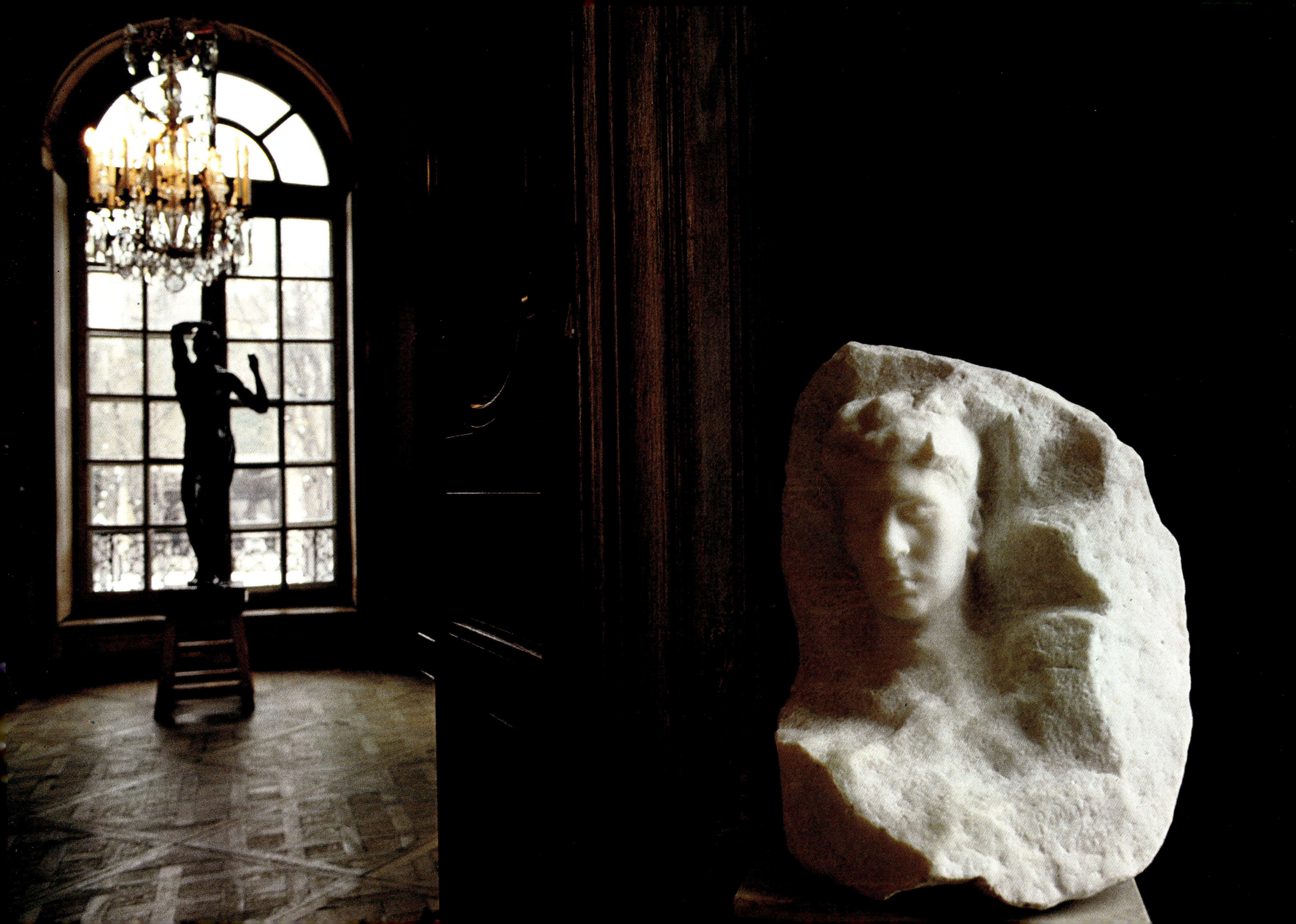

142 143

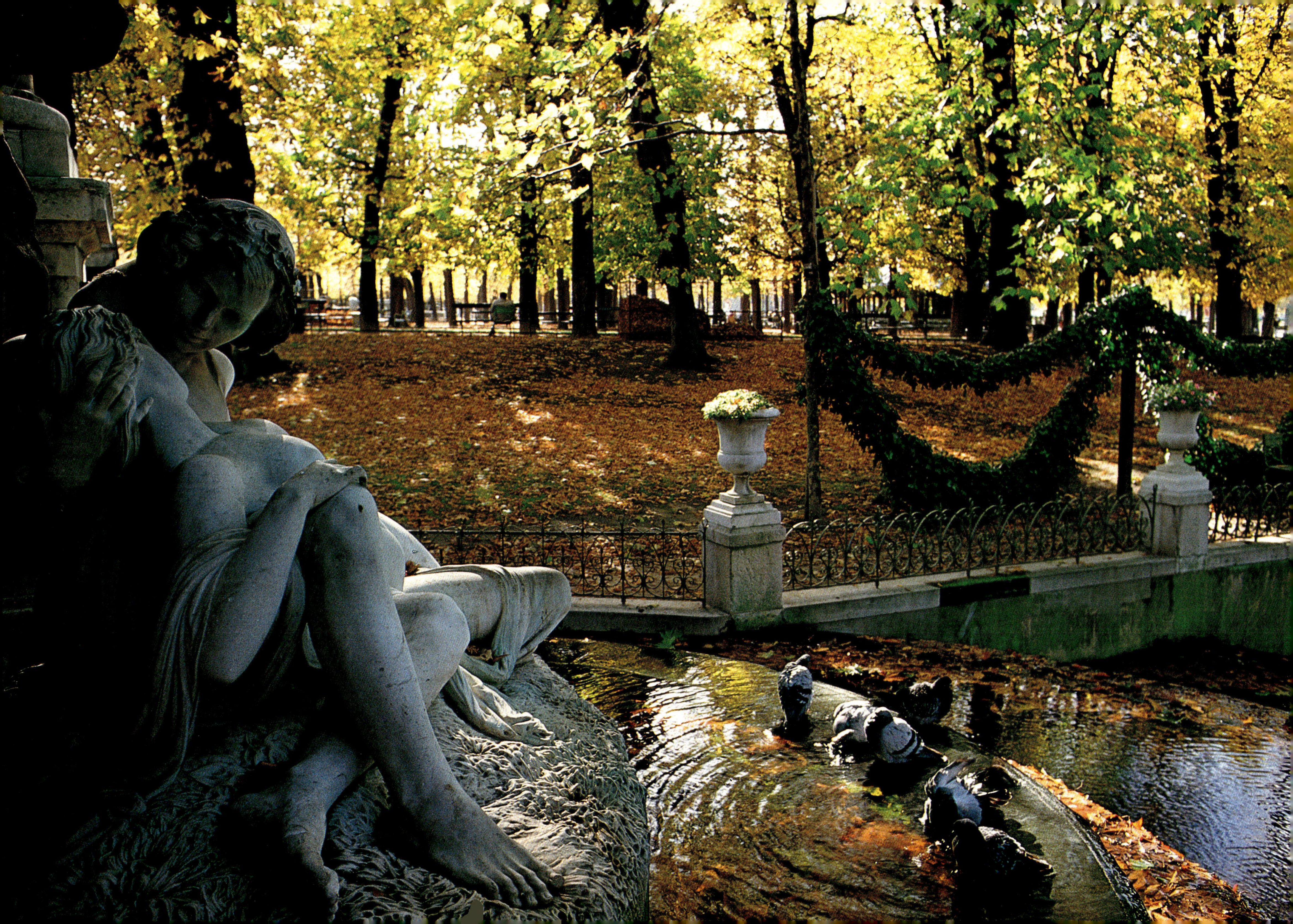

144 145

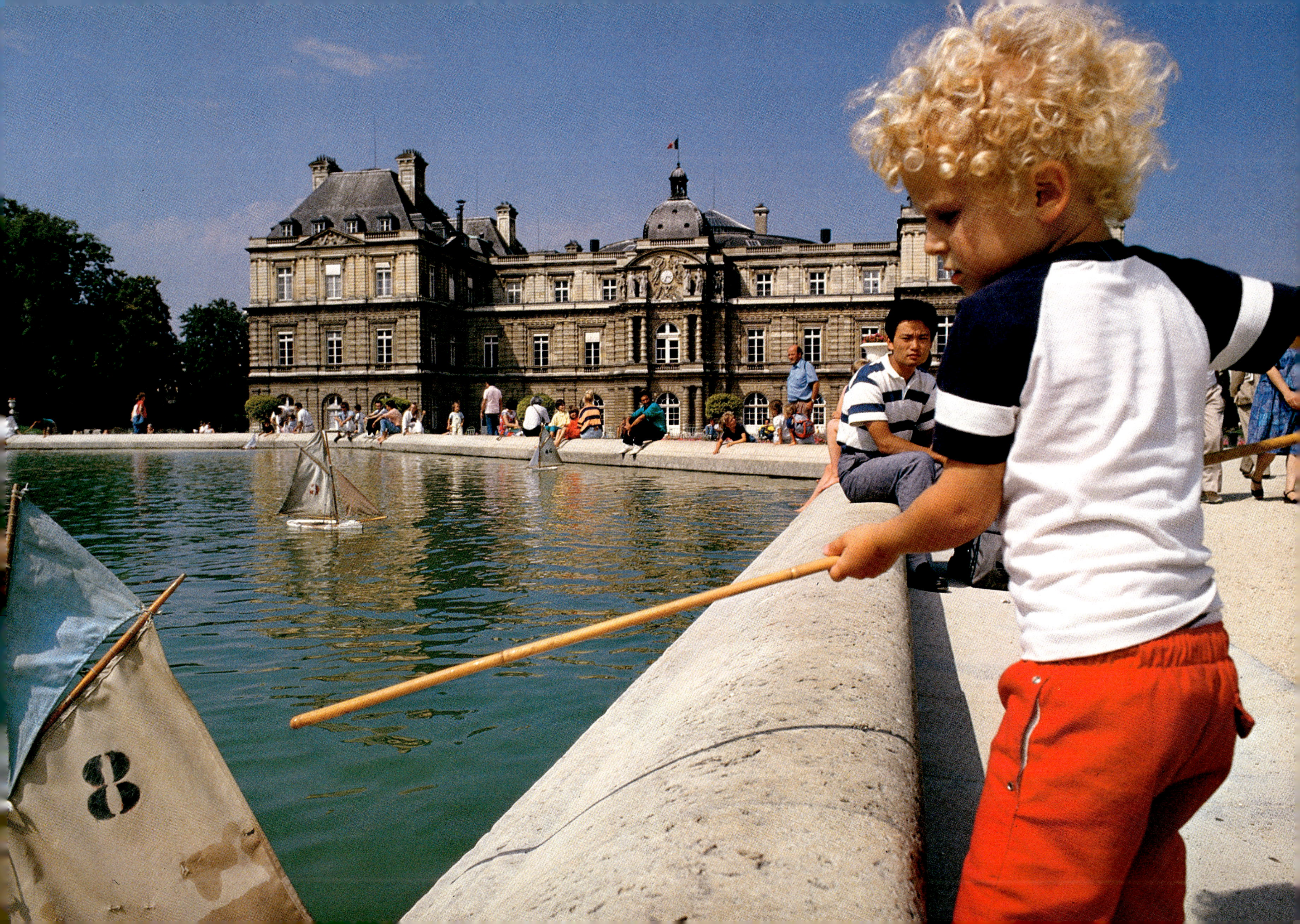
8

146 147

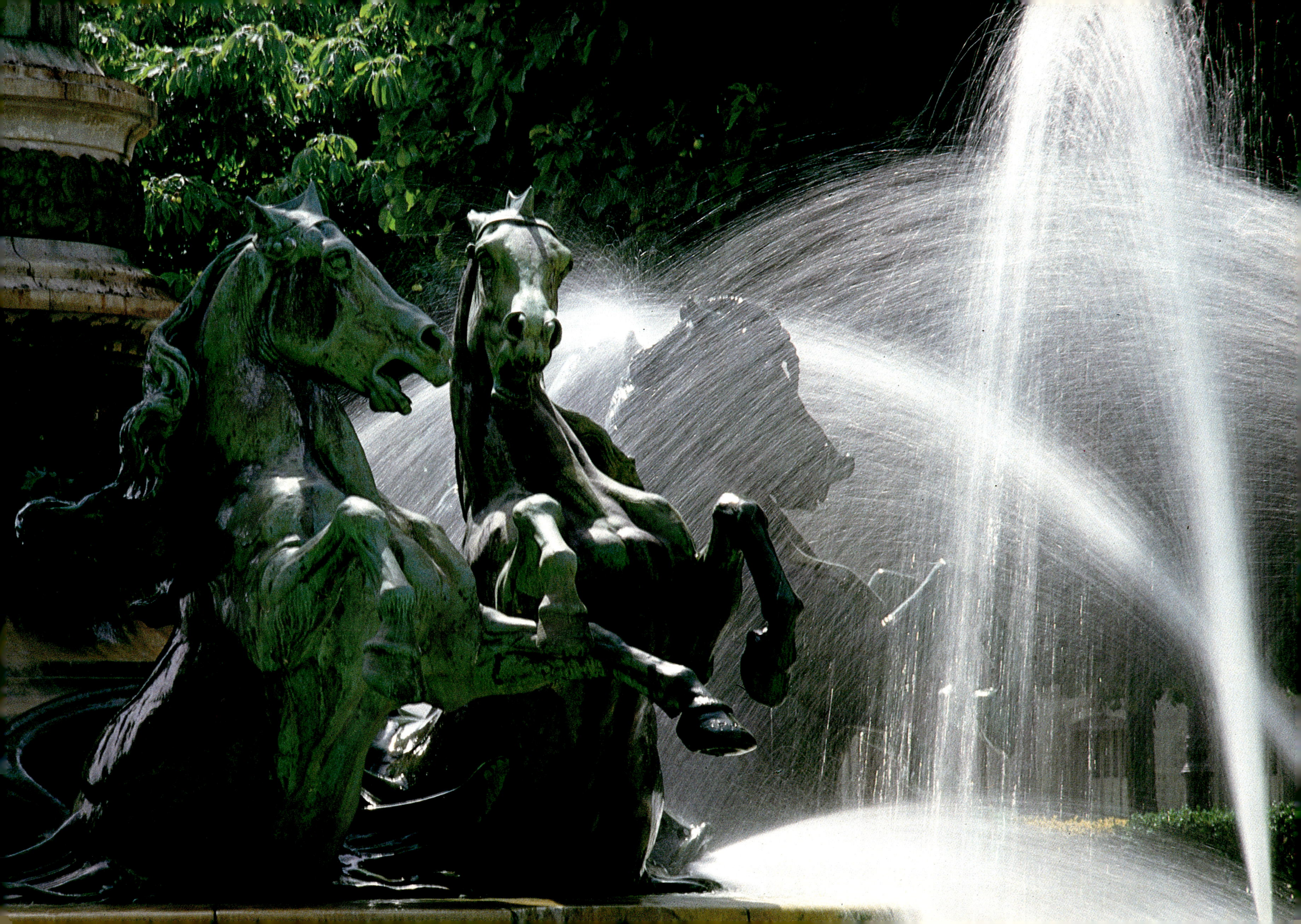

148 149

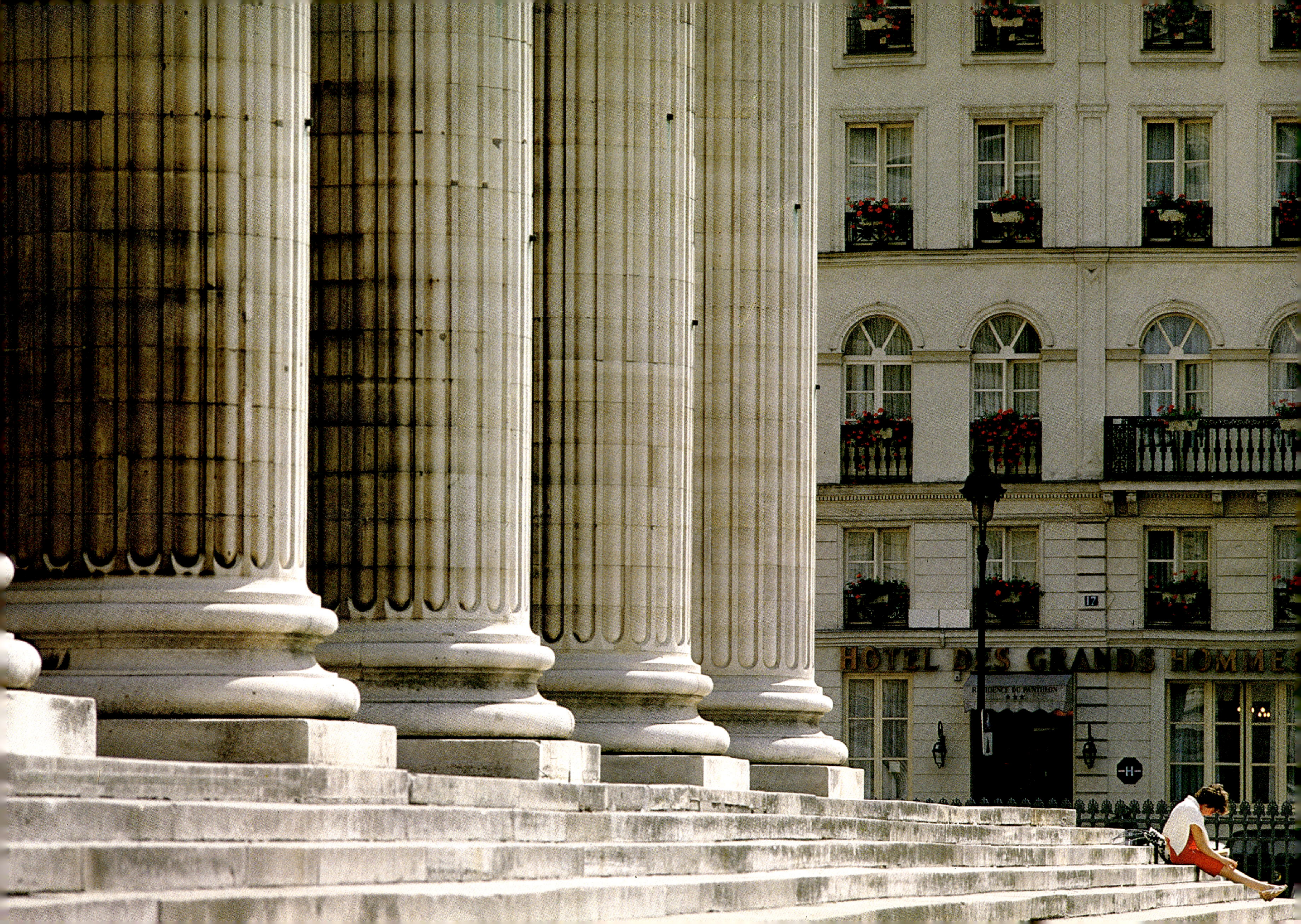
17
HOTEL DES GRANDS HOMMES

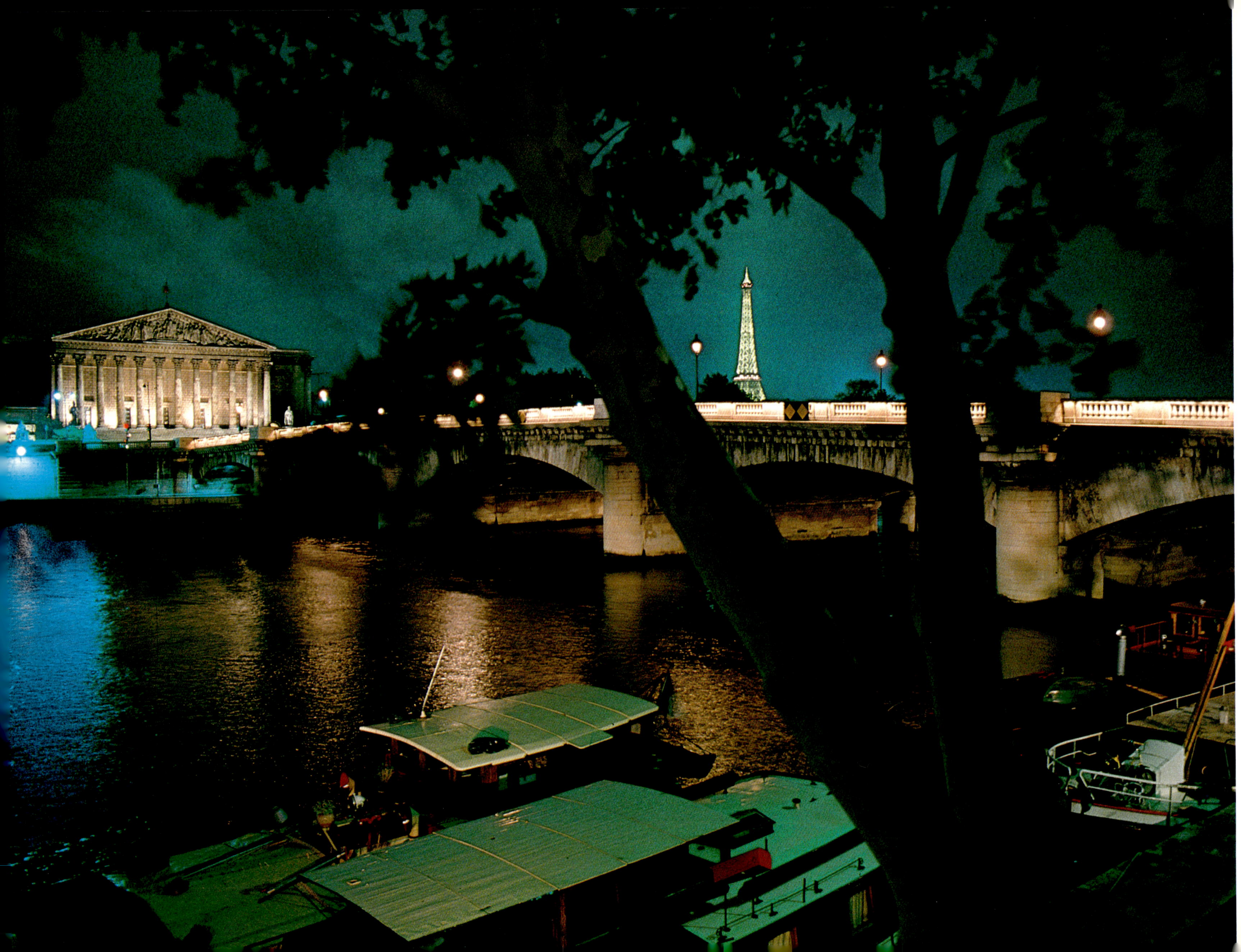

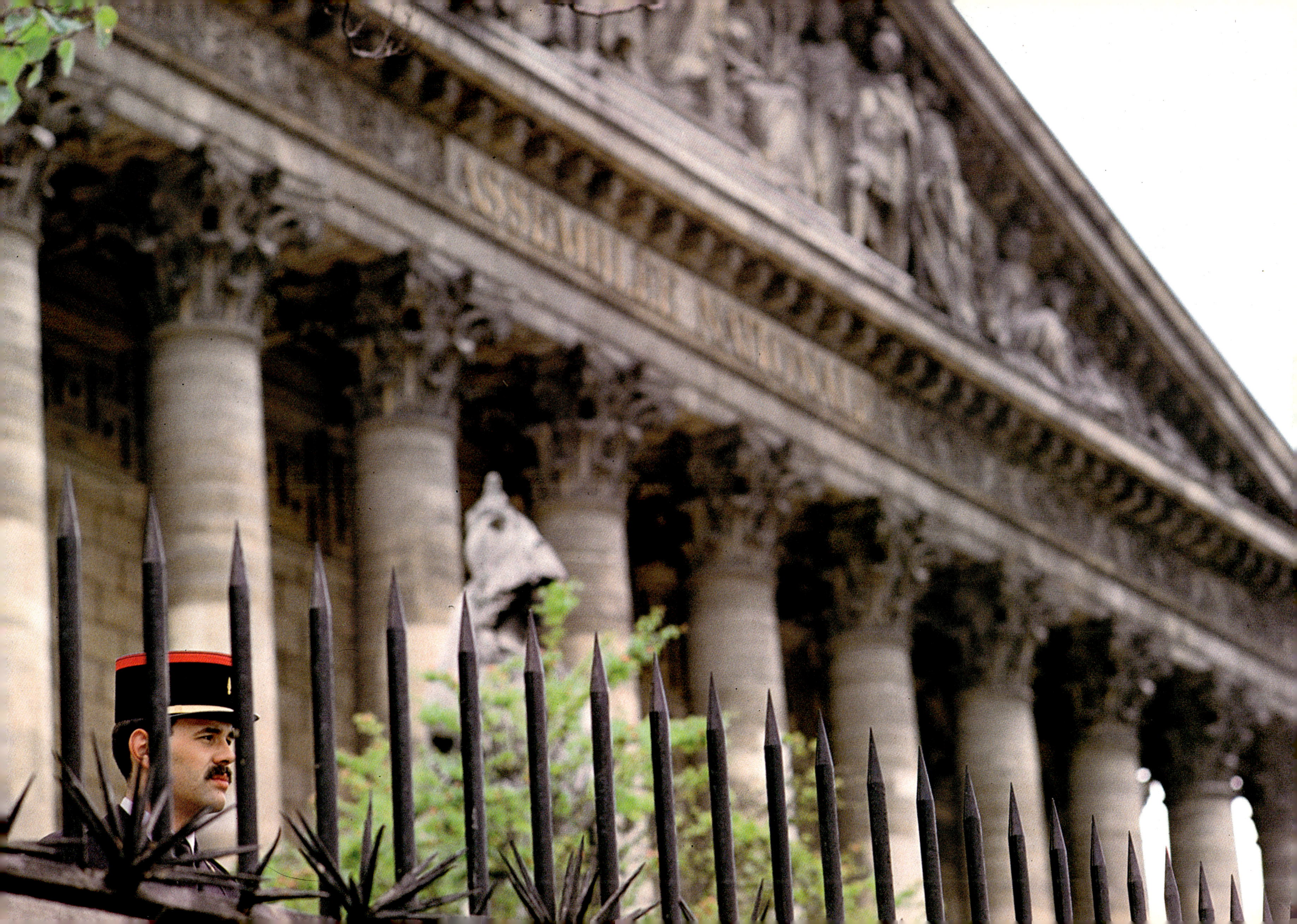

152 153

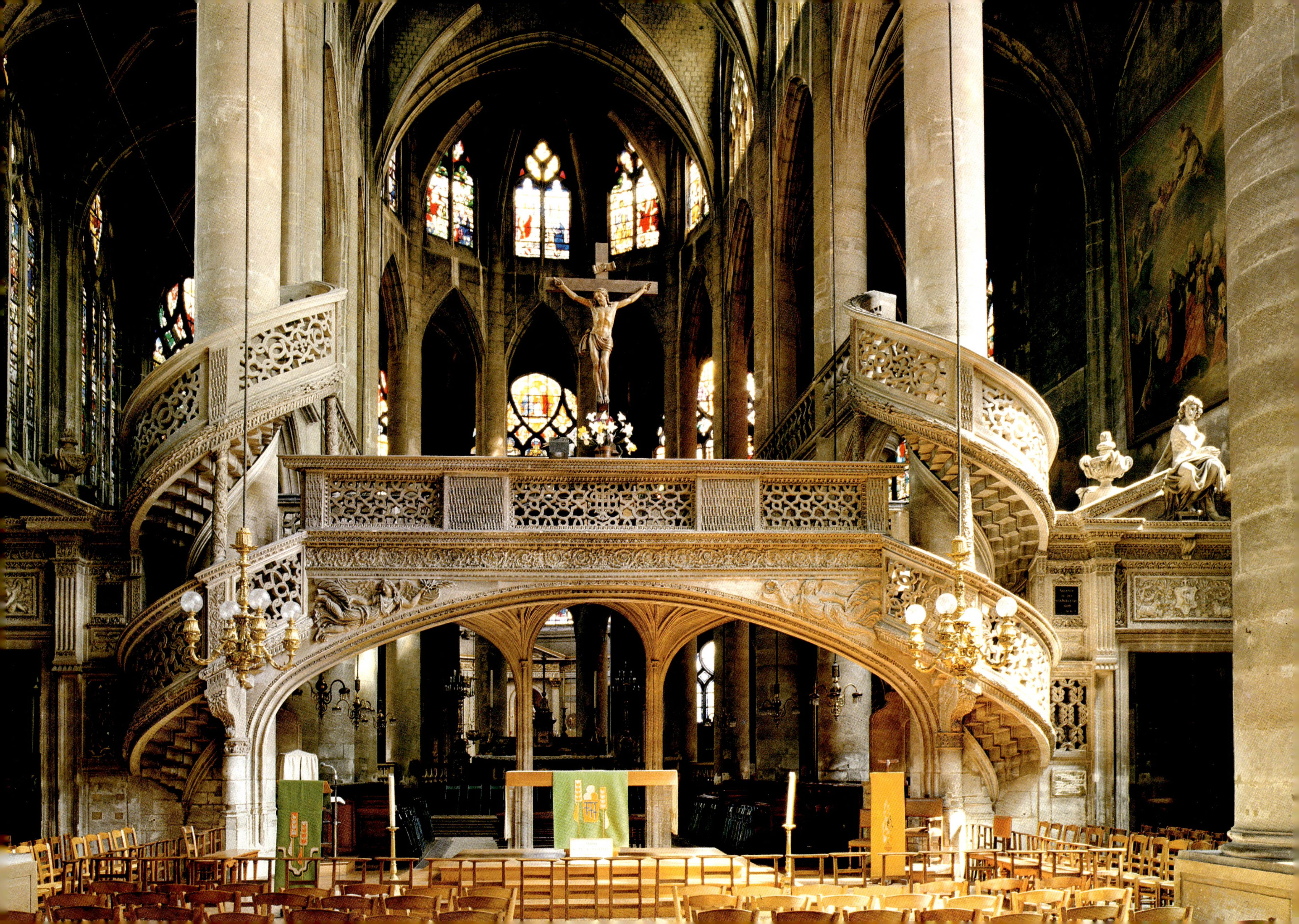

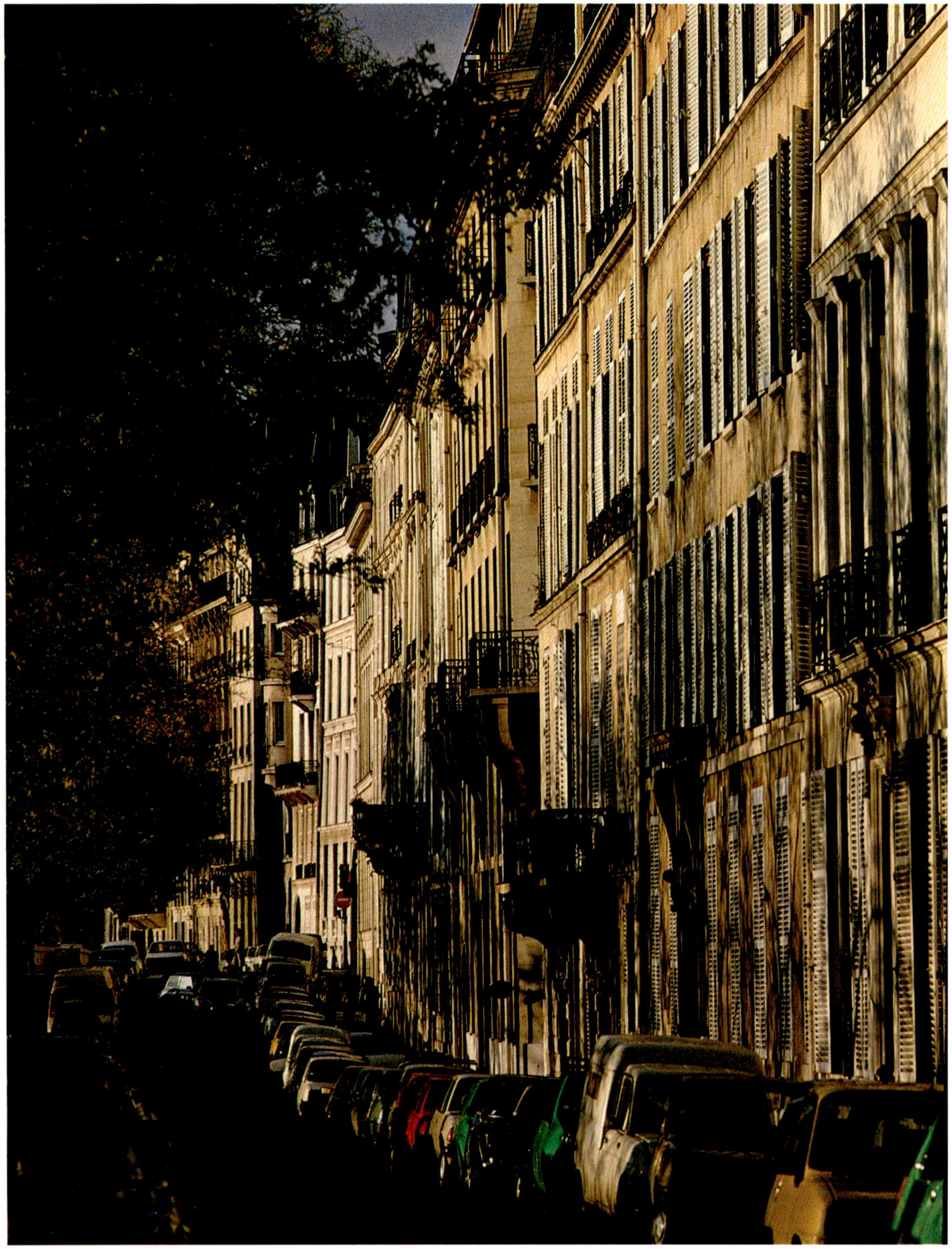

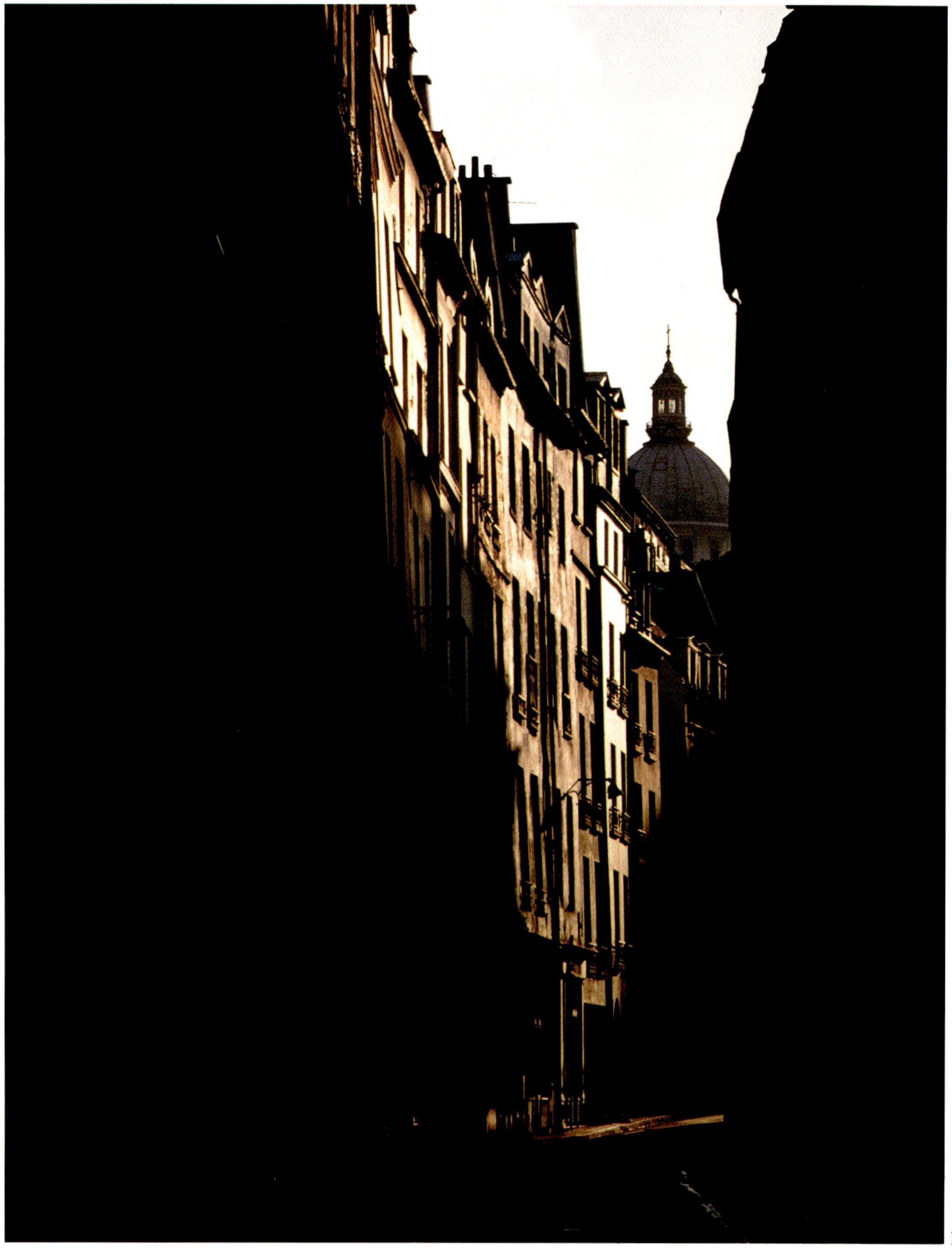

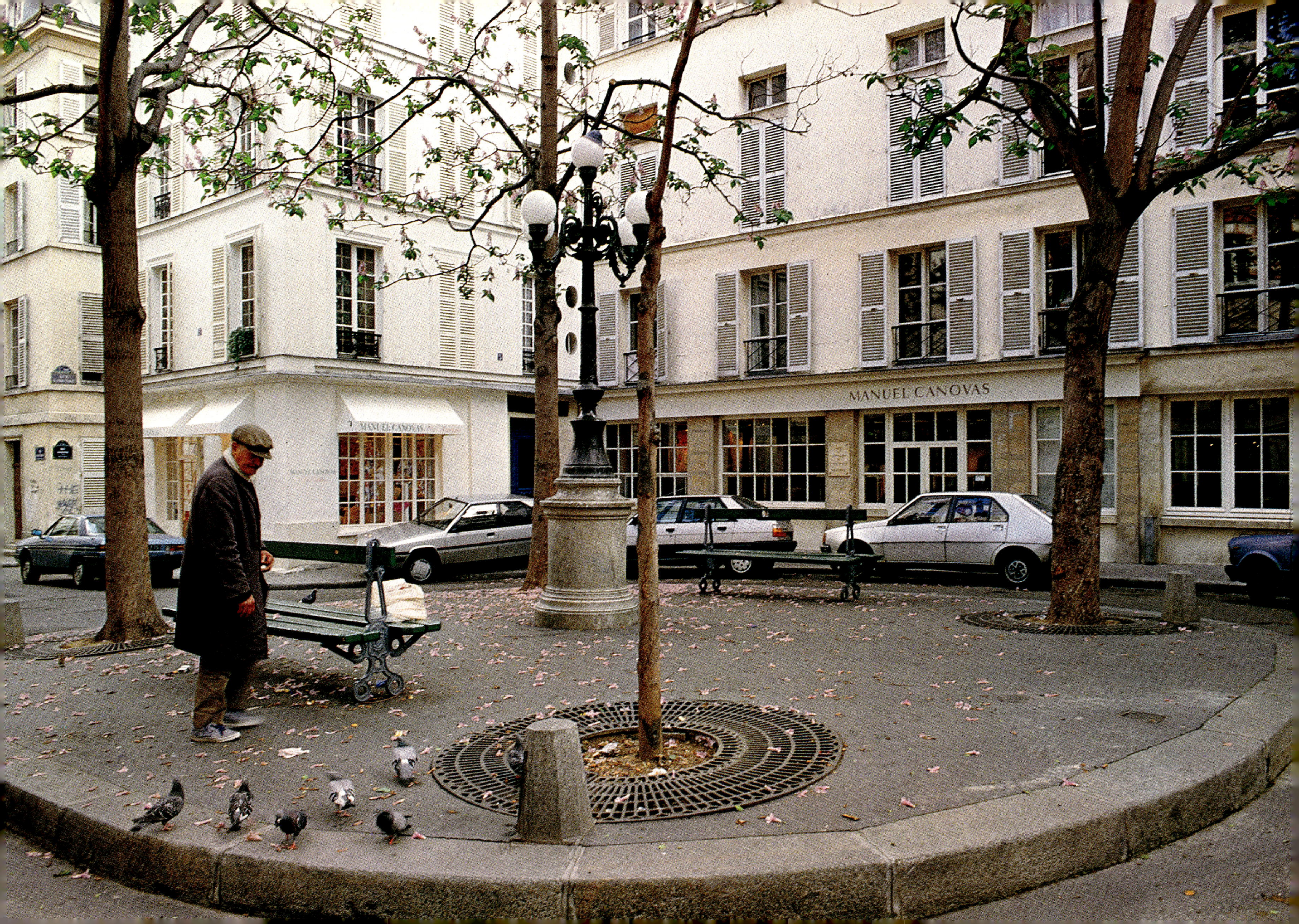
MANUEL CANOVAS
MANUEL CANOVAS

157 158

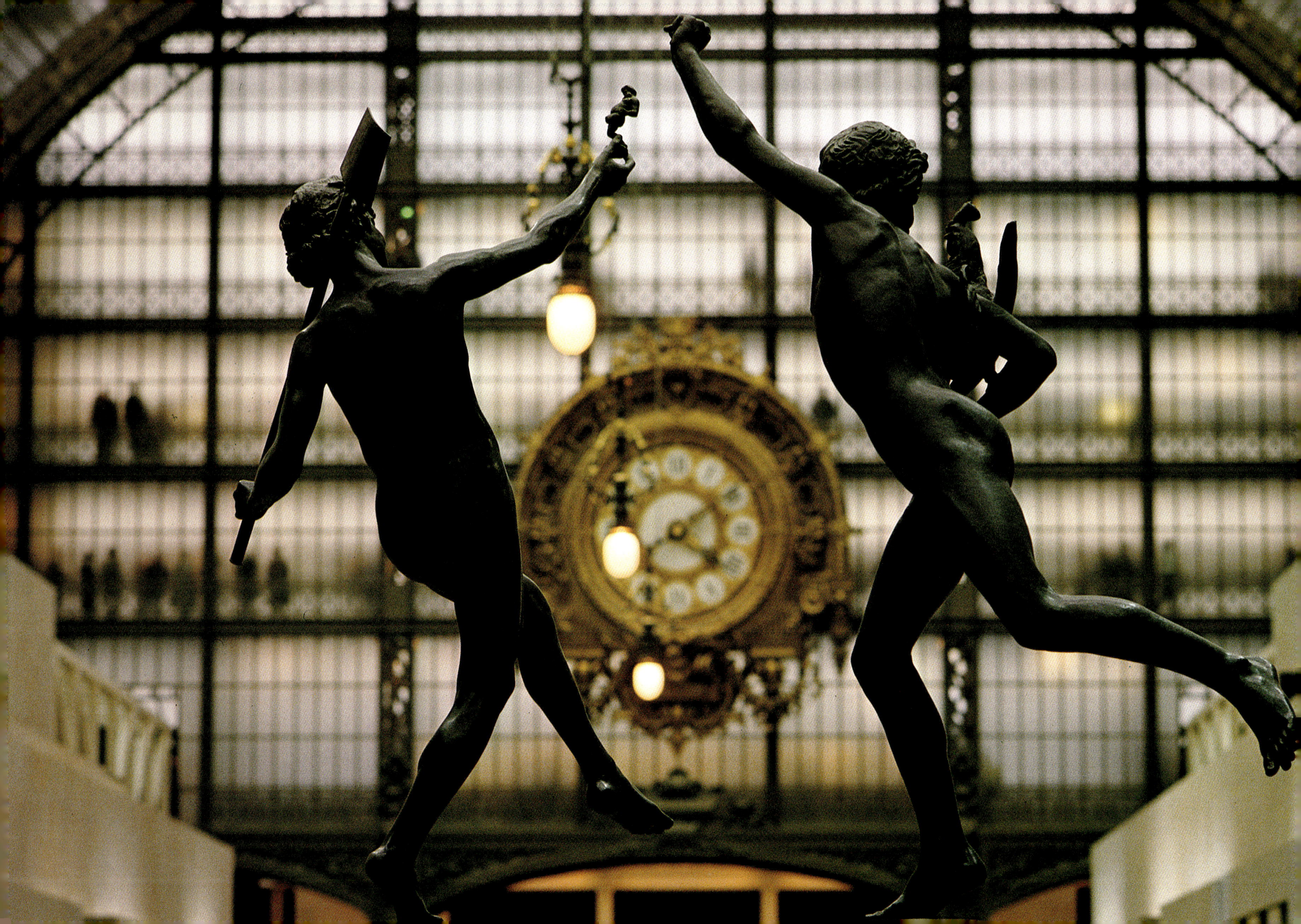

159 160

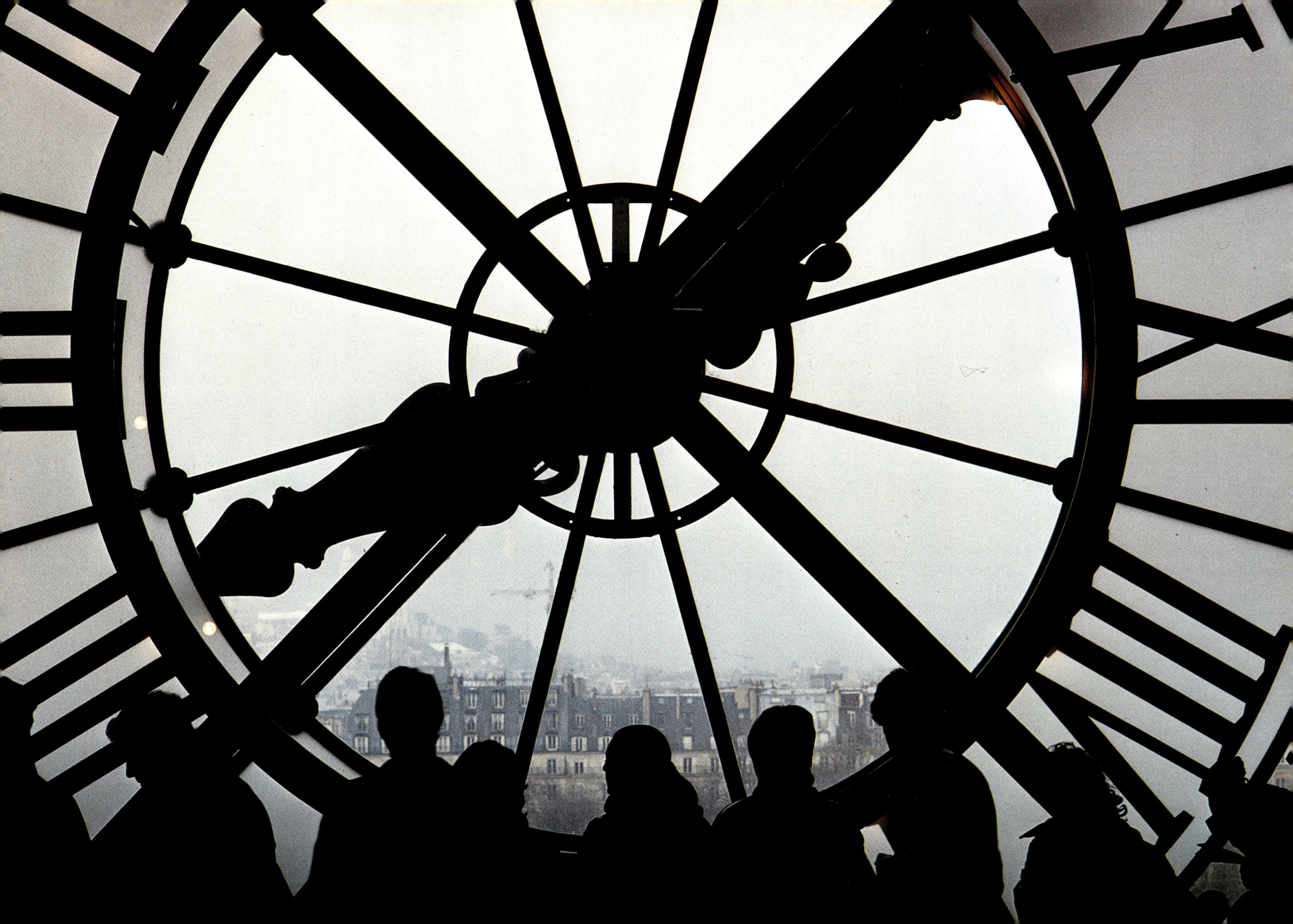

161 162

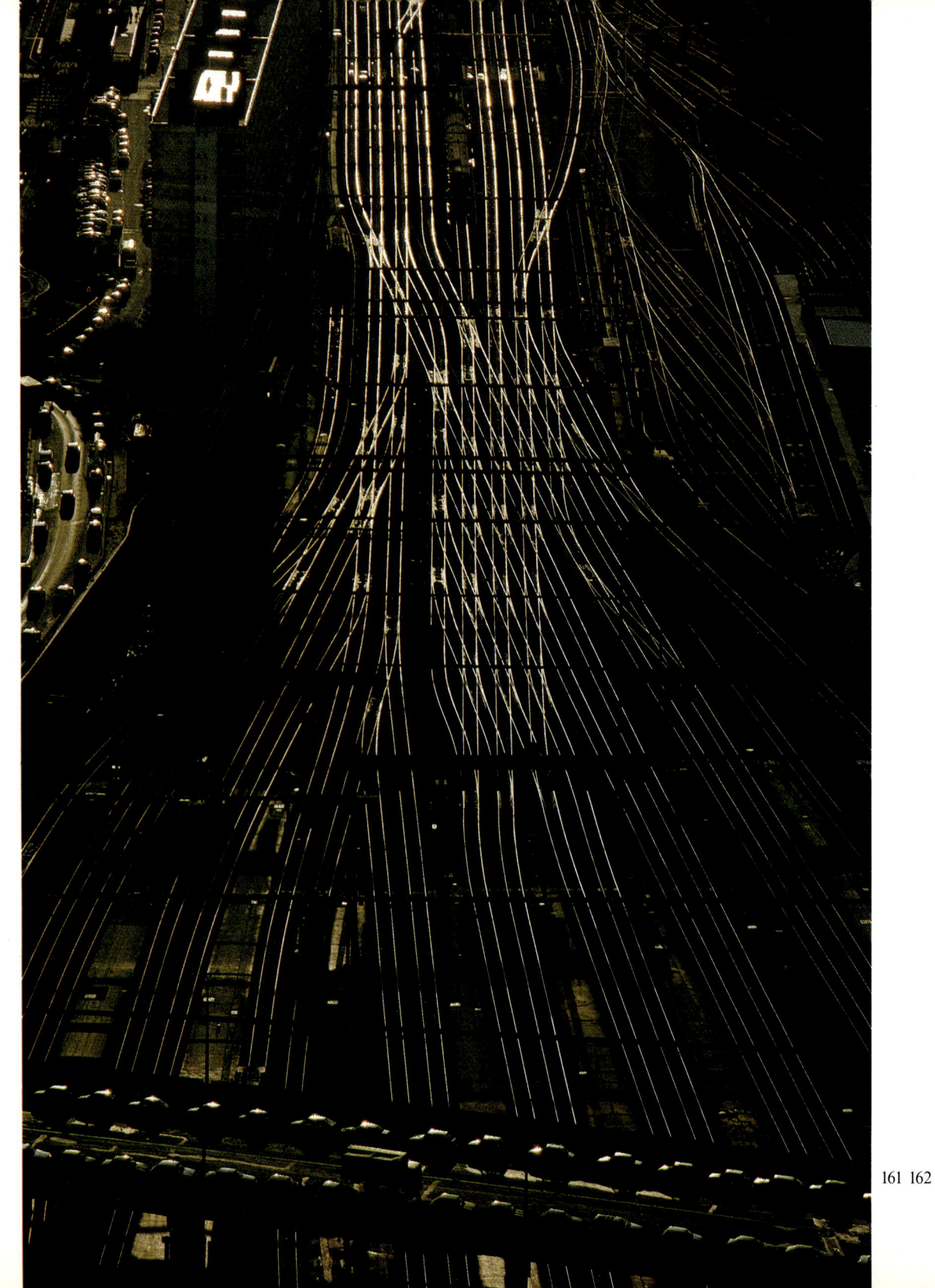

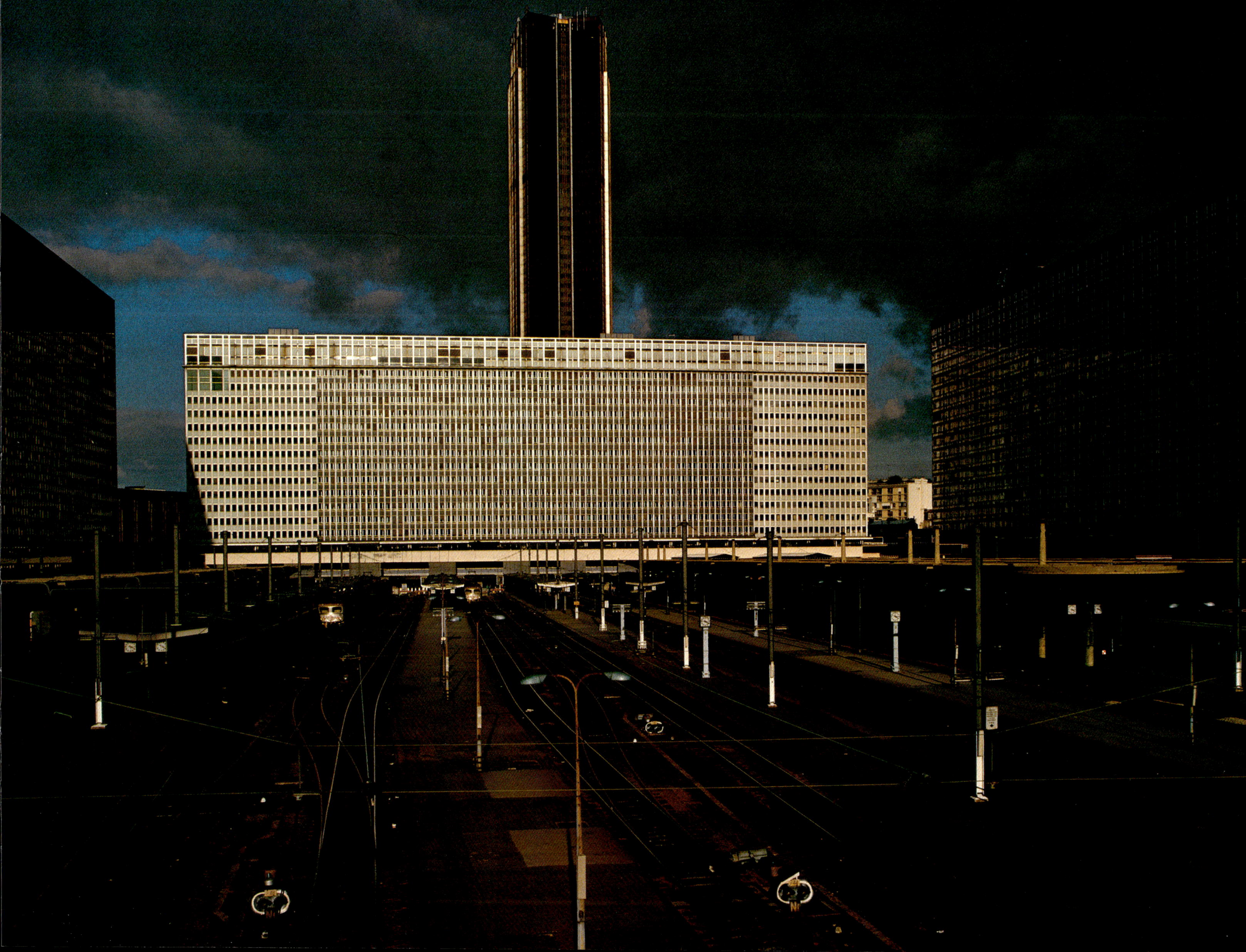

163 164

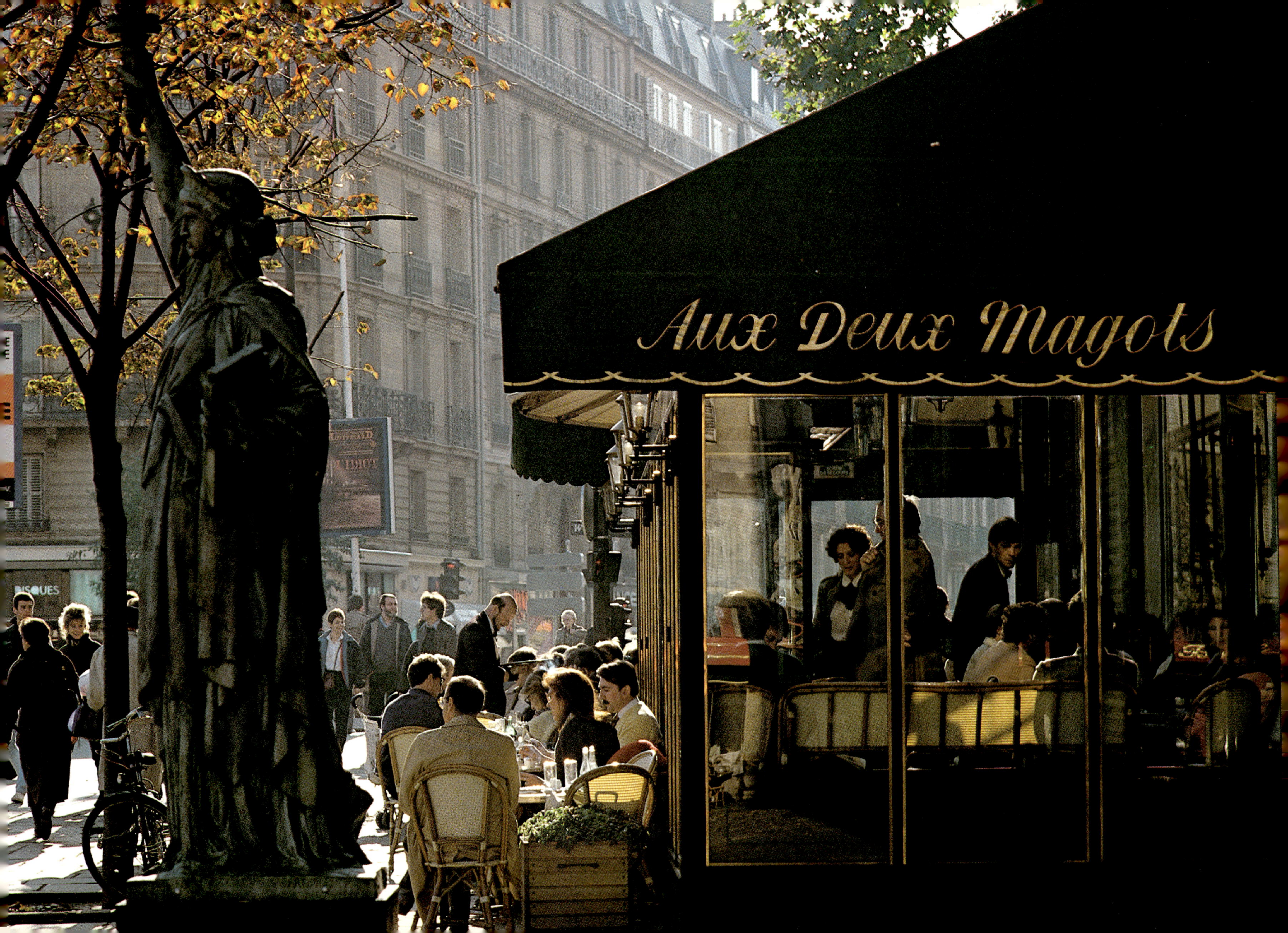
Aux Deux Magots
DISQUES

165 166

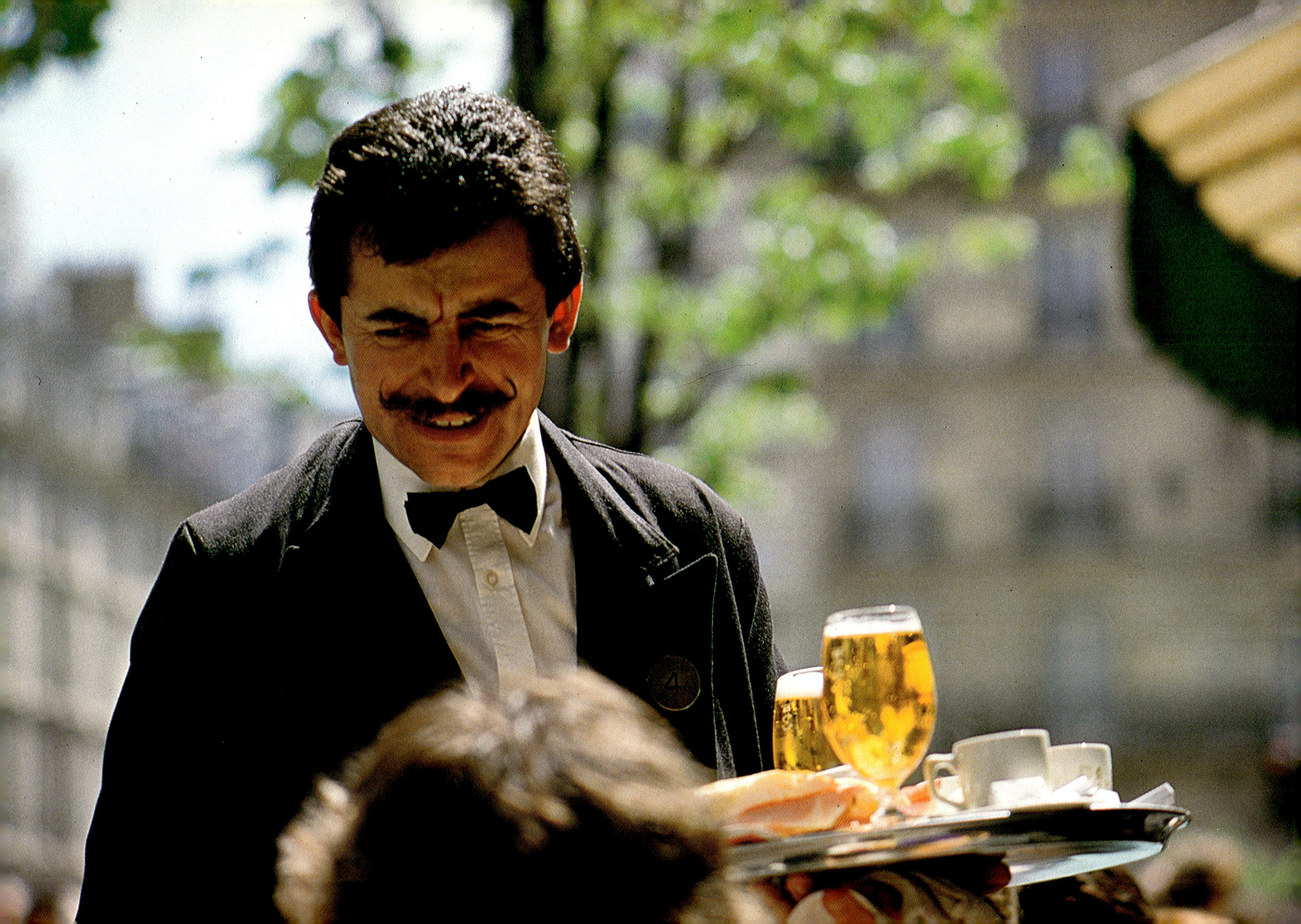
4

167 168 169

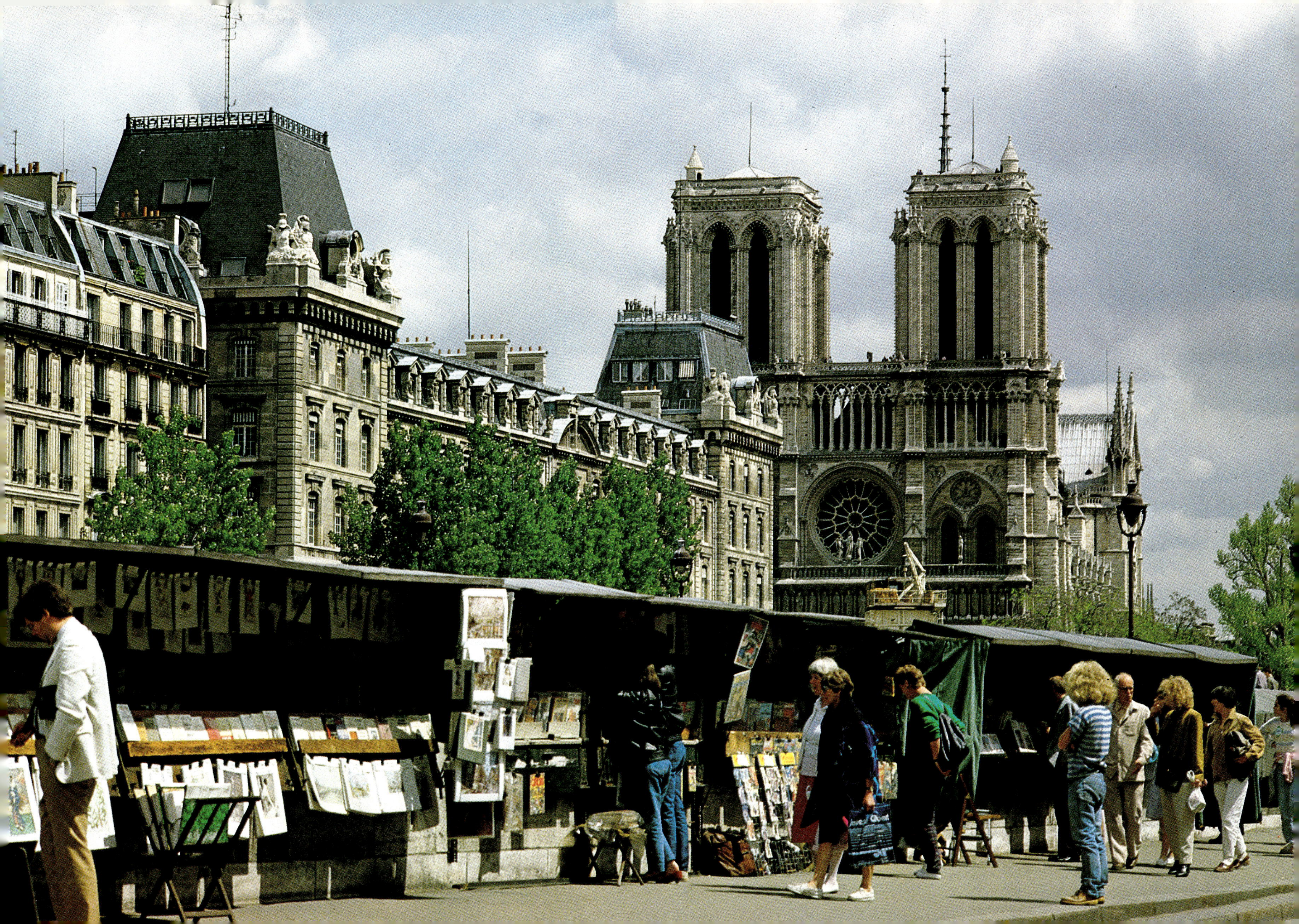

M 4 SAINT-GERMAIN-DES-PRÉS
RATP MÉTRO

DIS·CHARBONS
MAZOUT·GAZ
Mon R.ORLIAC
5 r. du Général BEURET · PARIS XV
53, Rue PERNETY
27, Rue ASSELINE
75014 PARIS
828-
8-78

Le Kilogramme
28,00 F
Le Kilogramme
Le Kilogramme
Le Kilogramme

MUSÉUM NATIONAL D'HISTOIRE NATURELLE
CONSIGNES GÉNÉRALES
RELATIVES A LA POLICE DE L'ETABLISSEMENT

173 174

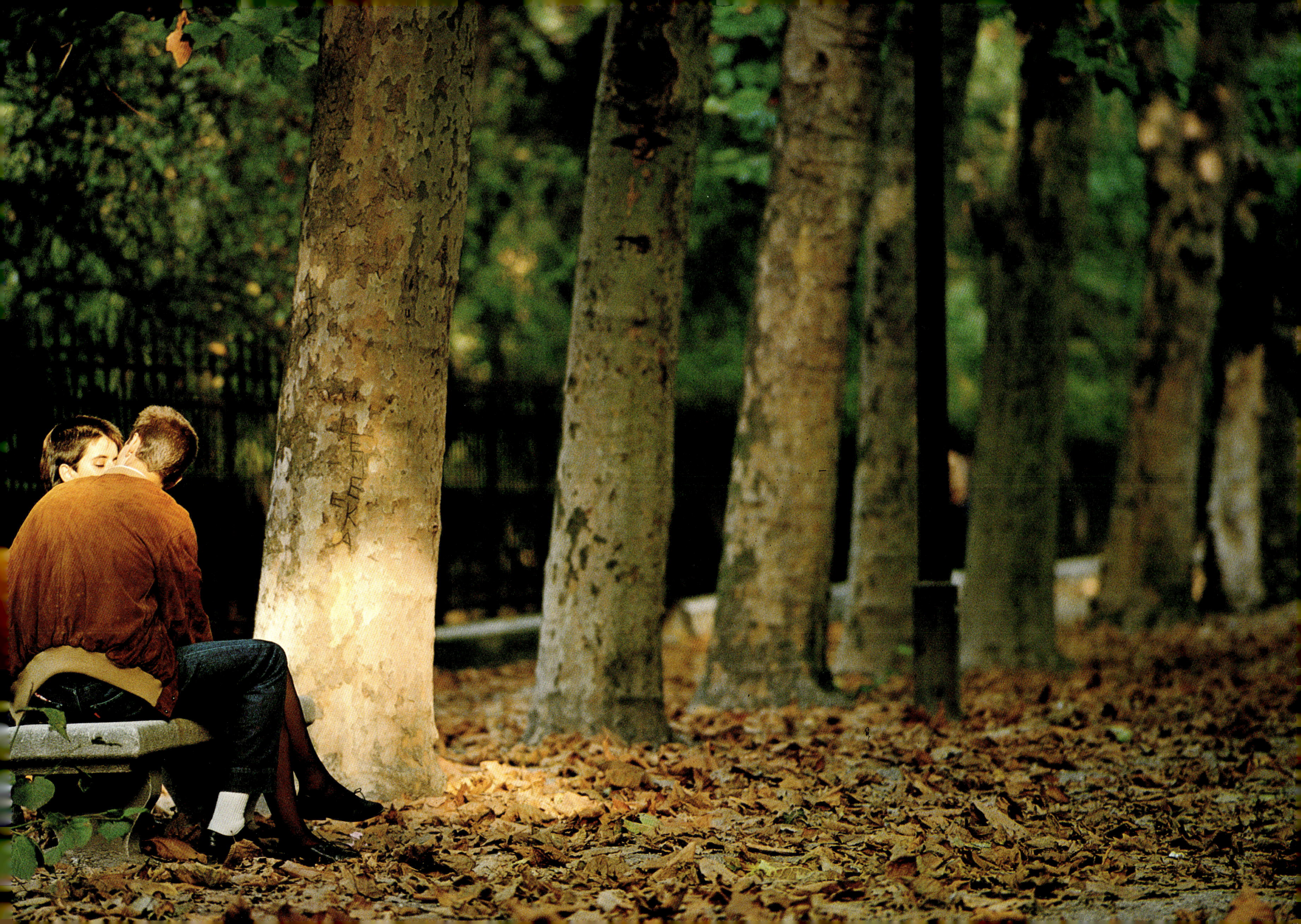

175 176

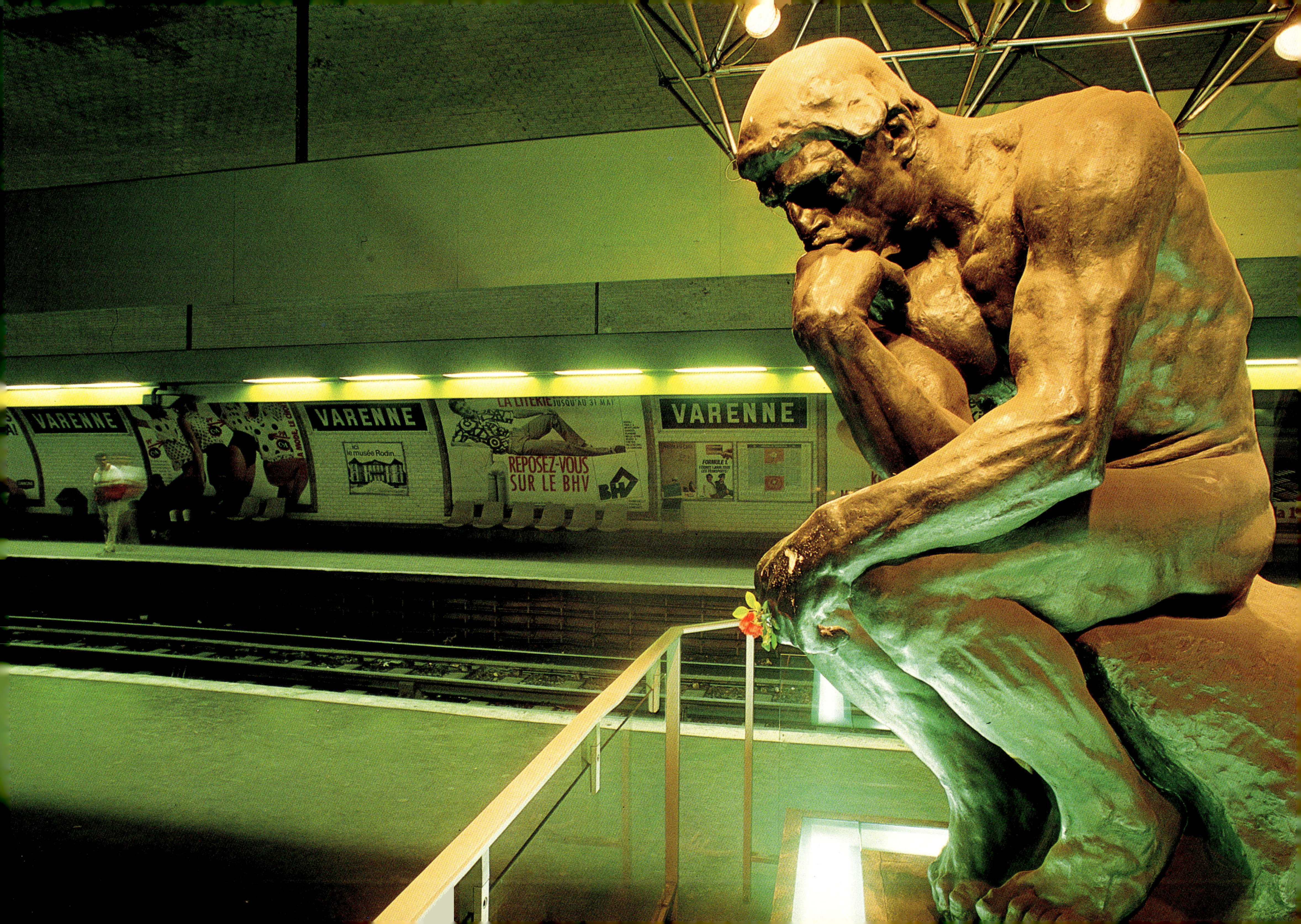
VARENNE
VARENNE
VARENNE
REPOSEZ-VOUS
SUR LE BHV

LIBERTÉ

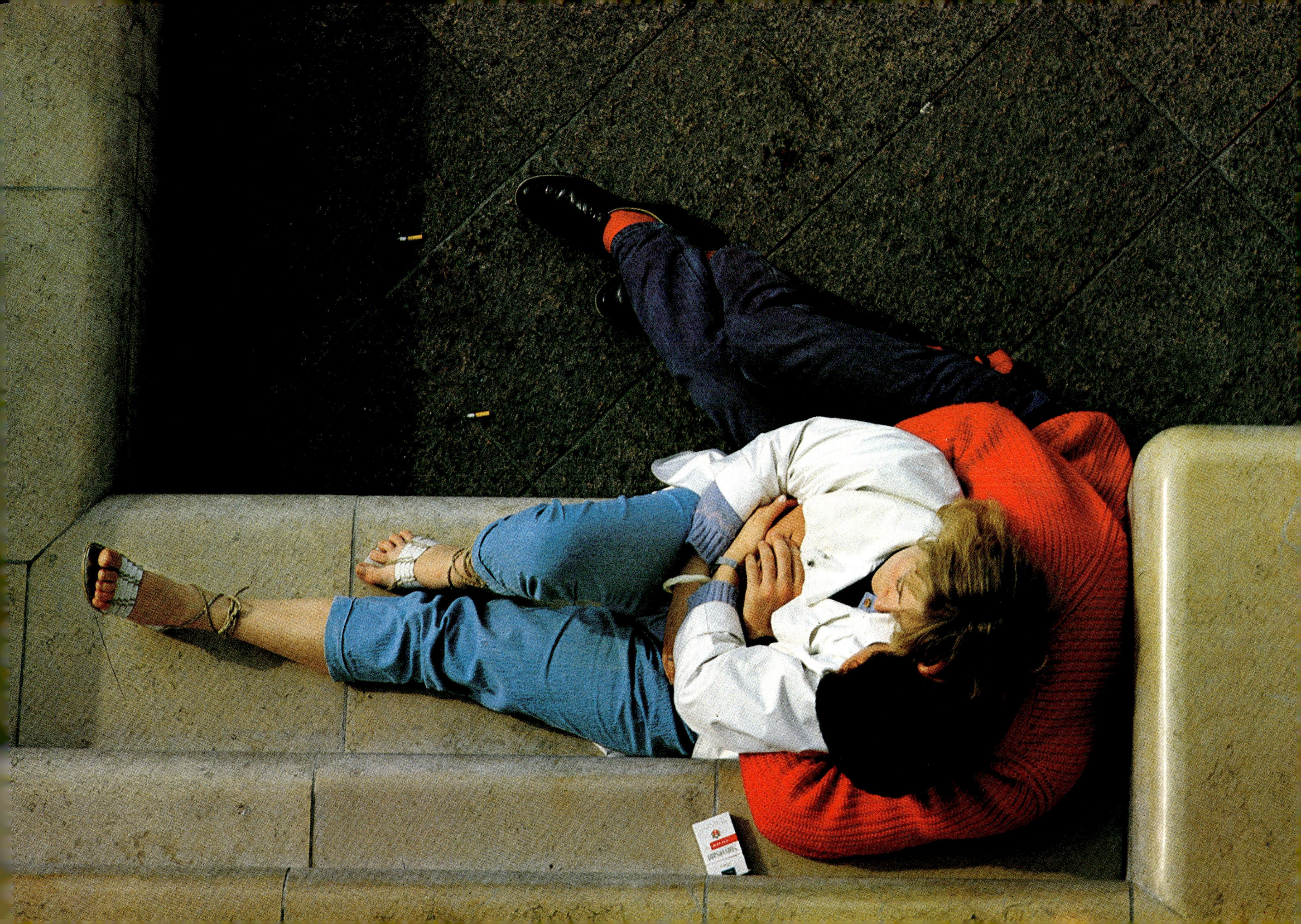

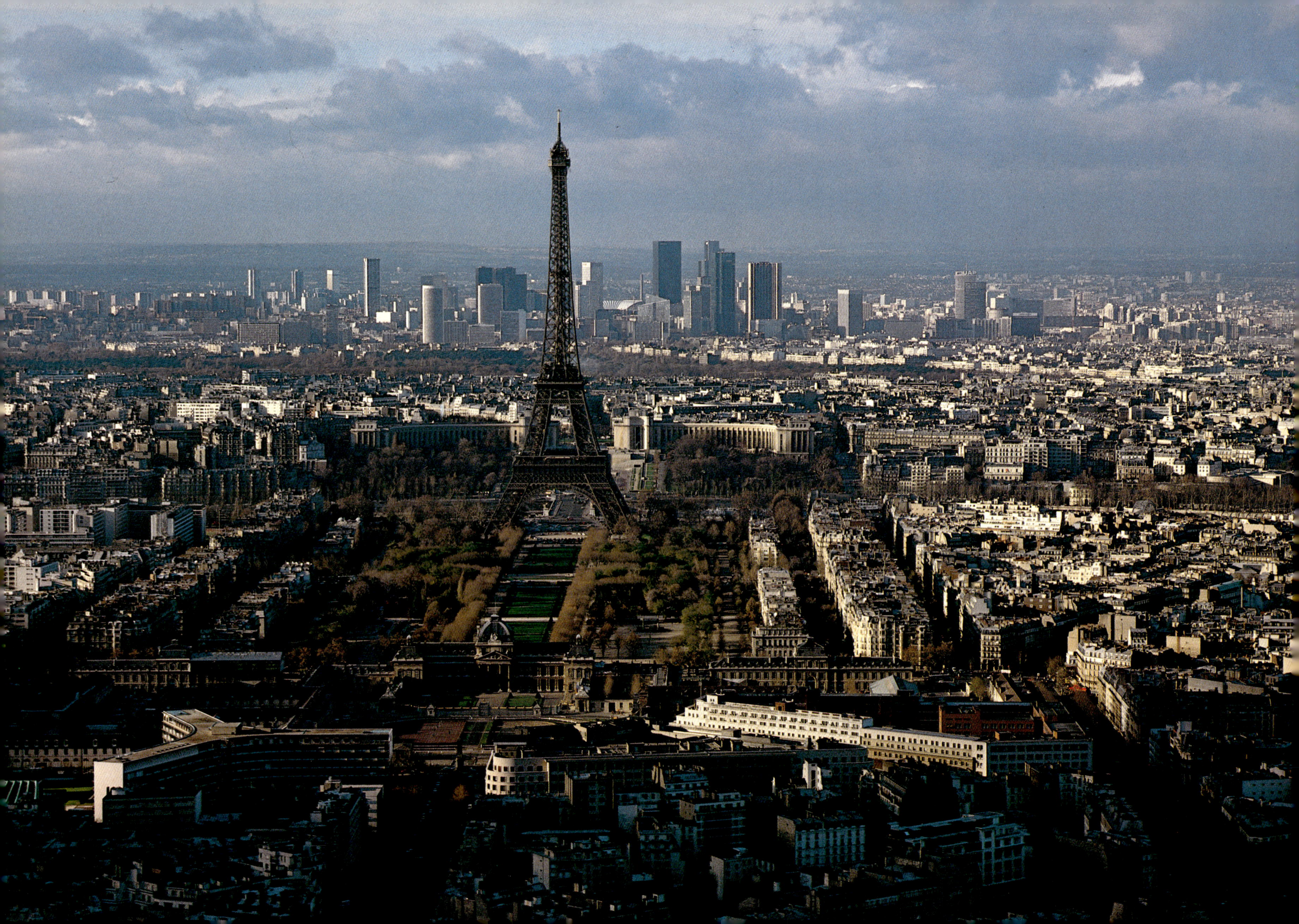

130   Silhouetted at sunset beyond the Pont Alexandre III, with its exuberant Neo-Baroque decoration, are the spire of the American Church in Paris, built in a revived Flamboyant Gothic style, and beyond it the Eiffel Tower, demonstrating a passion for pure construction without any consideration of style.

131, 132   Seen from below, the Eiffel Tower looks like an image in a kaleidoscope, or a Vasarely. From the Pont Alexandre III, it looks like an exquisite metallic web hung with a golden chain.

133   The view eastward from the Eiffel Tower shows a city built for the most part between 1860 and 1914, on the lines established by Haussmann when he demolished countless ancient houses to create great new straight streets through the dense urban fabric. Notable monuments visible here are the Sacré Coeur, brilliantly sunlit on the skyline at the left; in the centre, the glass roof of the Grand Palais; to the right of that, the towers of the Pont Alexandre III and, behind the trees, Gabriel's classical façades in the Place de la Concorde. Their line is continued by the Rue de Rivoli, which leads past the Louvre. At the extreme right, across the river from the Louvre, is the long dark roof of the trainshed of the former Gare d'Orsay, now the Musée d'Orsay (see Pl. 158).

134   Looking eastward from the Maine-Montparnasse Tower (the tall, dark office building visible in the distance in Pl. 135), the eye ranges as far as the Bois de Vincennes across a Paris that has been much changed. The high-rise social housing of the Porte d'Italie is the home of many immigrants, chiefly Asian, who form a little self-contained Hong Kong, with restaurants and shops run by Chinese for Chinese.

135   The Maine-Montparnasse Tower presents a sinister full stop at the end of the vista down the Champ de Mars from the Eiffel Tower. It claims attention more insistently than do the Ecole Militaire or the domed Val de Grace (see Pl. 138) to the left – not to mention the distant Saint-Sulpice beyond the Val de Grace, Notre Dame to the left of it, and the Panthéon to the right. The only compensation, if one chooses to regard it as such, is that the office tower with its 56 storeys and its height of 209 m (686 ft) is the tallest in Europe.

136, 137   Its thousand windows flaming in the evening sun or darkened, heralding a storm, the Maine-Montparnasse Tower reflects the sky from dawn until the last rays of light have faded.

138   The Val de Grace grew out of a vow made by the childless thirty-seven-year-old queen of Louis XIII, Anne of Austria. If she had a child, she promised, she would build a church near the house of the Benedictine nuns. She gave birth to a son in 1638, and the future Louis XIV laid the first stone in 1645. The church, modelled on St Peter's in Rome, was begun by François Mansart and completed by Jacques Lemercier, and is decorated inside with a fresco by Pierre Mignard. Until its desecration during the Revolution, the Chapel of St Anne received the heart-burials of members of the royal family and the house of Orléans.

139–141   The magnificent Hôtel Biron is devoted to the work of the greatest French sculptor of modern times, Auguste Rodin, who lived here until his death in 1917. Since then the State has maintained it as a museum, where his most famous works are displayed: *The Kiss*, *Sorrow*, *Balzac*, the *Burghers of Calais* of 1885 (Pl. 139), the *Gates of Hell*, on which the sculptor worked during the last years of his life, and *The Thinker* of 1880. Many of these are placed in the gardens, including *Ugolino*, which is sited in the middle of the ornamental lake.

The house, built in 1731 by Gabriel and Aubert, also contains furniture, pictures and memorabilia associated with Rodin. The grounds were restored in 1927 to commemorate the Maréchal de Biron, who spent vast sums in the eighteenth century on their layout and on the cultivation of flowers.

142, 143   Stone lovers and living lovers seek solitude, away from the roar of traffic and the crush of crowds. They find it in exposed places like the terraces in front of the Palais de Chaillot, or in the leafy intimacy of the autumnal Parc Monceau.

144–146   At the Palais du Luxembourg Marie de Médicis hoped to find splendour with a Florentine flavour; but Salomon de Brosse, the architect, gave her a building that is unmistakably French in outline, with its corner pavilions and high roofs. More Italian are the fountains dotted about the gardens.

First a royal palace and then a princely dwelling, during the Revolution the Luxembourg became a prison. It was then elevated again to house the government – the Directoire, the Consulate, the Chamber of Deputies under Louis XVIII, and since 1879 the Senate. To fit it for its new role, the palace was extended towards the gardens in the nineteenth century in a style copying the early seventeenth-century original.

The gardens, now a public park, are a favourite haunt of students from the Latin Quarter. On the ornamental pond serious children sail little boats, dreaming, perhaps, of the time when they will be round-the-world yachtsmen. Elsewhere, the mood is right both for energetic jogging and for brooding reflection.

147   Frémiet's quivering seahorses form the base of the superb fountain at the end of the Avenue de l'Observatoire, designed by Davioud and completed in 1874. They support a composition in which a globe is held aloft by figures of the four continents, by Carpeaux – who excluded Australasia in the interests of symmetry. That group is now in the Musée d'Orsay, and has been replaced by a copy.

148, 149   The Panthéon was begun in 1764 by Jacques-Germain Soufflot as a church dedicated to St Genevieve, the patron saint of Paris. Turning his back on Baroque richness, the architect sought effects which were lighter and more austere. He did not live to see the finished building: it was completed by his followers in 1790, ten years after his death.

The Revolutionary Assembly decreed that the church should become a Pantheon for the ashes of great men, among them the philosophers Voltaire and Rousseau. In the years that followed the building was in turn again a church, a burial place, and – under the Third Republic – a 'secular temple'.

On the pediment carved by David d'Angers is the inscription, 'Aux grands hommes la Patrie reconnaissante' (dedicated to great men by their grateful fatherland). If you stay at the hotel next door you needn't wait until you are dead to be a 'grand homme'.

150, 151   The Palais Bourbon was confiscated from its owner, the Prince de Condé, at the Revolution, first to house the Conseil des Cinq Cents and then to store archives. In 1807 Napoleon gave it a new façade with a pedimented portico to echo the design of the Madeleine, facing it across the river at the end of the Rue Royale.

The building was briefly returned to the Condé family, and then under the Restauration it was purchased by the government for the legislative body. It is now the seat of the National Assembly.

Twelve Corinthian columns support the pediment filled with sculpture by Cortot, and there are statues by Houdon, Roland, Rude and Pradier. None of these features existed – nor, rather more crucially, did the special guards and the high spiked railings – when the Revolutionary *sans-culottes* captured the palace of the Prince de Condé.

152   With its vaulting ribs sprouting from the pillars, the ambulatory of Saint-Séverin is like an extraordinary exotic forest, magically illuminated by rays transmuted by the fifteenth- and sixteenth-century stained glass and the modern windows by Jean Bazaine seen here. The architect of this late medieval work of genius is, tantalizingly, unrecorded.

153   Saint-Etienne-du-Mont is the epitome of Parisian church architecture of the sixteenth century. It was constructed between 1492 and 1586 by a succession of masters working in Flamboyant Gothic and Renaissance styles. Its most remarkable feature is the *jubé*, which is more than just a rood-screen: this unique structure, attributed to Philibert de l'Orme, comprises double spiral staircases, of which the lower pair lead to the rood-loft while another pair rise higher, to a gallery that runs right round the choir. Saint-Etienne is also notable for the Flamboyant vault over the crossing, the seventeenth-century organ with its ninety-two stops, paintings by De Troy and Largillière, and the tombs of Racine and Pascal in the ambulatory.

154, 155   The Ile Saint-Louis was formed out of two uninhabited islands, the Ile aux Vaches and the Ile Notre-Dame, between 1614 and 1630 by three speculators, Le Regratier, Poulletier and Jean-Christophe Marie. The latter linked it to the shore by a pretty hump-backed bridge that bears his name. The streets were laid out on a regular plan, and certain basic rules were laid down for the design of the houses, but no attempt was made to achieve the sort of grand uniformity that characterized some of the public squares of the same date, such as the Place des Vosges (Pl. 64). The island has retained a provincial charm that is surprising indeed in the heart of Paris.

156   The Place de Furstemberg is like a little stage-set all ready for the actors to appear. In the middle are the props: one streetlamp with frosted glass shades, two benches. In the wings to one side, Rue Jacob; to the other, Rue de l'Abbaye. At No. 6 in the square was the studio of the painter Eugène Delacroix, leader of the French Romantics, which is now a museum.

157   The Quai des Augustins is the oldest in Paris. Along it there are publishers, booksellers and antique dealers, the headquarters of the city's transport system (the Régie Autonome des Transports Parisiens) housed in the old depot of the Compagnie Générale des Omnibus, and still a few fine seventeenth-century houses. In one of them is Lapérouse, a restaurant long regarded as a shrine of Parisian gastronomy.

158–160   The Gare d'Orsay was opened on 14 July 1900, at the time of the Exposition Universelle, and served the area south-west of Paris. In later years, electrification and changes in track design left the enormous building unused. Victor Laloux's magnificent glass-roofed trainshed became a white elephant. There were plans for a great modern hotel, and in the meantime the space was shared between the old hotel, a theatre, a saleroom and a film studio. Le Corbusier and other architects drew up elaborate schemes which were greeted with horror and eventually abandoned. The building, neglected, decayed.

A change in its fate came when Jacques Duhamel, then Minister for Cultural Affairs, put forward the idea of listing the station as a historic monument and transforming it into a museum of the nineteenth century. His project was approved by President Pompidou. In 1978 President Giscard d'Estaing declared himself in favour, and in 1981 the listing was confirmed. Despite changes of government, the scheme and its funding survived.

The Musée d'Orsay became a reality on 9 December 1986. Its collections of fine and decorative art from 1848 to 1914 are displayed in a setting created within the old station by the Italian designer Gae Aulenti – a setting which many have found unsympathetic both to the building and to the works exhibited. But the museum is *chic*, like the Pompidou Centre, and like the equally controversial glass pyramid of the 'Grand Louvre' it is a declaration of Paris's intention to be in the forefront of cultural life.

161, 162   The old building of the Gare Montparnasse, which serves the western regions of Maine and Brittany, was destroyed when the neighbourhood was rebuilt; the most prominent of the new structures is the Maine-Montparnasse Tower (see Ill. 135), from which the railway lines look like those of a child's train set. Yet not far away the cafés of Montparnasse survive – the Coupole, Dôme, Rotonde and Select, those famous meeting places of Modigliani, Soutine, Léger, and other painters and poets of the Ruche.

163–166   Saint-Germain-des-Prés goes back to the sixth century, when Childebert I, son of Clovis, returned from Spain with a fragment of the True Cross and the tunic of St Vincent. To house those relics he founded a monastery in the fields close to the river, and was buried there in 558 near the tomb of St Germain or Germanus, Bishop of Paris.

The great monastery and its church have been much altered over the centuries, and the neighbourhood is now known not for its spiritual but for its intellectual character – though that too is perhaps a thing of the past. The famous Café des Deux Magots, Flore and Lipp, with their black-clad waiters in long white aprons, carry on the tradition of the cafés of the *grands boulevards* like the long-vanished Tortoni, Madrid and Napolitain, where writers, journalists and bohemians gathered amid the smoke of pipes and Havana cigars.

The small version of Bartholdi's Statue of Liberty, set up on the hundredth anniversary of the erection of its giant sister in New York harbour, holds her torch aloft to see if she can find a single survivor from Saint-Germain's great days as the centre of Existentialism.

167   The flea market at the Porte de Vanves, unlike its more pretentious rival at the Port Saint-Ouen, offers genuine junk; and, with that, the possibility of making a genuine discovery.

168   The bookshops of the Rue de l'Odéon have a venerable ancestry. This was the location of Sylvia Beach's Shakespeare and Company, frequented by Scott Fitzgerald, Hemingway and Joyce, whose *Ulysses*

was first sold there. In a shop higher up the street, Adrienne Monnier in her flowing grey dress welcomed the French writers Paul Valéry, Léon-Paul Fargue, Paul Morand and François Mauriac, who often held readings of their works.

169   The stalls of the *bouquinistes* are like magic chests where, among out-of-print books, copies of deceased magazines, and yellowing prints you just might find exactly what you were looking for. Or perhaps it was just an excuse for a stroll along the river . . .

170   The Metro map is like an x-ray of the arteries and veins of the city. There are 1,663 stops on 55 lines with 509 km (316 miles) of track, all interconnecting to allow an easy passage from one side of the city to the other.

171   The coal merchant is now a rare sight in the streets of Paris, as oil and gas systems replace the cast-iron or ceramic stoves that stood in the living room, and the kitchen ranges forever burning under their massive hoods. Traditionally the coal merchants or *bougnats* were rough but sterling characters from Auvergne, and they kept little wine-shops next to their stocks of coal and wood, under the sign 'Vins et Charbons'.

172   The Rue Mouffetard links the Place de la Contrescarpe with Saint-Médard, originally the church of a little village on the banks of the Bièvre. Every day the street is the scene of a lively market, and the old shops lining it, some with quaint signs, show that its commercial activity goes back for centuries.

173, 174   The Jardin des Plantes began life as the Royal Physic Garden, established by Louis XIII's court doctor, Gui de La Crosse. Its collection was enlarged first under Louis XIV by Tournefort, the Jussieu brothers, and other botanist-explorers; and then, most notably, by Buffon, who was director from 1739 to 1786. During the Revolution the director was Bernardin de Saint-Pierre, better known as the author of *Paul et Virginie*, and the complex of the gardens became the 'Muséum d'Histoire Naturelle'. Great scientists associated with the Jardin des Plantes and its museums include Lamarck and Cuvier.

The Revolution also led to the creation of a zoo (started with animals from the royal menagerie), to the delight of the populace. It had to be re-stocked, however, after the Parisians had been reduced to eating the animals during the siege of the city by the Prussians in 1870. There is a small collection of animals here again today, though the main zoo of Paris is at Vincennes.

175   The Paris Metro system was laid out at the end of the nineteenth century by Baron Edouard Empain's Compagnie Générale de Traction, under the engineer Fulgence Bienvenüe. The first line opened on 19 July 1900, to coincide with the Universal Exposition: it ran from the Porte de Vincennes to the Porte Maillot, a distance of 10 km (6 miles), and served eighteen stations. The present system (see Pl. 170), which carries more than one and a half million passengers each year, is crucial to the economic, social and cultural life of the metropolis.

176   The first Metro station to be given a facelift suggestive of a neighbouring museum was that of the Louvre, where since 1968 the trains have drawn up opposite replicas of works of art from ancient

Egypt, the Classical world, the French Middle Ages and the Far East. In 1978 the same idea was applied to the station of Varennes, near the Musée Rodin. Here the central platform was transformed into a gallery with reproductions of Rodin's sculptures (such as *The Thinker*), watercolours and drawings, and photographs. To everyone's surprise, the exhibits have remained untouched by the graffiti and mess usually found in underground stations.

177, 178   Red, white and blue: Liberty, equality, fraternity. It was Louis XVI, in the early days of the Revolution, who decided on the use of these colours on the flag; the motto originated in a more vigorous Revolutionary spirit. The quais of the Seine give all lovers equal liberty to fraternize in peace . . .

179   The Maine-Montparnasse Tower is the only beacon to give an eye-level view of the top of that more famous beacon of Paris, the Eiffel Tower. The view north-west extends across the Unesco Building with its three curving wings, by Zehrfuss, Breuer and Nervi, to the Ecole Militaire and up the Champ de Mars, past the Eiffel Tower to the Palais de Chaillot, then on to the trees of the Bois de Boulogne before reaching the forbidding palisade of tall buildings at La Défense. For views in the opposite direction, see Pls. 135 and 181.

Outskirts and environs

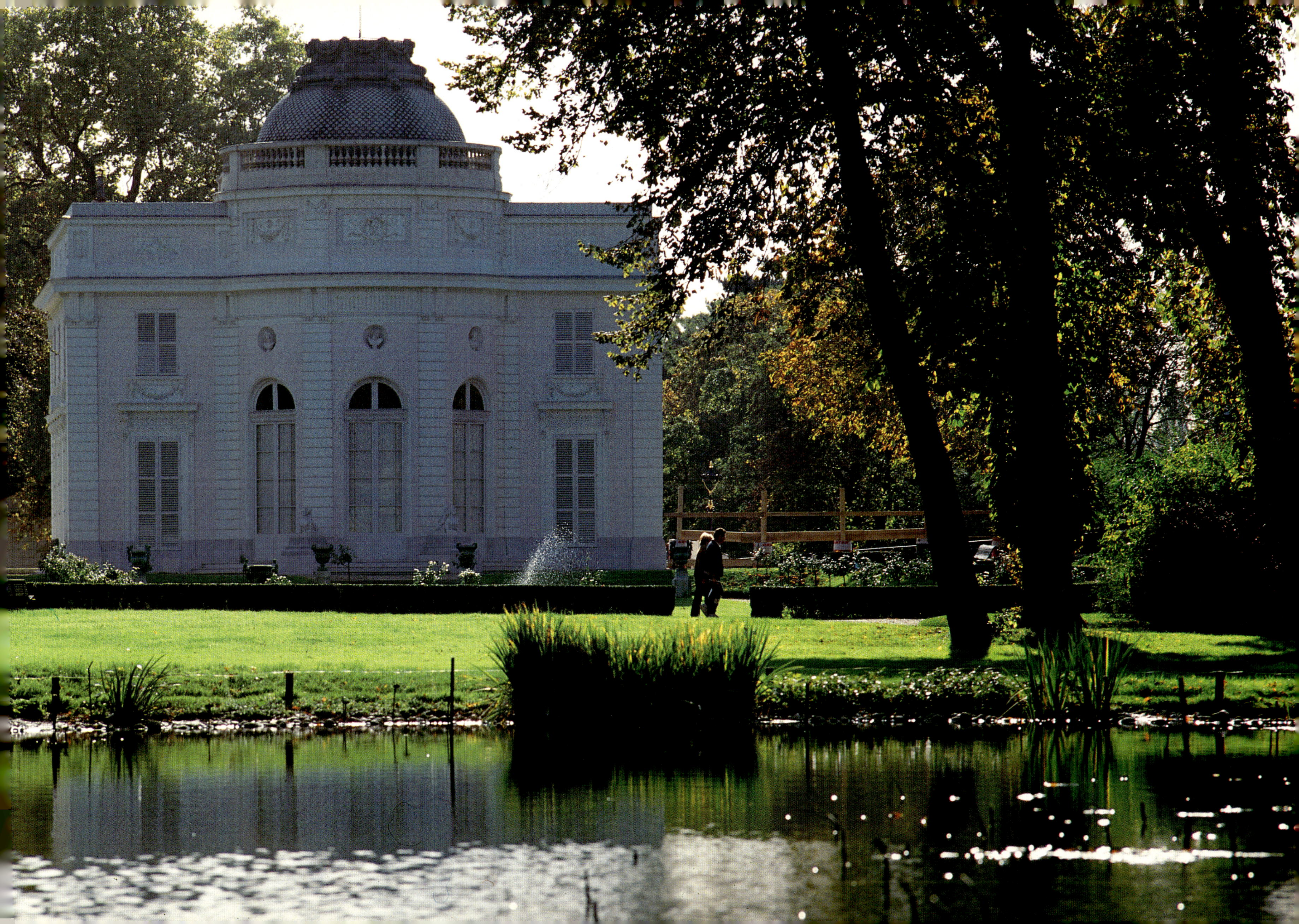

181 182

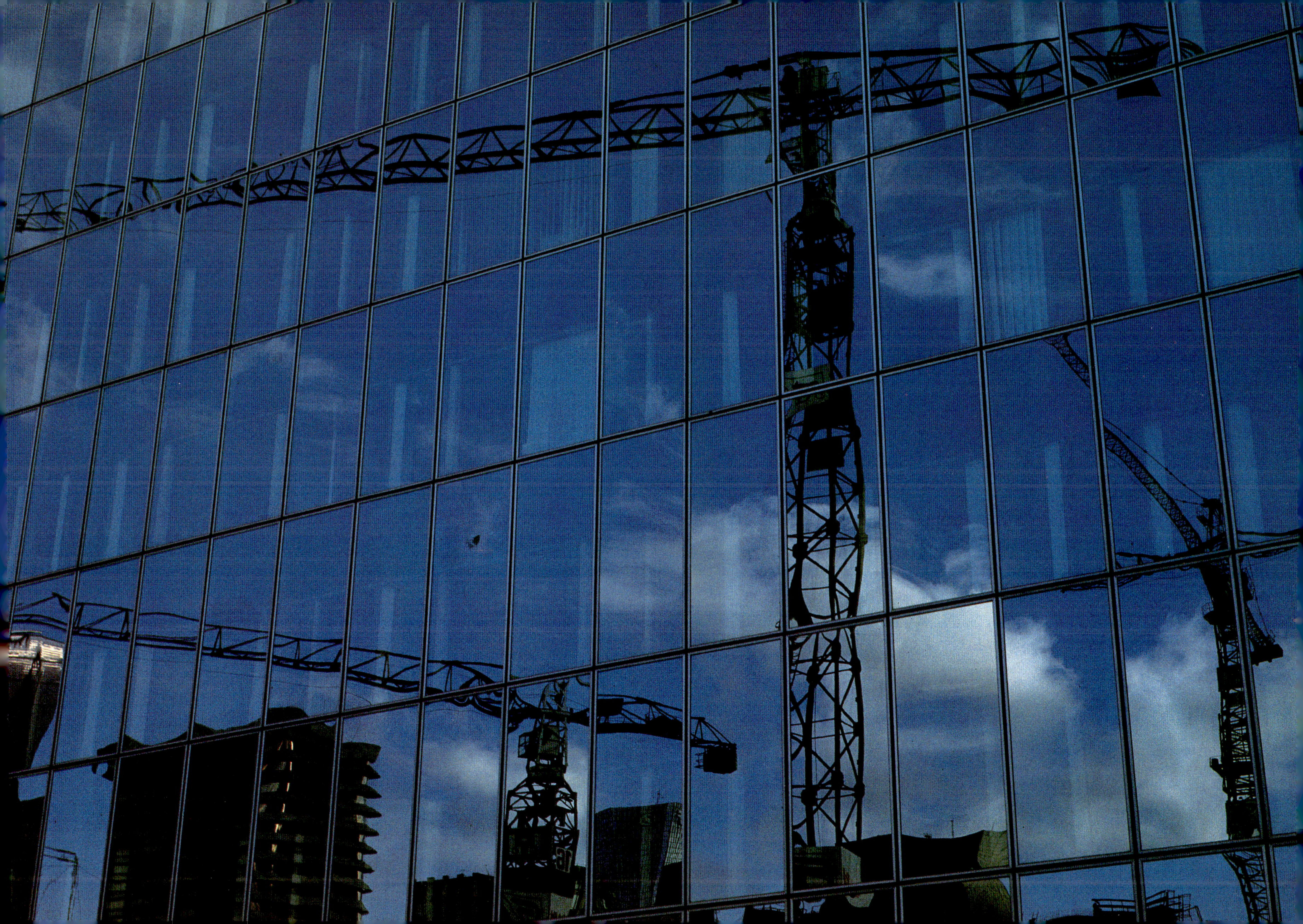

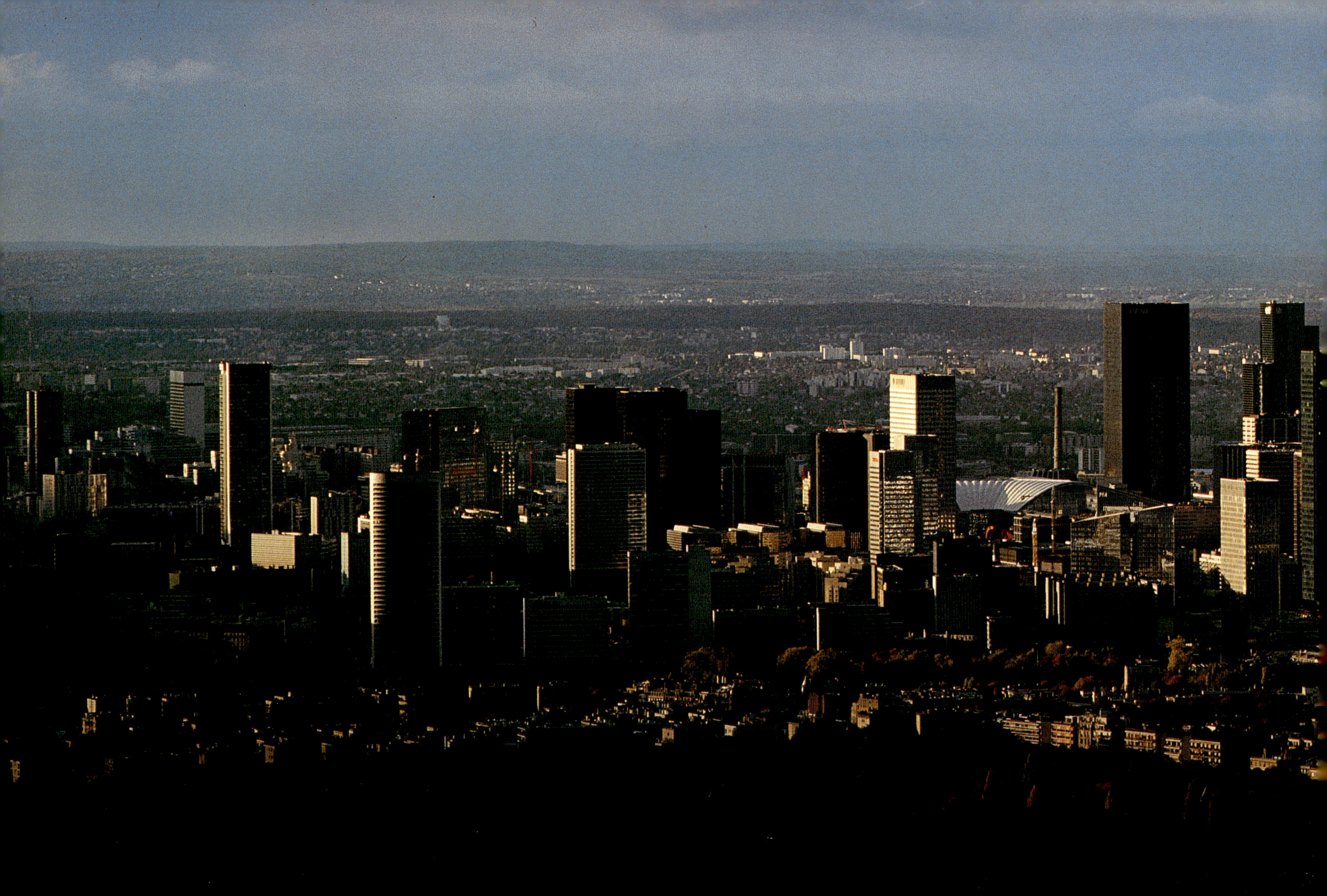

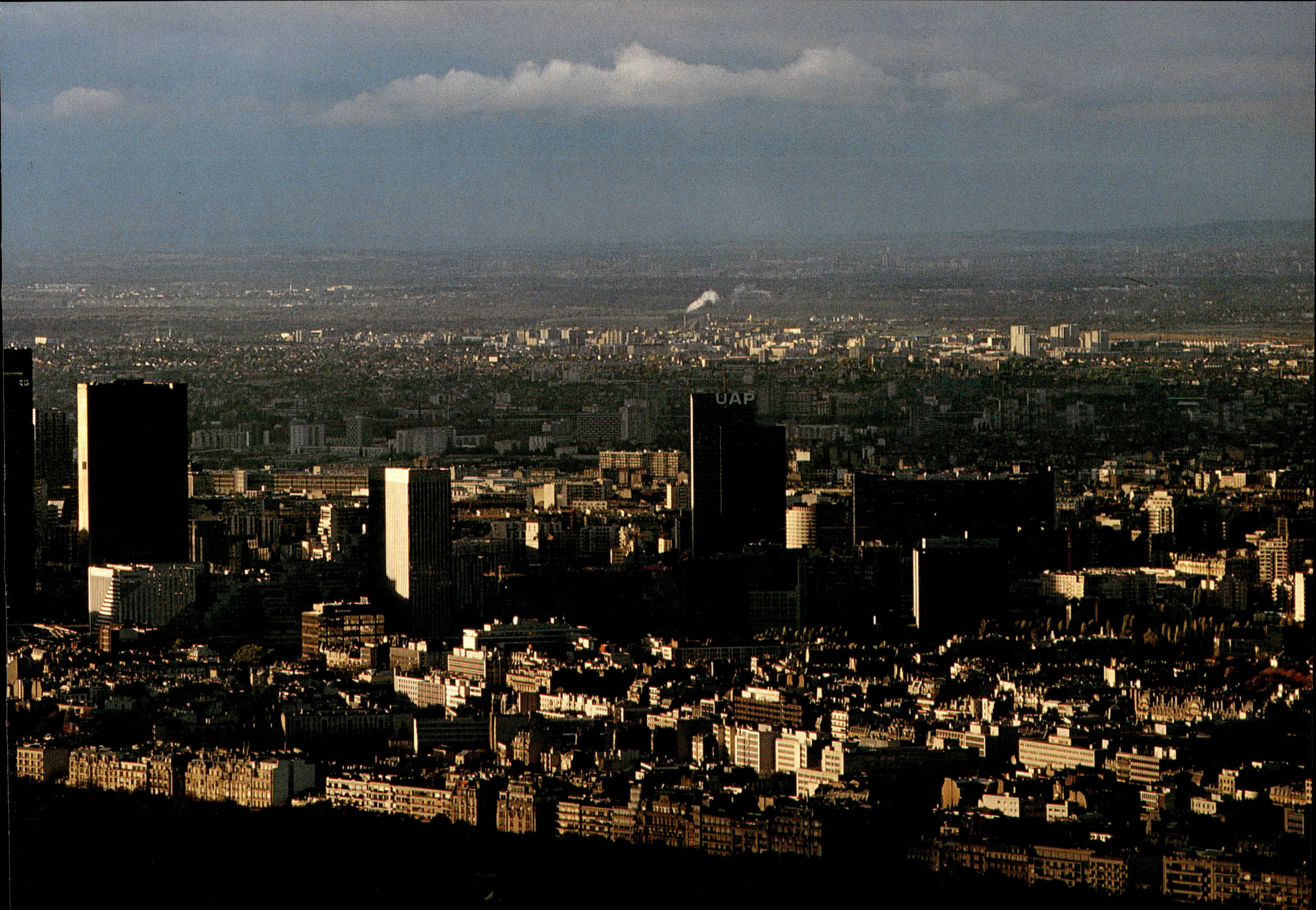
UAP

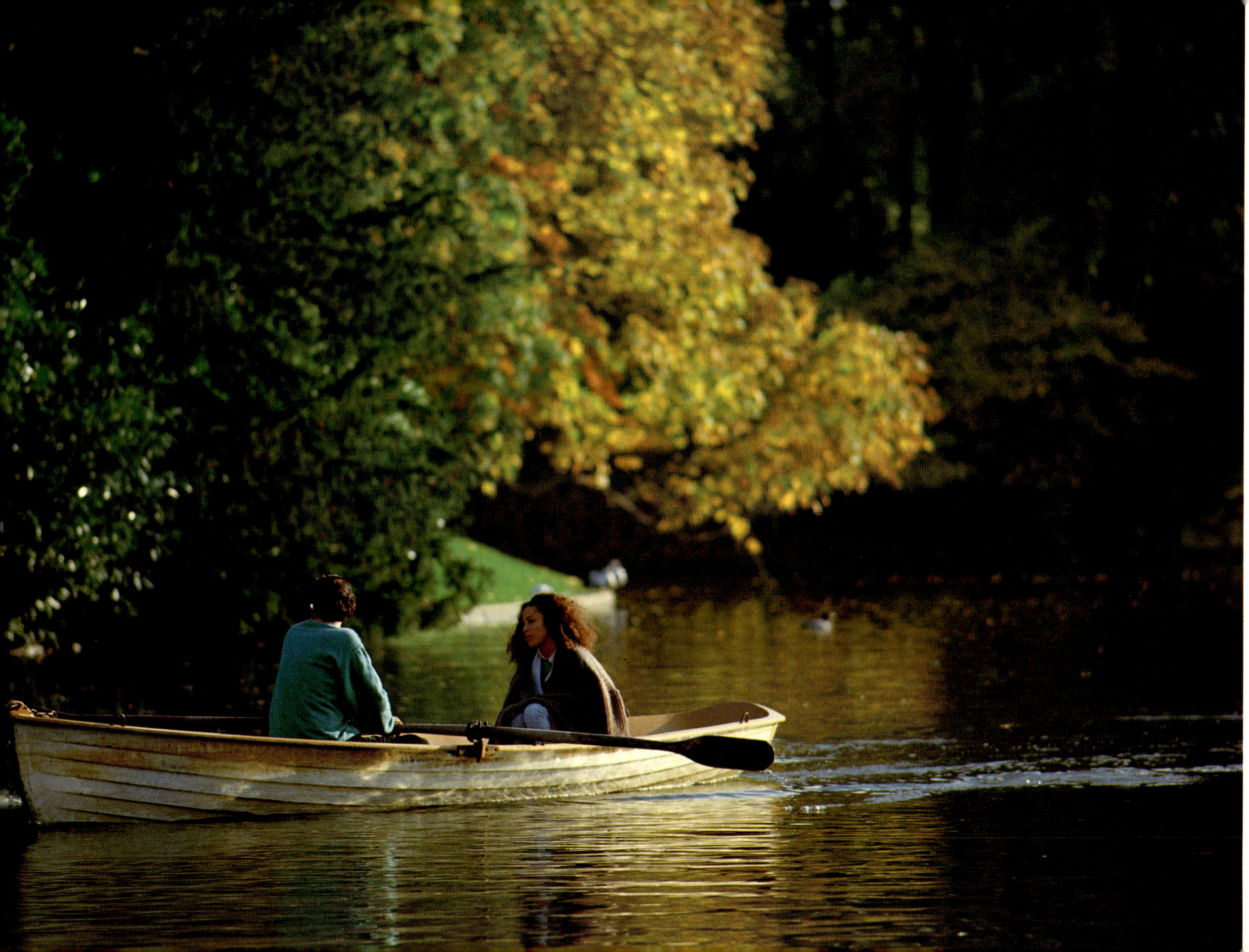

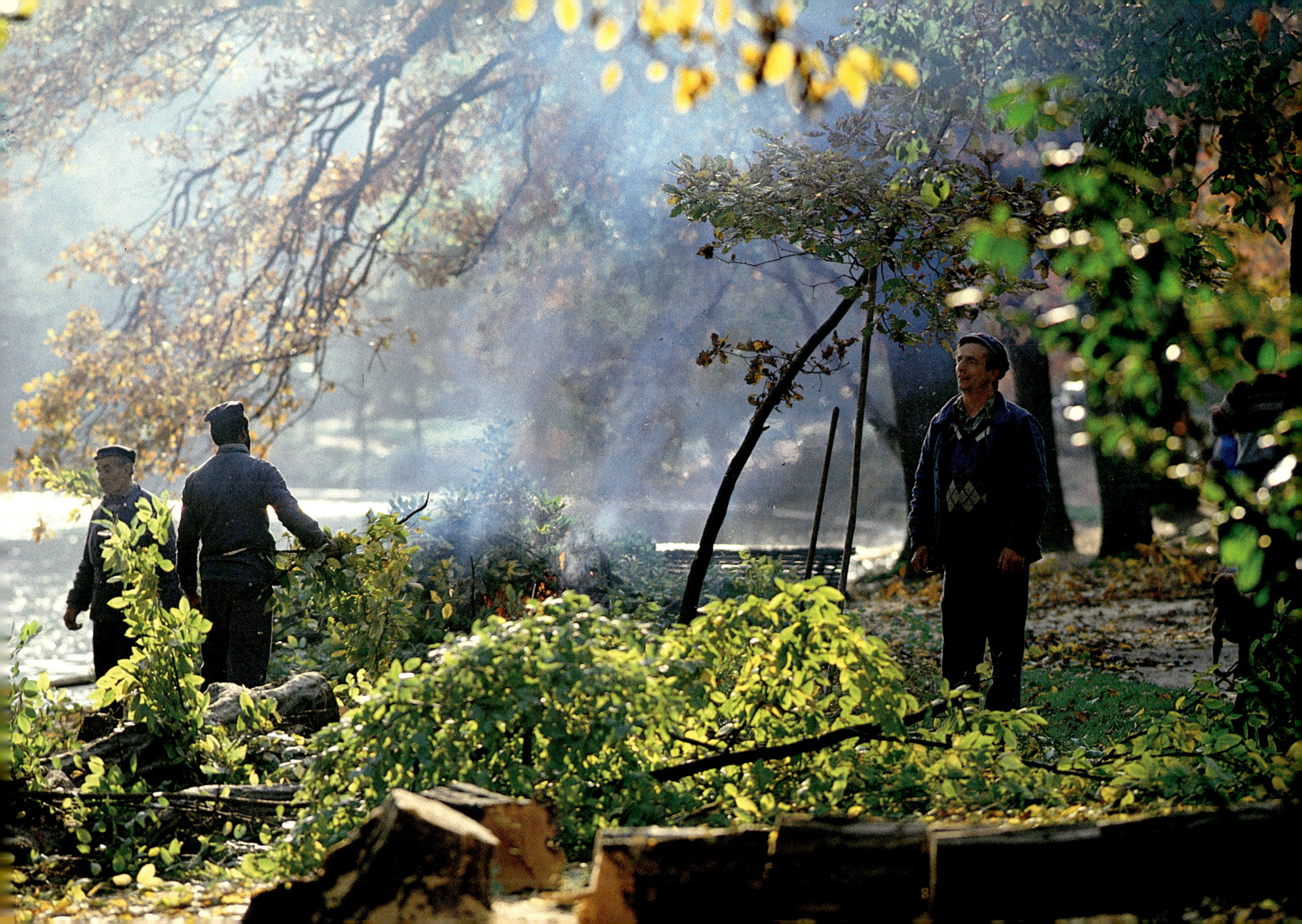

186 187

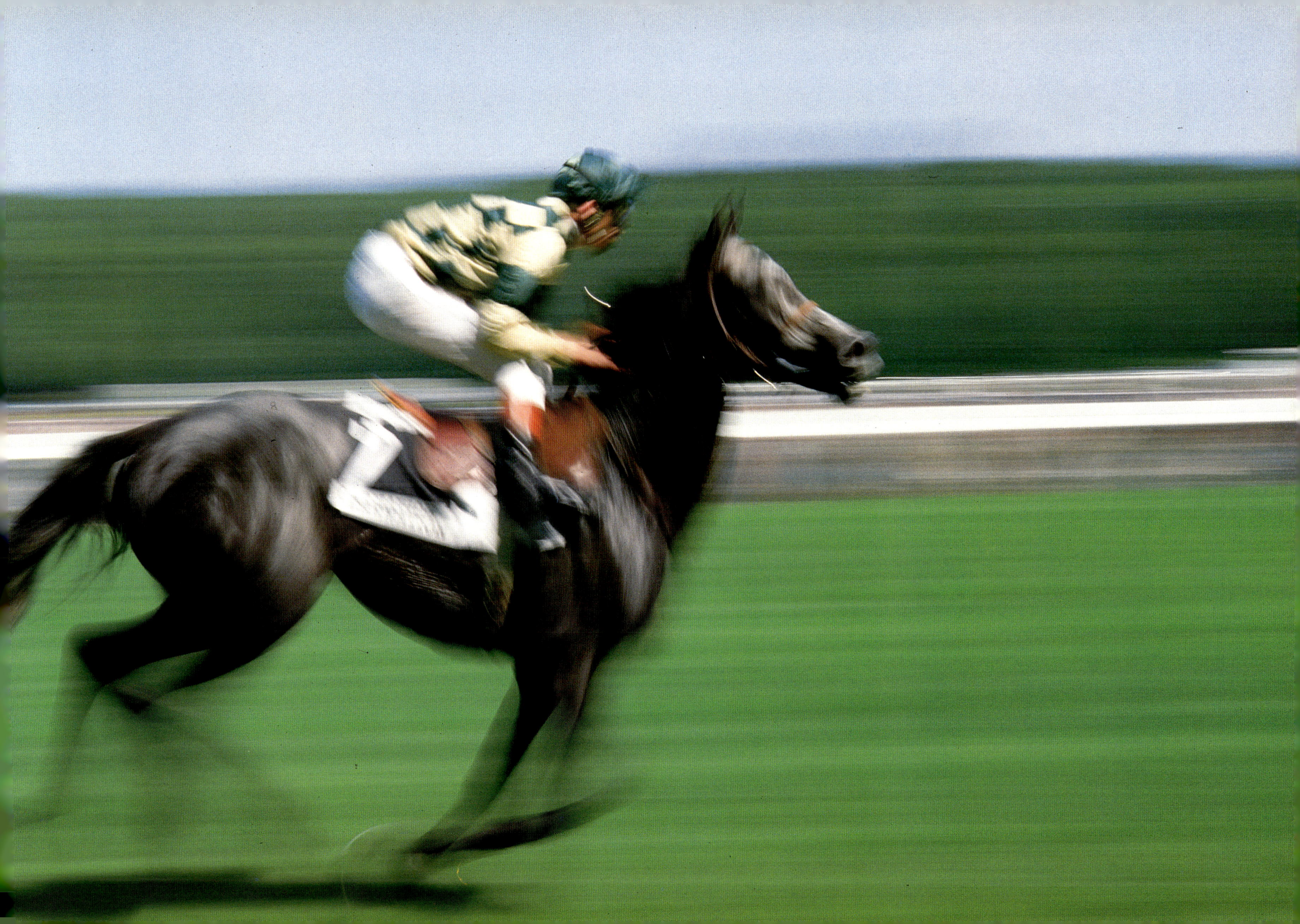

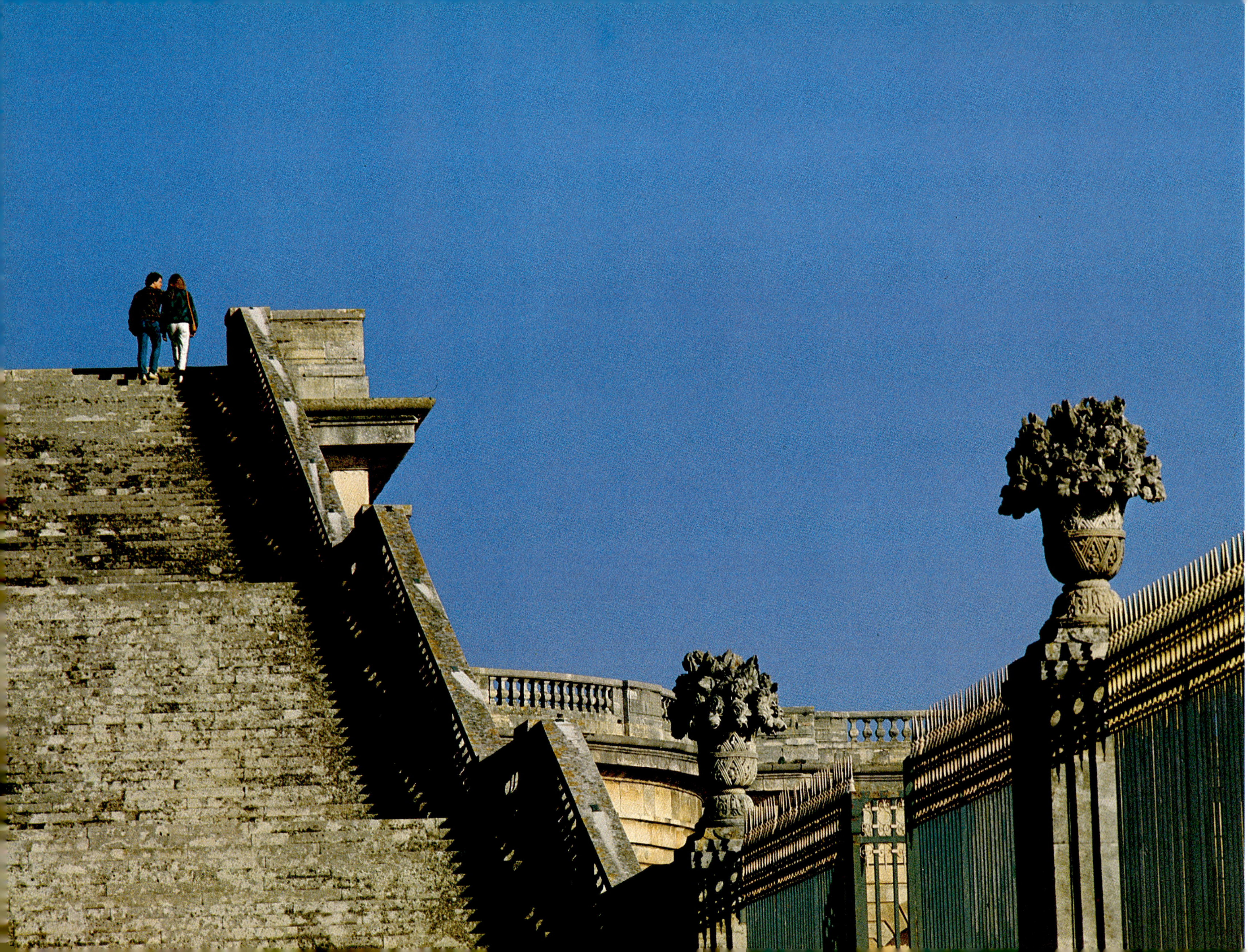

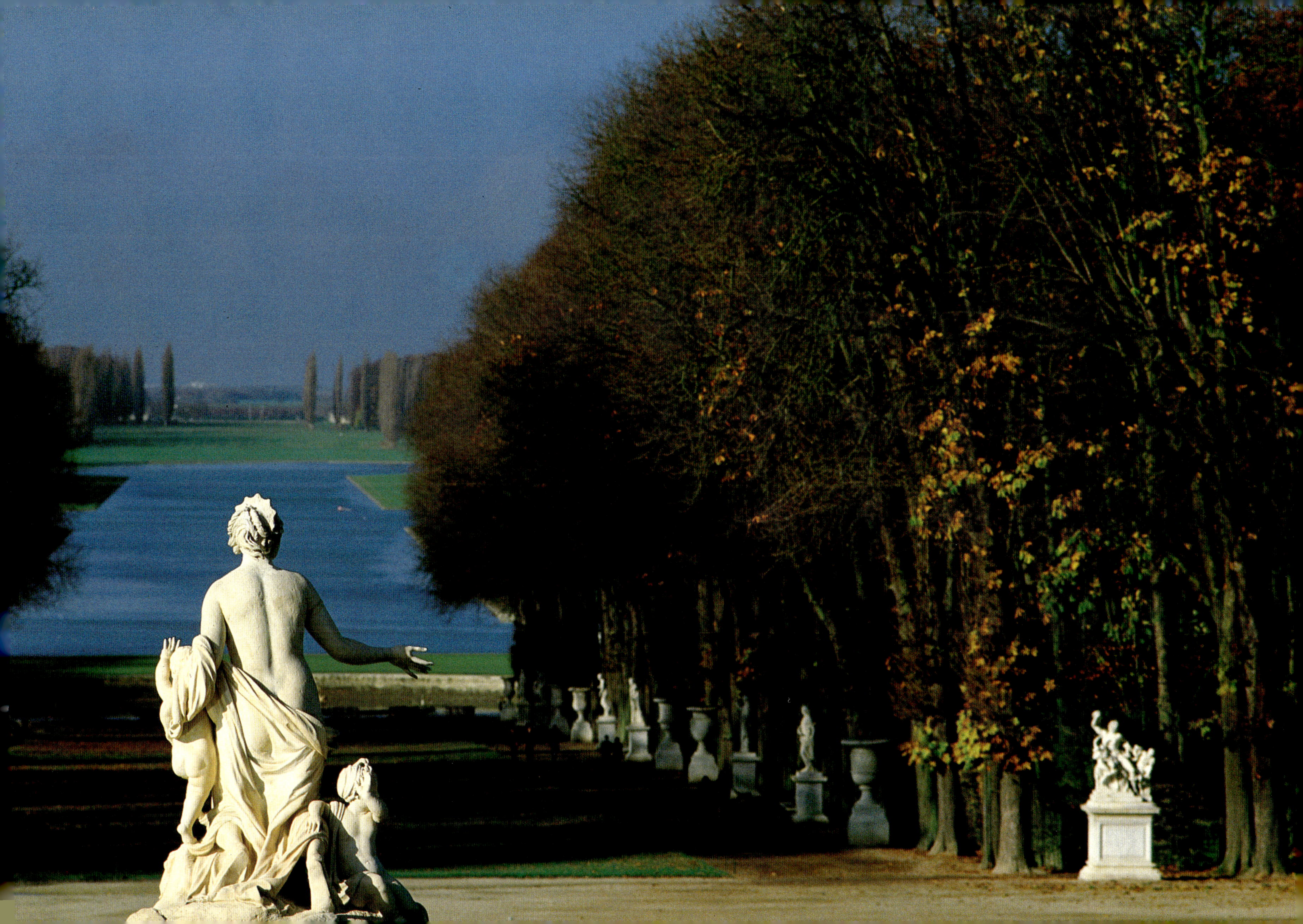

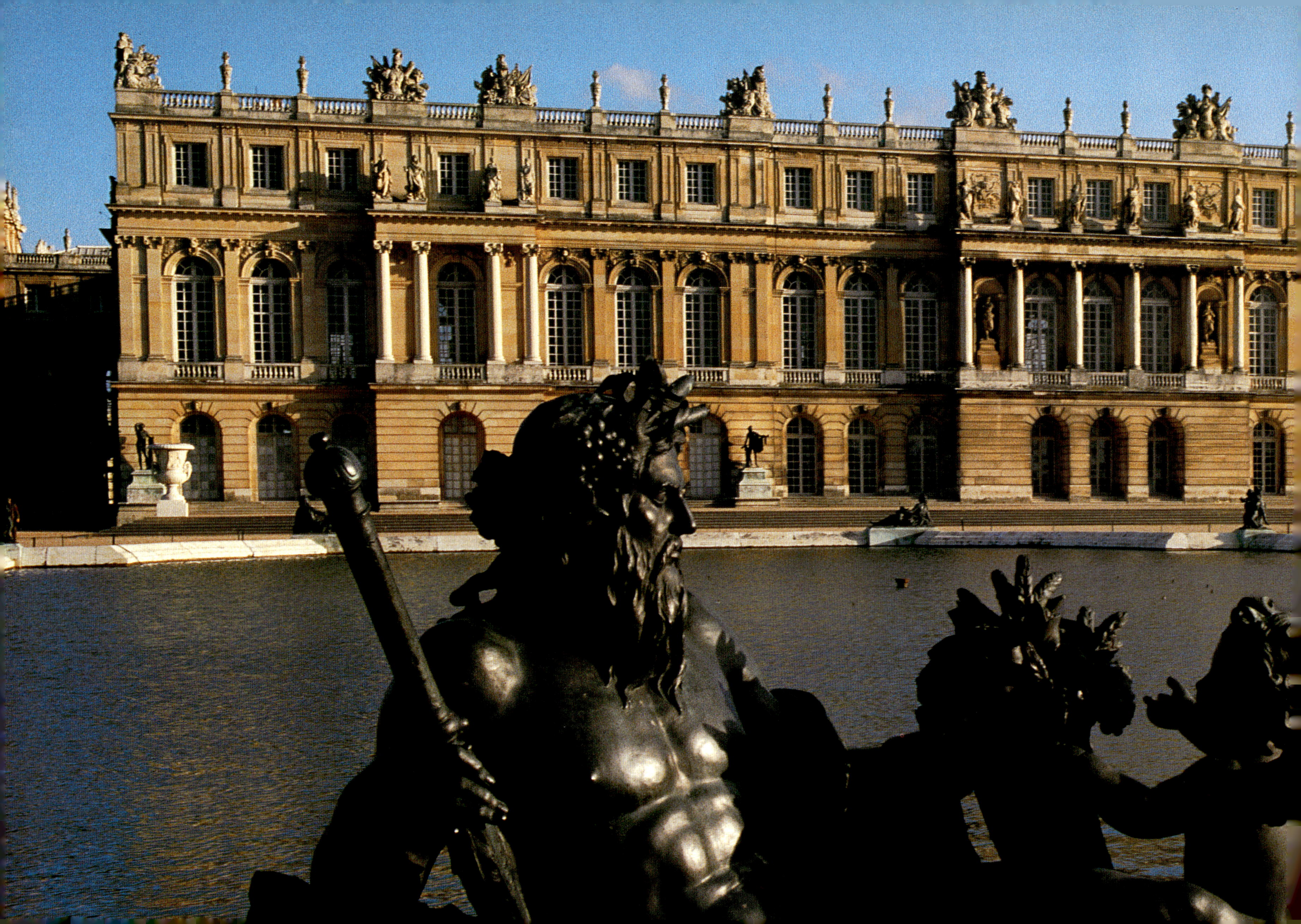

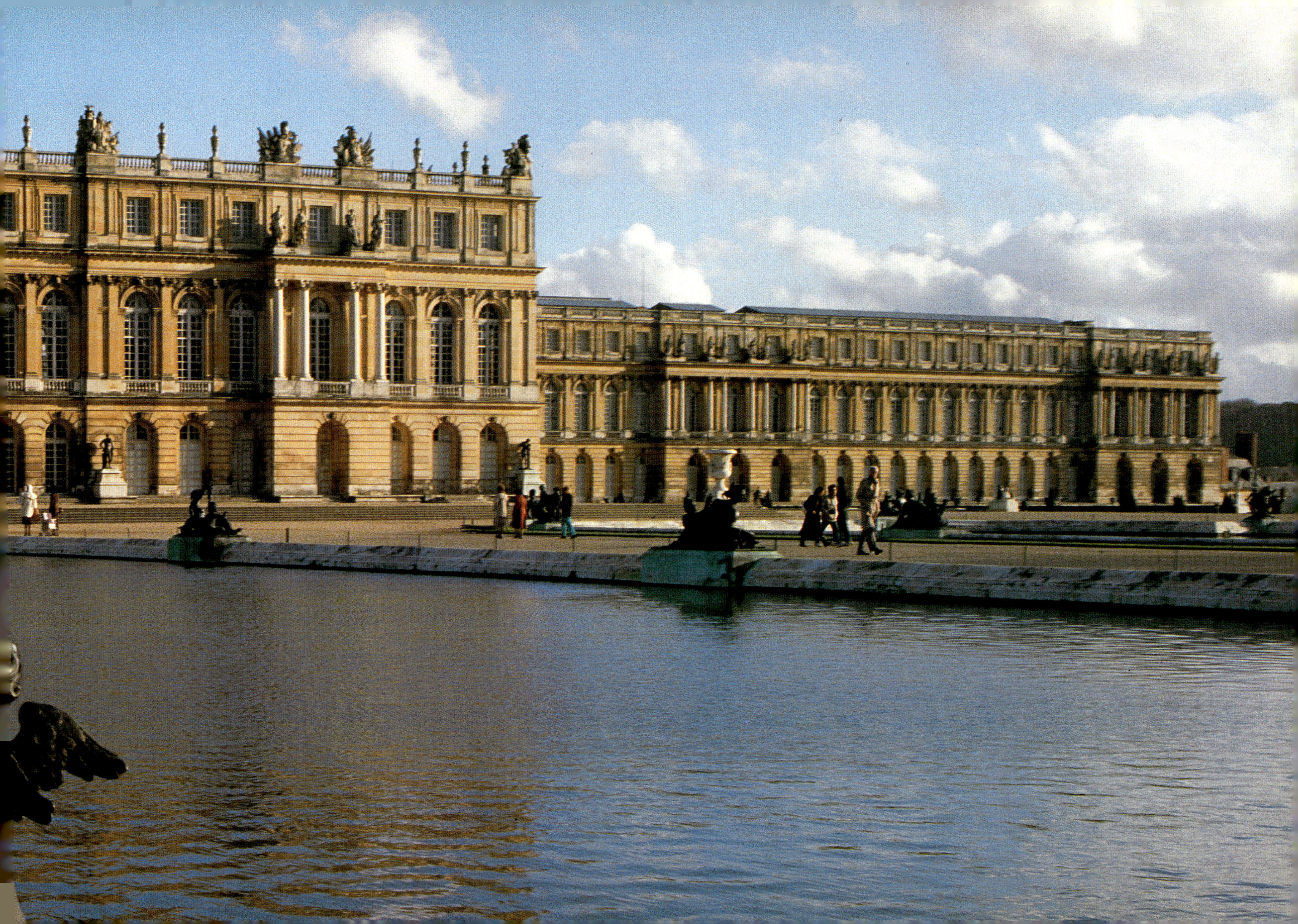

191 192

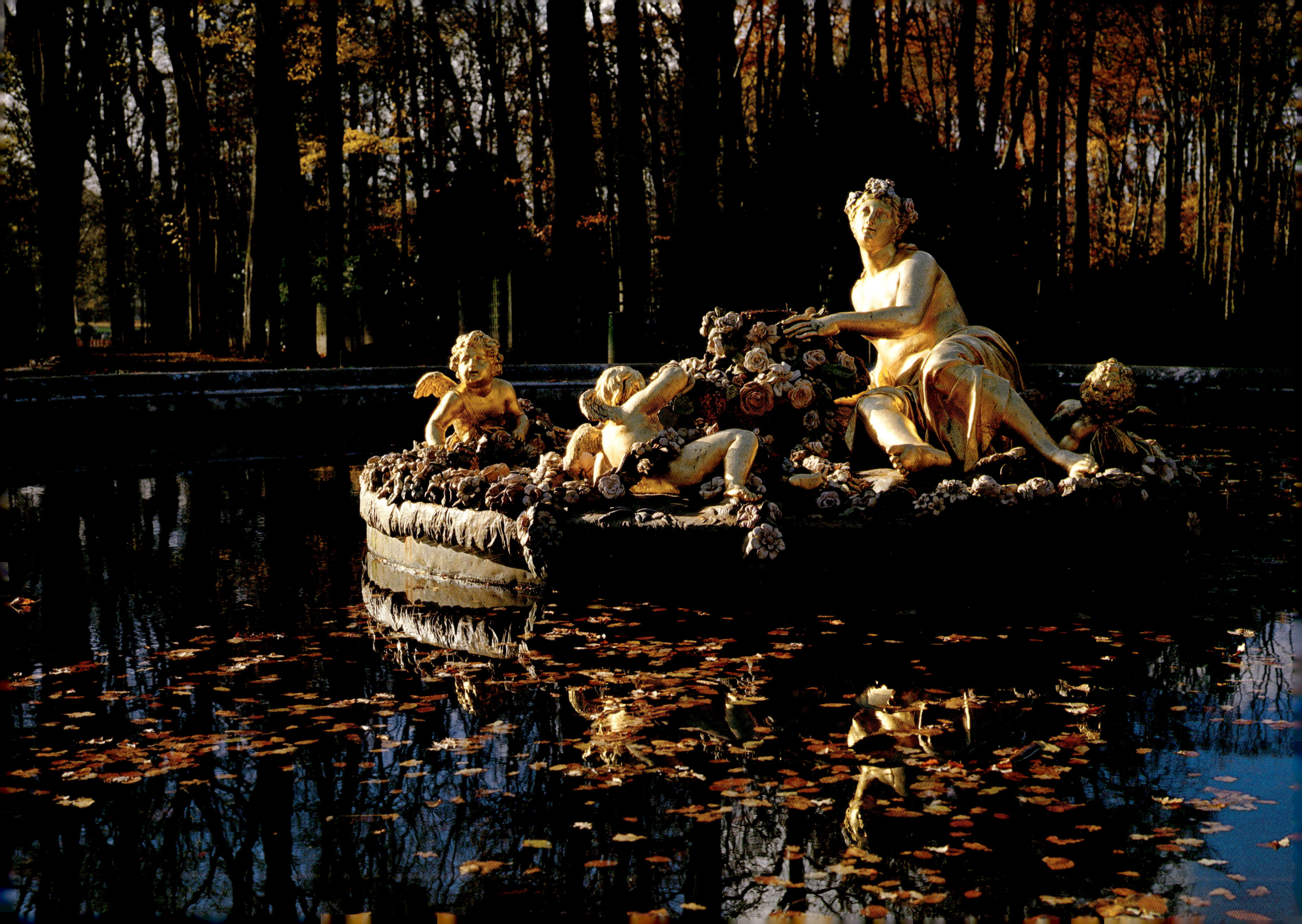

LES GLOIRES DE LA FRANCE

180   The little house of Bagatelle, in the Bois de Boulogne, was the subject of a bet made in 1775 between the Comte d'Artois (the future Charles X) and his sister-in-law, Marie Antoinette. He had bought a ruin, and promised her that a new building would be completed within three months. He won his bet: his architect, Bellanger, drew up the plans in twenty-four hours, and the house was built in sixty-three days.

   Luckily, Bagatelle escaped unharmed at the Revolution. Napoleon made it into a palace for his infant son, the King of Rome. The Duc de Berry recovered his family property at the Restauration, and it then passed into the hands of the expatriate Englishman Richard Wallace, who was a great art collector and also a benefactor of Paris, to which he presented a city-wide network of drinking-water fountains (known to Parisians as 'Wallaces'). Finally, in 1905, the City of Paris bought the estate from his heirs.

   The charm of the house itself is further enhanced by its enchanting setting. Much of the park laid out by a British gardener in the informal style fashionable in the later eighteenth century survives; and there are also notable tulip beds, a rose garden, and waterlilies fine enough to please Monet.

181   The old centre of Paris is sandwiched between high-rise and high-rise, and the Eiffel Tower, so shocking in its day, has become a friendly symbol compared with the 'engineer's architecture' of today.

182, 183   The satellite development of 'La Défense' was begun in 1960 around the Porte de la Défense, which lies at the western end of the great axis from the Louvre up the Champs Elysées, under the Arc de Triomphe and down the Avenue de la Grande Armée. Seen from the top of the Eiffel Tower, the buildings rise as in an architect's vision of the 'city of tomorrow'. In the distance is the little town of Pontoise.

184   The Bois de Boulogne is the Parisians' countryside. At the first hint of spring lovers are out boating on the lower lake or seeking seclusion on the islands; others play tennis or polo, or go riding, or lounge by the swimming pools building up a tan for their summer holidays. There are picnics on the grass, siestas in the shrubbery, and games of *pétanque* that go on late into the evening by the light of car headlamps. There is the French Garden and the Shakespeare Garden, the Rose Garden, the 'Japanese Mirror', the waterlily lake and the great rock.

   But the Bois de Boulogne is even more than all that. It includes the race-tracks of Auteuil and Longchamp, the latter surrounded by a track for cyclists and marathon runners, and the Parc des Princes, with its football matches. From the Porte Maillot a special train goes to the Jardin d'Acclimatation, a tiny zoo, where children are enraptured by the otters' water-ballet. Nearby is the Musée des Arts et Traditions Populaires, which holds exhibitions connected with folk life and popular culture. And beyond that is the Roland Garros stadium, which every year grows bigger to make more room for the fans of international tennis superstars.

185   The City of Paris employs a whole army of gardeners in squares, formal parks, the Bois de Boulogne and the Bois de Vincennes to set out bedding plants, prune trees and mow lawns. There are also uniformed park guardians, the mere sight of whom keeps small children in order.

186, 187   Winners and losers – feelings run high at Longchamp and Auteuil as the horses come out into the final straight. Standing in his stirrups, the jockey demands and gets a supreme effort from his animal that takes them victorious across the finishing line. A certain percentage of the money from bets goes to the Société d'Encouragement pour l'Amélioration de la Race Chevaline (a society to encourage improvements in horse-breeding) and to the State through the totalizator betting system known as the Pari Mutuel Urbain, or PMU, which is one of the most profitable businesses in France.

188–193   Versailles

188   The famous Cent Marches lead to the palace from the orangery. There, in the days of Louis XIV, some nine thousand orange and palm trees were kept in tubs, and brought out to give a novel exotic accent in the rooms and halls of the palace. It is said that the 'hundred steps' are now used by showgirls to practice for a stately descent on sets like those of the Folies-Bergère.

189   The Tapis Vert or 'green carpet' slopes gently away from the palace, between the Bassin de Latone and the Bassin d'Apollon. It is flanked by giant urns carved with classical scenes and by statues, which include a copy of the *Laocoön* (far right).

190   Versailles might well, like Narcissus, fall in love with its own reflection. Conceived by Le Vau, d'Orbay and Hardouin Mansart for the Sun King, it is the image of French Classicism, and Le Nôtre's stately gardens, with their terracing and disciplined stands of trees, provide the perfect setting for it.

191   This little cupid-triton holds his trident like a gondolier's oar, a reminder that the Doge of Venice presented Louis XIV with a flotilla of gondolas in which courtiers could glide elegantly on the formal lakes.

192   Under the direction of the painter Charles Le Brun, the gardens were filled with sculptures by the greatest artists of the day, among them Girardon, Coysevox, and Jean-Baptiste Tuby. Here Flora reclines on an island in the Bassin de Flore. Ceres, Bacchus and Saturn stand at the major intersections of the park, and elsewhere we glimpse Latona, Diana, Apollo, Aurora and Cephalus, allegorical figures whose individual significance and precise position in the gardens had a special meaning for the King and his guests.

193   Louis-Philippe in the early nineteenth century transformed part of the palace into a historical museum dedicated 'To all the Glories of France'. Many alterations were made to rooms on the ground floor, and upstairs the Galerie des Batailles was created to display martial paintings. Outside, in the Cour des Ministres, before you reach the Cour Royale, you are received by the Sun King on horseback. Versailles, in the words of Pierre Gaxotte, represents the union of classical and modern civilizations; it is a symbol of humanism, and the pattern of a noble style of life.

Technical notes

The photographs were all taken on Fujichrome film. Except for those on double-page spreads, they were realized with Nikon bodies (F³ and FE²) and Nikkor lenses (16–500 mm).
The technical indications give the following information: the camera body (Nikon F³ or FE²; Mamiya 645) – lens, shutter speed, aperture, and film (RFP 50 ASA/ISO; RDP 100 ASA/ISO; RTP 50 ASA/ISO).

Endpapers: Fujica G.617–Fujinon 8/105 mm, 1/250, f/16, RFP

1. F³ – Nikkor 2.5/105 mm, 8 sec., f/5.6, RDP
2. FE² – Nikkor 2.5/105 mm, 1/125, f/8, RFP
3. FE² – Nikkor 2.5/105 mm, 1/125, f/8, RFP
4. Mamiya 645 – Sekor shift 4/50 mm, 16 sec., f/8, RTP
5. F³ – Nikkor 2.5/105 mm, 4 sec., f/4, RFP
6. F³ – Nikkor 1.8/50 mm, 4 sec., f/2.8, RFP
7. FE² – Nikkor P.C. 3.5/28 mm, 8 sec., f/11, RFP
8. F³ – Nikkor 2.8/180 mm, 1/250, f/4, RFP
9. F³ – Nikkor 2.8/180 mm, 1/500, f/4, RDP
10. F³ – Nikkor 2.5/105 mm, 1/250, f/8, RDP
11. F³ – Nikkor 2.8/180 mm, 1/1000, f/2.8, RDP
12. F³ – Nikkor 2.5/105 mm, 1/500, f/4, RDP
13. FE² – Nikkor 2.5/105 mm, 1/125, f/8, RFP
14. FE² – Nikkor 8/500 mm, 16 sec., f/8, RFP
15. F³ – Nikkor 2.8/180 mm, 1/250, f/5.6, RDP
16. F³ – Nikkor 2.5/105 mm, 1/500, f/4, RDP
17. F³ – Nikkor 2.8/180 mm, 1/125, f/8, RDP
18. FE² – Nikkor 2.5/105 mm, 1/60, f/11, RDP
19. FE² – Nikkor 2.5/105 mm, 1/30, f/2.5, RFP
20. F³ – Nikkor 2.8/28 mm, 1/125, f/5.6, RDP
21. FE² – Nikkor 2.8/180 mm, 2 sec., f/4, RDP
22. F³ – Nikkor 2.8/180 mm, 1/250, f/4, RFP
23. F³ – Nikkor 2.8/180 mm, 1/500, f/4, RDP
24. F³ – Nikkor 2.8/180 mm, 1/125, f/5.6, RDP
25. FE² – Nikkor 2.8/20 mm, 1/60, f/11, RFP
26. FE² – Nikkor 2.8/180 mm, 1/60, f/2.8, RDP
27. FE² – Nikkor 2.5/105 mm, 1/30, f/4, RDP
28. FE² – Nikkor 2.8/28 mm, 1/15, f/4, RDP
29. FE² – Nikkor 2.8/180 mm, 1/8, f/4, RDP
30. F³ – Nikkor 2.5/105 mm, 1/125, f/2.5, RFP
31. F³ – Nikkor 2.8/180 mm, 1/250, f/5.6, RDP
32. FE² – Nikkor 2.5/105 mm, 1/125, f/5.6, RFP
33. F³ – Nikkor 2.8/180 mm, 1/250, f/4, RDP
34. F³ – Nikkor 8/500 mm, 1/125, f/8, RDP
35. FE² – Nikkor 2.8/180 mm, 1/250, f/5.6, RFP
36. F³ – Nikkor 2.8/20 mm, 1/60, f/2.8, RDP
37. F³ – Nikkor P.C. 3.5/28 mm, 8 sec., f/11, RDP
38. FE² – Nikkor 2.8/28 mm, 1/60, f/8, RFP
39. F³ – Nikkor 1.8/50 mm, 1/30, f/5.6, RFP
40. F³ – Nikkor 2.8/16 mm, 1/4, f/5.6, RFP
41. F³ – Nikkor 2.8/16 mm, 1/8, f/8, RFP
42. FE² – Nikkor 2.5/105 mm, 1/250, f/5.6, RDP
43. F³ – Nikkor 2.8/180 mm, 8 sec., f/4, RFP
44. FE² – Nikkor 1.8/50 mm, 1/15, f/1.8, RDP
45. FE² – Nikkor 2/35 mm, 1/2, f/4, RDP
46. FE² – Nikkor 1.8/50 mm, 2 sec., f/4, RDP
47. Mamiya 645 – Sekor 3.5/35 mm, 1/60, f/11, RDP
48. F³ – Nikkor 2.8/20 mm, 1/60, f/5.6, RDP
49. F³ – Nikkor 2.8/180 mm, 1/125, f/5.6, RFP
50. FE² – Nikkor 2.8/16 mm, 1/60, f/4, RFP
51. F³ – Nikkor 2.8/28 mm, 1/60, f/5.6, RFP
52. F³ – Nikkor 2.8/28 mm, 1/60, f/5.6, RFP

53. FE² – Nikkor 2.8/180 mm, 1/250, f/2.8, RDP
54. F³ – Nikkor 2.8/28 mm, 1/30, f/4, RFP
55. F³ – Nikkor 2.5/105 mm, 1/125, f/8, RDP
56. FE² – Nikkor 1.8/50 mm, 1/4, f/5.6, RDP
57. FE² – Nikkor 2.8/28 mm, 1/8, f/5.6, RFP
58. F³ – Nikkor 2.8/180 mm, 1/60, f/11, RFP
59. F³ – Nikkor 2.8/16 mm, 1/60, f/8, RDP
60. FE² – Nikkor 2.8/180 mm, 1/125, f/4, RDP
61. F³ – Nikkor P.C. 2.8/35 mm, 1/60, f/11, RFP
62. F³ – Nikkor 1.8/50 mm, 1/125, f/5.6, RFP
63. FE² – Nikkor 2.8/28 mm, 1/60, f/11, RFP
64. Mamiya 645 – Sekor shift 4/50 mm, 1/60, f/16, RDP
65. F³ – Nikkor 2.8/28 mm, 1 sec., f/5.6, RFP
66. F³ – Nikkor 2.8/20 mm, 1/30, f/5.6, RFP
67. FE² – Nikkor 2.8/28 mm, 1/60, f/11, RFP
68. FE² – Nikkor 2.8/180 mm, 1/250, f/4, RFP
69. FE² – Nikkor 2.5/105 mm, 1/2, f/8, RFP
70. F³ – Nikkor 1.8/50 mm, 1/60, f/11, RDP
71. F³ – Nikkor 2.5/105 mm, 1/125, f/5.6, RDP
72. F³ – Nikkor 2.8/180 mm, 1/500, f/2.8, RDP
73. FE² – Nikkor 1.8/50 mm, 1/30, f/4, RDP
74. F³ – Nikkor 2.5/105mm, 1/125, f/5.6, RFP
75. Mamiya 645 – Sekor shift 4/50, 1/60, f/11, RFP
76. F³ – Nikkor 2.8/28 mm, 1/125, f/2.8, RDP
77. F³ – Nikkor 2.5/105 mm, 1/60, f/4, RDP
78. F³ – Nikkor 2.5/105 mm, 1/125, f/8, RDP
79. FE² – Nikkor 2/35 mm, 1/30, f/5.6, RFP
80. FE² – Nikkor 2.8/180 mm, 1/250, f/2.8, RFP
81. F³ – Nikkor 2.8/180 mm, 1/500, f/4, RDP
82. FE² – Nikkor 2.8/28 mm, 1/125, f/4, RDP
83. F³ – Nikkor 2.5/105 mm, 1/60, f/5.6, RFP
84. F³ – Nikkor 2.8/28 mm, 1/125, f/5.6, RFP
85. F³ – Nikkor 2.5/105 mm, 1/125, f/8, RFP
86. FE² – Nikkor 2.5/105 mm, 1/125, f/11, RDP
87. F³ – Nikkor 2.5/105 mm, 1/60, f/8, RFP
88. FE² – Nikkor 2.8/28 mm, 1/60, f/11, RDP
89. F³ – Nikkor 2.8/180 mm, 1/250, f/4, RFP
90. Mamiya 645 – Sekor 3.5/35 mm, 1/60, f/11, RFP
91. Mamiya 645 – Sekor shift 4/50 mm, 1/30, f/16, RFP
92. FE² – Nikkor 2.5/105 mm, 1/125, f/4, RFP
93. F³ – Nikkor 2.8/180 mm, 1/250, f/2.8, RDP
94. FE² – Nikkor 2.8/180 mm, 1/250, f/4, RDP
95. FE² – Nikkor P.C. 2.8/35 mm, 16 sec., f/5.6, RFP
96. F³ – Nikkor 2.8/180 mm, 1/125, f/4, RFP
97. FE² – Nikkor 1.8/50 mm, 1 sec., f/2.8, RDP
98. Mamiya 645 – Sekor 3.5/35 mm, 1/30, f/5.6, RDP
99. FE² – Nikkor 2.8/180 mm, 1/125, f/8, RFP
100. F³ – Nikkor 2.8/180 mm, 1/250, f/5.6, RFP
101. Mamiya 645 – Sekor shift 4/50 mm, 1/60, f/11, RFP
102. FE² – Nikkor 2.8/180 mm, 1/125, f/8, RFP
103. F³ – Nikkor 2.8/180 mm, 1/250, f/5.6, RDP
104. FE² – Nikkor 2.8/28 mm, 1/30, f/4, RDP
105. FE² – Nikkor 2.8/28 mm, 1/60, f/4, RDP
106. F³ – Nikkor 2.8/20 mm, 1/125, f/4, RFP
107. F³ – Nikkor 2.8/20 mm, 1/30, f/8, RFP
108. F³ – Nikkor 2.8/20 mm, 1/60, f/4, RDP
109. FE² – Nikkor 2.8/180 mm, 1/250, f/4, RFP
110. FE² – Nikkor 2.5/105 mm, 1/125, f/8, RFP
111. FE² – Nikkor 2.8/180 mm, 1/60, f/5.6, RDP
112. F³ – Nikkor 2.8/28 mm, 1/60, f/11, RFP
113. FE² – Nikkor 2.8/28 mm, 8 sec., f/11, RDP
114. Mamiya 645 – Sekor 3.5/35 mm, 1/60, f/8, RFP
115. F³ – Nikkor 2.8/180 mm, 1/250, f/4, RFP
116. FE² – Nikkor, 2.8/20 mm, 1/60, f/8, RFP
117. FE² – Nikkor, 2.5/105 mm, 1/250, f/4, RDP
118. F³ – Nikkor 2.8/180 mm, 1/500, f/4, RFP
119. Mamiya 645 – Sekor shift 4/50 mm, 1/60, f/11, RFP
120. F³ – Nikkor 8/500 mm, 1/125, f/8, RFP
121. FE² – Nikkor 2.5/105 mm, 1/250, f/4, RFP
122. FE² – Nikkor 2.5/180 mm, 1/250, f/5.6, RDP
123. FE² – Nikkor 2.8/180 mm, 1/500, f/4, RDP
124. F³ – Nikkor 2.5/105 mm, 1/125, f/4, RFP
125. FE² – Nikkor 2.8/28 mm, 1/8, f/5.6, RDP
126. FE² – Nikkor 2.8/180 mm, 1/4, f/5.6, RFP
127. Mamiya 645 – Sekor 3.5/35 mm, 1/60, f/11, RFP
128. F³ – Nikkor 2.8/20 mm, 1/30, f/8, RFP
129. F³ – Nikkor 2.8/28 mm, 1/60, f/5.6, RFP
130. FE² – Nikkor 2.8/28 mm, 1/60, f/4, RFP
131. FE² – Nikkor 2/35 mm, 1/125, f/8, RDP
132. F³ – Nikkor 8/500 mm, 1/2, f/8, RDP
133. Mamiya 645 – Sekor shift 4/50 mm, 1/60, f/11, RFP
134. FE² – Nikkor 2.5/105 mm, 1/125, f/4, RFP
135. FE² – Nikkor 2.8/28 mm, 1/125, f/5.6, RFP
136. FE² – Nikkor 2/35 mm, 1/60, f/11, RDP
137. FE² – Nikkor 2/35 mm, 1/60, f/5.6, RDP
138. F³ – Nikkor 2.8/180 mm, 1/250, f/4, RFP
139. FE² – Nikkor 2.8/28 mm, 1/60, f/5.6, RFP
140. FE² – Nikkor 2.8/28 mm, 1/15, f/4, RFP
141. FE² – Nikkor 2.8/28 mm, 1/30, f/2.8, RFP
142. FE² – Nikkor 2.8/180 mm, 1/250, f/4, RFP
143. F³ – Nikkor 2.8/28 mm, 1/60, f/5.6, RFP
144. FE² – Nikkor 2.8/180 mm, 1/500, f/4, RDP
145. F³ – Nikkor 2.8/28 mm, 1/125, f/5.6, RFP
146. F³ – Nikkor 2.8/180 mm, 1/250, f/4, RDP
147. FE² – Nikkor 2.5/105 mm, 1/8, f/16, RFP
148. F³ – Nikkor 2.8/180 mm, 1/125, f/5.6, RFP
149. F³ – Nikkor 2.8/180 mm, 1/60, f/11, RFP
150. FE² – Nikkor 2.8/28 mm, 4 sec., f/4, RDP
151. FE² – Nikkor 2.5/105 mm, 1/250, f/2.5, RFP
152. F³ – Nikkor P.C. 2.8/35 mm, 2 sec., f/8, RFP
153. F³ – Nikkor P.C. 2.8/35 mm, 2 sec., f/11, RFP
154. FE² – Nikkor 2.8/180 mm, 1/250, f/5.6, RFP

155. FE² – Nikkor 2.5/105 mm, 1/125, f/8, RFP
156. F³ – Nikkor 2.5/28 mm, 1/30, f/4, RFP
157. FE² – Nikkor 2.8/28 mm, 1/30, f/4, RFP
158. F³ – Nikkor 2.5/105 mm, 1/15, f/5.6, RDP
159. FE² – Nikkor 2.8/16 mm, 1/8, f/8, RFP
160. F³ – Nikkor 2.5/105 mm, 1/60, f/5.6, RDP
161. FE² – Nikkor 2.8/180 mm, 1/250, f/4, RDP
162. F³ – Nikkor P.C. 2.8/35 mm, 1/60, f/8, RDP
163. F³ – Nikkor 2.5/105 mm, 1/60, f/8, RDP
164. F³ – Nikkor 2.5/105 mm, 1/60, f/11, RDP
165. FE² – Nikkor 2.8/28 mm, 1/125, f/4, RFP
166. FE² – Nikkor 2.5/105 mm, 1/250, f/2.5, RFP
167. F³ – Nikkor 2.8/28 mm, 1/30, f/5.6, RDP
168. F³ – Nikkor 2.8/28 mm, 1/60, f/8, RDP
169. FE² – Nikkor 2.5/105 mm, 1/125, f/5.6, RFP
170. FE² – Nikkor 2.8/28 mm, 1/60, f/4, RFP
171. F³ – Nikkor 2.8/180 mm, 1/250, f/4, RFP
172. FE² – Nikkor 2.5/105 mm, 1/60, f/5.6, RDP
173. F³ – Nikkor 2.8/180 mm, 1/250, f/4, RFP
174. F³ – Nikkor 2.8/180 mm, 1/125, f/2.8, RFP
175. FE² – Nikkor 2.8/28 mm, 2 sec., f/2.8, RDP
176. FE² – Nikkor 2.8/20 mm, 4 sec., f/5.6, RFP
177. F³ – Nikkor 2.8/180 mm, 1/250, f/4, RFP
178. FE² – Nikkor 2.5/105 mm, 1/60, f/5.6, RDP
179. F³ – Nikkor 2.5/105 mm, 1/125, f/4, RFP
180. F³ – Nikkor 2.8/180 mm, 1/60, f/5.6, RFP
181. FE² – Nikkor 2.8/180 mm, 1/125, f/4, RFP
182. FE² – Nikkor 2.8/28 mm, 1/30, f/2.8, RFP
183. Mamiya 645 – Sekor 3.5/150 mm, 1/125, f/5.6, RDP
184. F³ – Nikkor 2.8/180 mm, 1/125, f/4, RFP
185. F³ – Nikkor 2.5/105 mm, 1/250, f/4, RFP
186. FE² – Nikkor 2.8/28 mm, 1/60, f/4, RDP
187. FE² – Nikkor 2.5/105 mm, 1/4, f/11, RDP
188. F³ – Nikkor 2.5/105 mm, 1/125, f/8, RFP
189. F³ – Nikkor 2.8/180 mm, 1/250, f/4, RDP
190. Mamiya 645 – Sekor shift 4/50 mm, 1/60, f/11, RDP
191. F³ – Nikkor 2.5/105 mm, 1/500, f/5.6, RFP
192. FE² – Nikkor 2.5/105 mm, 1/30, f/5.6, RFP
193. F³ – Nikkor 2.8/180 mm, 1/60, f/11, RFP

Printed and bound in Italy by Grafiche Lema - Maniago/Pordenone
in June 1988